Month-by-Month
Reading Instruction
for the Differentiated Classroom

Maria P. Walther
Katherine A. Phillips

■SCHOLASTIC

New York • Toronto • London • Auckland • Sydney
Mexico City • New Delhi • Hong Kong • Buenos Aires

Dedication

To Katie:

I wish for you the power to dream, the knowledge that you can do anything, and the whisper inside your head saying you are smart, you are capable, you are strong. —MPW

To Brynne, Jake, and Lauren:

May your eyes be filled with wonder, your hearts be filled with stories, and your shelves be filled with books. —KAP

Acknowledgments

This book is brimming with ideas because we are fortunate to be surrounded by people who nudge and support us as we spend countless hours trying to do what's best for kids. Thanks to…

- Katie DeSotell, Kathy Pease, Linda Tyrell, and Paula Loret de Mola for taking time to read our manuscript—your comments and suggestions spurred our thinking.
- all our friends and book enthusiasts who work at Anderson's Bookshop in Naperville, Illinois— you are our partners as we work diligently to put exceptional books in the hands of teachers and children.
- the following publishers: Albert Whitman, Disney/Hyperion, Egmont, HarperCollins, Lee & Low, Lerner, Macmillan Publishing Group, and Marshall Cavendish, who help us stay on top of the latest and greatest literature for kids.
- the Indian Prairie District 204 Language Arts Committee members past and present, including Paula (Schoenfelder) Jensen, Katie DeSotell, and Pat Hitt, for shaping our vision of powerful reading instruction.
- our first graders at Gwendolyn Brooks Elementary School in Aurora, Illinois, whose dazzling words and shining faces are our inspiration.
- Joanna Davis-Swing, our editor, thank you for your patience as you answered our many questions and for your insightful suggestions. You helped us to fine-tune and shape a distinctive resource for primary grade teachers.
- our families and friends who understand that for us, spending extra time at school together is fun!

Scholastic Inc. grants teachers permission to photocopy the reproducible pages in this book only for personal classroom use. No other part of this publication may be reproduced in whole or in part, or stored in a retrieval system, or transmitted in any form or by any means, electronic, mechanical, photocopying, recording, or otherwise, without written permission of the publisher. For information regarding permission, write to Permissions Department, Scholastic Inc., 557 Broadway, New York, NY 10012.

Editor: Joanna Davis-Swing
Cover design: Scott Davis
Interior design: LDL Designs
Cover photos: Leonard and Maria Walther
Interior photos: Maria Walther

ISBN: 978-0-545-28069-3
Copyright © 2012 by Maria P. Walther and Katherine A. Phillips
All rights reserved. Published by Scholastic Inc.
Printed in the U.S.A.

3 4 5 6 7 8 9 10   40   19 18 17 16 15

CONTENTS

Introduction 4
    Morning Message Menu 5
    Mini-Lesson Menu 5
    Ten Things You Might Choose to Do Before School Begins 8

CHAPTER 1: Powerful Reading Instruction 9

CHAPTER 2: SEPTEMBER—Setting the Stage 37

CHAPTER 3: OCTOBER—Making Meaningful Connections 79

CHAPTER 4: NOVEMBER & DECEMBER—Predicting in Real and
Make-Believe Stories 107

CHAPTER 5: JANUARY—Retelling, Comparing, and Contrasting Stories 131

CHAPTER 6: FEBRUARY—Questioning and Determining Importance to
Understand Biographies 153

CHAPTER 7: MARCH—Visualizing and Inferring to Peek Into Poetry 177

CHAPTER 8: APRIL & MAY—Questioning and Determining Importance to
Navigate Nonfiction 195

Professional Resources Cited 215

Children's Literature Cited 216

CD Print Resources 223

CD Interactive Whiteboard Resources 224

INTRODUCTION

We Need More Pages!

As we were putting the finishing touches on *Month-by-Month Trait-Based Writing Instruction* we thought to ourselves, "That was fun—let's write a book about reading instruction." Great idea! So we started gathering ideas, and the manuscript began to take shape and grow, and grow, and grow. After the first summer of writing, we called our editor and said, "Joanna, we need more pages!" After writing all fall and winter, we pleaded again, "We still need more room." What we soon realized, as we compiled over 40 years of ideas into one resource, is that primary-grade reading instruction is complex and multifaceted. With that said, what you hold in your hands today constitutes our "best thinking" right now. As you are reading this book, we'll be working in our classrooms to continue to revise our thinking and instruction based on our students' needs, our reflection, and our new learning.

We were raised as teachers in a school district that valued professional development. In fact, in the early years of our careers, our district, thanks to Dr. Joan Maute, had its own professional development system where teachers earned salary schedule credit for taking in-house PD sessions led by our own literacy experts. So, the content in this book is a result of layer upon layer of learning from our dear friends and literacy experts like Paula (Schoenfelder) Jensen, Katie DeSotell, Bob Allison, Kathy Klees, and so many more that we can't name them all. Sadly, as leadership priorities and funding have changed, that system is no longer in place. But the lessons we learned along the way have become part of who we are as primary-grade teachers. While some compare education to a swinging pendulum, we view it as a colorful patchwork quilt. We believe that thoughtful teachers take the best of each "trend" and weave the research-based yet sensible practices into the fabric of their teaching to blanket their students with powerful reading instruction. So that is what we've done in this book. In Chapter 1, we define powerful reading instruction and attempt to answer three big questions: "What do I teach? How do I teach it? When do I find time?" Chapter 2 is the longest chapter because it lays out a comprehensive plan for launching a reading workshop. Then, in chapters 3 through 8, we share a month-by-month guide for teaching reading through morning messages, targeted mini-lessons, comprehension conversations, vocabulary-building activities, genre studies, and much more! It is our hope that this book helps to bring more joy and laughter into your classroom as you read, think, and converse with your students. Let the reading begin!

MORNING MESSAGE MENU

	Self-Monitoring/ Decoding Messages	Comprehension Messages	Vocabulary-Building Messages	Reading-Response Messages
September Launching Reading-Related Morning Messages (p. 38)	Picture Clues (p. 39)	Knock, Knock! Who's There? (p. 39)	Labeling the Parts of a Book (p. 40)	What Kinds of Books Do You Prefer? (p. 40)
October	Skip and Read Through (p. 80)	Can You Comprehend This Sentence? (p. 80)	Compound Words (p. 81)	Thinking About Books (p. 82)
November & December	Look for Chunks (p. 108)	Predict the Title (p. 109)	Using Adjectives to Describe Our Favorite Characters (p. 110)	Can You Guess the Character? (p. 110)
January	Get Your Mouth Ready (p. 132)	Story Elements (p. 132)	Familiar Words with New Meanings (p. 133)	Using Key Words and Phrases to Retell (p. 134)
February	Introducing Prefixes (p. 154)	Introducing Question Words (p. 155)	What Is Chronological Order? (p. 155)	A Timeline of Our Day (p. 156)
March	Decoding Two-Syllable Words (p. 178)	Words That Evoke Images (p. 178)	Quiet Words and Noisy Words (p. 178)	Creating List Poems (p. 179)
April & May	Decoding Multisyllabic Content-Related Words (p. 196)	Understanding Text Features (p. 197)	"Text Structure Signal Words (p. 197)	True or False (p. 198)

CD Resource I.1

MINI-LESSON MENU: LAUNCHING THE READING WORKSHOP

	Mini-Lessons for Creating a Community of Book Lovers	Procedural Mini-Lessons for Reading, Thinking, and Talking in a Whole Class Setting	Procedural Mini-Lessons for Establishing Independent Reading	A Menu of Mini-Lessons for Reading Response	A Guide for Exploring the W.O.R.L.D. Time
September: Setting the Stage	We Are Readers! (p. 43) Reading Makes Us Feel Good (p. 44) We Read to Laugh! (p. 44) We Read to Learn (p. 45) We Read to Ponder (p. 46) Readers Have Their Favorite Kinds of Books (p. 47) Have I Got a Book for You! (p. 48)	Are You Listening? (p. 50) You Talk While I Listen; I Talk While You Listen (p. 51) Let's Link Our Thinking (p. 52) How to Politely End a Conversation (p. 53)	Let's Read, Think, and Talk About the Pictures (p. 55) Let's Retell a Folktale, Fairy Tale, or Nursery Rhyme (p. 56) Let's Use Picture Clues to Help Us Read the Words (p. 56) Let's Read the Words (p. 57) Independent Reading—What Are You Doing? What Are You Learning? (p. 57) Independent Reading—Choosing Just-Right Books (p. 59)	What Do Readers Do? R-E-R-E-A-D, Reread, Reread (p. 61) What Do Readers Do? Read Book, After Book, After Book . . . (p. 62) What Do Readers Do? Read, Think, and Talk With a Friend (p. 63) What Do Readers Do? Read, Think, and Write (p. 64) Read-Alouds With Rich Vocabulary (p. 72) **Words Introduced:** *admiration, captivated companion, compromise, desperately, disturbed, immense, journey, mighty*	Be a Writer (p. 66) Be an Observer (p. 67) Be a Reader (p. 68) Be a Listener (p. 69) Be a Word Detective (p. 70) Genre Study: Read-Aloud Favorites for the Beginning of the School Year (p. 72) Sensible Strategies for Struggling Readers: The Reading Boost Bag (p. 75) Targeting Talented Readers: My Reading Autobiography (p. 76)

MINI-LESSON MENU

	Self-Monitoring/ Decoding Strategy Mini-Lessons	Comprehension Strategy Mini-Lesson	Vocabulary-Building Activities	Reading Response Mini-Lessons	Genre Study: Meeting the Needs of ALL Learners'
October: Making Meaningful Connections	Get Your Mouth Ready (p. 85) Skip and Read Through (p. 86) Look Through the Word for Sounds You Know (p. 87) Look for Chunks—Foundation Lesson (p. 88) Word Family Chunks—Follow-Up Lesson (p. 89)	The ABCs of Schema—Foundation Lesson (p. 90) Making Connections: Read-Aloud/Think-Aloud—Foundation Lesson (p. 92) Text-to-Self Connections: Read-Aloud/Think-Together—Follow-Up Lesson (p. 93) Making Meaningful Connections—Follow-Up Lesson (p. 94) Using Your Schema to Make Text-to-Self Connections (p. 95)	Introducing Compound Words—Foundation Lesson (p. 98) Compound Word Webs—Follow-Up Lesson (p. 99) Read-Alouds With Rich Vocabulary (p. 100) **Words Introduced:** *aloft, clambered, dandy, gingerly, inspired, permanent, plummeted, sulked, waded*	My Schema/ My New Learning (p. 101) The Character and Me (p. 102)	Genre Study—Personal Narratives (p. 102) Sensible Strategies for Struggling Readers: Series Books (p. 104) Targeting Talented Readers: Studying Series Books (p. 106)
November & December: Predicting in Real and Make-Believe Stories	Pause, Think, and Check for Understanding—Foundation Lesson (p. 112) Integrating the Decoding Strategies—Foundation Lesson (p. 113) Integrating the Decoding Strategies—Follow-Up Lesson (p. 114)	Predicting—Peek & Predict (p. 116) Preview & Predict: Read-Aloud/Think-Aloud—Foundation Lesson (p. 116) Preview & Predict: Read-Aloud/Think-Together—Follow-Up Lesson (p. 117) Using Visual Information to Set Purpose for Reading and Predicting (p. 119) Using Schema and Connections to Predict (p. 120)	Verbs—Shades of Meaning (p. 122) Adjectives—Making Connections (p. 122) Read-Alouds With Rich Vocabulary (p. 123) **Words Introduced:** *capture, concoction, contemplate, craving, critters, eerie, fetched, parlor, scrumptious*	Creating Character Webs (p. 124) Noticing the Beginning, Middle, and End (p. 125) Writing a Book Blurb (p. 126)	Genre Study—Real and Make-Believe Stories (p. 127) Sensible Strategies for Struggling Readers: The Appeal of Graphic Novels (p. 129) Targeting Talented Readers: Let's Have a Debate! (p. 130)
January: Retelling, Comparing, and Contrasting Stories	Self-Monitoring at the Word Level (p. 137) Self-Monitoring—Present- and Past-Tense Verbs (p. 138)	Let's Retell a Story: Read-Aloud/Think-Aloud—Foundation Lesson (p. 139) Let's Retell a Story: Read-Aloud/Think-Together—Follow-Up Lesson (p. 140) Using Key Vocabulary to Sequence, Predict, and Retell (p. 140) Text-to-Text Connections: Read-Aloud/Think-Aloud—Foundation Lesson (p. 142) Text-to-Text Connections: Read-Aloud/Think-Together—Follow-Up Lesson (p. 143)	Learning About Synonyms (p. 146) Learning About Antonyms—Antonym Memory Game (p. 147) Read-Alouds With Rich Vocabulary (p. 148) **Words Introduced:** *exhausted, filthy, nimble, rascal, refreshed, sensitive, sympathetic, unison, useless*	Comparing/ Contrasting Texts (p. 148) Write a Book Review (p. 149)	Genre Study—Traditional Tales (p. 150) Sensible Strategies for Struggling Readers: Take-Home Book Club (p. 151) Targeting Talented Readers: Digital Retelling (p. 152)

MINI-LESSON MENU

	Self-Monitoring/ Decoding Strategy Mini-Lessons	Comprehension Strategy Mini-Lesson	Vocabulary-Building Activities	Reading Response Mini-Lessons	Genre Study: Meeting the Needs of ALL Learners
February: Questioning and Determining Importance to Understand Biographies	Look for Prefixes—Foundation Lesson (p. 159) Look for Prefixes—Follow-Up Lesson (p. 160)	Questioning Read-Aloud/Think-Aloud—Foundation Lesson (p. 161) Questioning Read-Aloud/Think-Together Follow-Up Lesson (p. 162) Questioning the Writer (p. 163) Determining Importance in Biographies: Read-Aloud/Think-Aloud—Foundation Lesson (p. 167) Determining Importance in Biographies: Read-Aloud/Think-Together—Follow-Up Lesson (p. 167) Asking Questions to Determine Important Information (p. 168)	Studying Root Words (p. 170) Studying Suffixes (p. 170) Read-Alouds With Rich Vocabulary (p. 171) **Words Introduced:** *debated, essentials, eventually, fumbling, glamorous, persuade, prevail, resourceful, respectable*	Asking Questions Before, During, and After Reading (p. 173) Creating a Time Line (p. 172)	Genre Study—Biographies (p. 173) Sensible Strategies for Struggling Readers: Pockets, Passwords, and Sticky Notes (p. 175) Targeting Talented Readers: Creating a Visual Time Line (p. 176)
March: Visualizing and Inferring to Peek Into Poetry	Understanding Multiple-Meaning Words—Foundation Lesson (p. 181) Understanding Multiple-Meaning Words—Follow-Up Lesson (p. 182)	Mental Images—Mind Music (p. 183) Mental Images—Using Senses to Describe (p. 183) Mental Images—Poetry (p. 184) Predicting vs. Inferring (p. 185) Using Schema, Connections, and Mental Images to Infer Big Ideas (p. 186)	Homophones—Foundation Lesson (p. 188) Homophones—Follow-Up Lesson (p. 189) Read-Alouds With Rich Vocabulary (p. 189) **Words Introduced:** *bellowed, clearing, dense, furiously, meandered, nonsense, piercing, splendid, still*	Using Poetry as a Response to Reading (p. 190) Inferring With Poetry—Revising Our Thinking (p. 191)	Genre Study—Poetry (p. 192) Sensible Strategies for Struggling Readers: Highlighting Word Endings (p. 194) Targeting Talented Readers: Puzzling Poetry Books (p. 194)
April & May: Questioning and Determining Importance to Navigate Nonfiction	Using Visual Information to Pause, Think, and Check for Understanding (p. 200)	Questioning in Nonfiction Read-Aloud/Think-Aloud—Foundation Lesson (p. 201) Questioning in Nonfiction Read-Aloud/Think-Together Follow-Up Lesson (p. 203) Determining Importance Using Nonfiction Features—Foundation Lesson (p. 203) Determining Importance Using Nonfiction Features—Follow-Up Lesson (p. 204) Inferring Big Ideas with Earth Day Books (p. 205)	Preview-Predict-Confirm (p. 207) Categorizing Content-Area Words (p. 208) Read-Alouds With Rich Vocabulary (p. 210) **Words Introduced:** *expedition, gumption, lamented, overheard, peered, perched, precisely, reluctantly, revolutionize*	Compile a Fact Web (p. 210) List the Top Ten Facts You Learned (p. 211)	Genre Study—Pairing Fiction and Nonfiction (p. 211) Sensible Strategies for Struggling Readers: Summer Reading List (p. 213) Targeting Talented Readers: Animal Research (p. 214)

CD Resource I.2

Ten Things You Might Choose to Do Before School Begins

1. Mail a letter introducing yourself to your students, along with a questionnaire for children's families (CD Resource I.4). We've used this open-ended questionnaire for years and always get helpful information and insights from our students' families. In addition, their answers may provide some background about your students' interests to help you as you guide them in selecting books for independent reading.

2. Prepare an anecdotal record sheet and/or conferring notebooks (CD Resources 1.10 and 1.11) so you can begin jotting your observations on the very first day of school.

3. Gather a varied collection of books to have at your fingertips so you are ready to read aloud a number of times each day. You will find many recommendations in the pages ahead.

4. Designate a spot for your read-aloud tally. See page 20 for a rationale supporting this practice.

5. Assemble whole-group book bins. See page 54 for book ideas to get you started.

6. Copy Read, Think, and Respond pages (CD Resources 1.2–1.7).

7. Create a comfortable space for young readers to gather together. In this "Place for Learning" they will listen to read-alouds and read, sing, and chant poems found in the pocket chart, displayed on an interactive whiteboard or via an overhead projector or document camera.

8. Collect the materials needed for Explore the W.O.R.L.D. time described on pages 65–70.

9. Charge your digital camera or video camera so you can take photos to display around the room or video clips to view.

10. Purchase a small notebook to record your thinking and reflections. You can organize it by adding sticky tabs labeled with the following categories:
    - Observations
    - Discussions/Charts
    - Books
    - Things to Do
    - Notes From Professional Development Sessions
    - Other

CD Resource I.3

CHAPTER 1

Powerful Reading Instruction

It is midsummer in Illinois. We've been out of school long enough that the hectic days with our students are slowly becoming a distant memory. Every July, we meet to think, reflect, and plan for the upcoming school year. We spend hours creating the "perfect" daily schedule and revisiting all of the lessons that we wanted to teach last year (but ran out of time to complete). We synthesize our shared learning from graduate classes, professional reading, and presentations by leaders in the field, including Debbie Miller, Sharon Taberski, Peter Johnston, Regie Routman, Linda Hoyt, Dick Allington, and many more. Their wise words reaffirm what our research-guided experience has taught us about effective core literacy instruction for young readers. Then we envision all the ways we want to improve our classroom instruction for the upcoming school year. Do you do this too? If so, then you know what comes next . . . WHOOOSH! It's August, you're setting up your room, then the first bell rings and, once again, school begins.

We know from decades of experience that once we meet our kids and jump into the fast-paced routines that characterize primary-grade teaching, our best intentions sometimes get sidetracked and a hint of frustration begins to creep in. You may find yourself in the same boat. To combat this feeling, it is our goal to support you by sharing an extensive compilation of classroom-tested ideas organized in a month-by-month sequence. This suggested sequence is designed to serve as a scaffold to help you design the best reading instruction for the young learners in your classroom.

This is an ideal time to share our unwavering belief that there is neither one right way, nor one professional book or packaged program that will teach a youngster how to read. You are the only one who can meet your students' reading needs, armed with the expertise you gain from engaging in the following practices:

- meaningful, school-embedded, ongoing professional development
- frequent conversations with students
- student-focused collaboration with your colleagues
- professional conversations about books, articles, and other up-to-date information
- honest reflection on your own teaching practices
- rejuvenating time away from school

Therefore, if we had the pleasure of visiting your classroom, we would hope to find this book on your desk among several other professional resources, along with a stack of well-loved picture books, anecdotal notes about your students, some photos of fun times with your family and friends, and all the other essentials that you need to have a successful school year. Equipped with this collection of resources, and the willingness to adjust your plans and thinking based on your conversations with students, you are ready to implement powerful reading instruction.

Packaged programs and professional books don't teach a child how to read—you do!

What to Teach: Balancing Instruction

As you know, there is only so much time in a school day, and with the increased pressure to do more, more, more, it is critical that we make informed decisions about the learning that is taking place in our classrooms. We want kids to leave our classrooms with the ability to think critically, solve problems, and collaborate with others so that they can be successful and self-confident. To meet this goal, we must answer the following questions: How do we make the best decisions about what to teach to our young readers? What are the essential skills that students need in order to be

> ## TYPES OF MINI-LESSONS
>
> **Inspiring and Motivating:** Helping Readers to Love Books!
>
> **Self-Monitoring/Decoding Strategies:** Helping Readers Figure Out Unknown Words
>
> **Comprehension Strategies:** Helping Readers to Read and Think at the Same Time
>
> **Fluency Fun:** Helping Readers Read With Style
>
> **Vocabulary Development:** Helping Readers Expand Their Vocabulary and Uncover Word Meanings
>
> **Reading Response:** Helping Readers Organize and Transform Thinking Into Conversations and Writing
>
> **Genre Awareness:** Helping Readers Understand Different Types of Books

proficient, interested readers? In this chapter, we will draw from our research-guided teaching experience, coupled with the thinking of other experts, to answer those questions. To ensure that the lessons and ideas included in the remaining chapters reflect the essential aspects of literacy instruction, we will also weave in the K–2 standards that are outlined in the Common Core State Standards (CCSS) for English Language Arts (NGA Center/CCSSO, 2010) and the learning and innovation skills found in the *Framework for 21st Century Learning* (Partnership for 21st Century Skills, 2009).

INSPIRING AND MOTIVATING: HELPING READERS TO LOVE BOOKS!

It seems so simple: teach students to love books. Think back for a moment. When was the last time you went to a professional development session that was focused on nurturing the *desire* to read or an RtI problem-solving meeting where you discussed the interventions you could implement to help a struggling reader find joy in the written word? In our conversations with teachers across the country, we hear more and more that the affective side of reading is being ignored. We can't let this happen. What is the point of teaching a child how to read if

You may be the one teacher who will instill the love of reading.

he or she is never going to pick up a book? In *Igniting a Passion for Reading* (2009), Steven Layne urges us to "raise our voices in faculty meetings . . . and at parent nights, and educate people about aliteracy" (p. 13). Then, in our classrooms, carve out time to savor, promote, and celebrate books. You may be the one teacher who will instill the love of reading in a child for the rest of his or her life. How can you pass up that chance?

SELF-MONITORING/DECODING STRATEGIES: HELPING READERS FIGURE OUT UNKNOWN WORDS

Of course, students who love books are going to want to read books. Part of our role as teachers of young readers is to guide students to discover an array of strategies that they can flexibly apply as they read for meaning and figure out tricky or unknown words. As with all the instruction that we will discuss in this section, decoding strategy instruction can occur in targeted whole-group mini-lessons, while guiding readers during small-group or independent reading conferences, or as a thread that runs through conversations that occur while you and your students are reading aloud, thinking about, and enjoying books together. It only takes an extra second or two to stop and articulate your thinking when you've made a reading miscue. For example, let's say while you are reading aloud you accidently skip a page. Instead of automatically going back to read the page you skipped, you might stop and say, "Wait! This isn't making sense, is it, girls and boys? I need to stop and figure out why. Oh, look, I've skipped a page, let's go back and read that page to see if it makes more sense—that's what readers do!" In each chapter that follows, we've included mini-lessons for raising students' awareness of the importance of self-monitoring and lessons that key in on the specific decoding strategies listed below.

Students who love books are going to want to read books.

You'll notice that the strategy "Pause, Think, and Check for Understanding" appears as both a self-monitoring/decoding strategy and a comprehension strategy. Our thinking behind placing the strategy on both lists is that we want to continually remind readers to monitor their comprehension, whether it be at the word level when they are using picture clues and beginning sounds to figure out an unknown word, at the sentence level as they use context to determine the meaning of a word, or the text level, when they are reading to understand the big idea, lesson, or moral of the story.

To provide students with a visual reminder of each decoding strategy, we've included a resource called a Decoding Strategy Wheel (CD Resource 2.4). We enlarge this wheel and display it near our meeting area so that we can refer to it as we teach the self-monitoring/decoding strategy mini-lessons. You can also display it on your whiteboard using IWB_Decoding_Wheel (see CD). You can also make small copies for students to keep in their individual book boxes or to use as you guide readers in small groups. Another collection of resources that you may find helpful when teaching the strategies are the decoding strategy songs. For each decoding strategy you will find a strategy song. We wrote these songs to highlight the key ideas that readers need to remember about the strategy. In the preparation section of the mini-lessons, we've reminded you to locate and/or make copies of the song. We usually begin the mini-lesson by singing the song, and then review the song at the end of the lesson. In addition, we give students their own copy of the song to place in their poetry notebooks. Each song is written to a familiar tune so that you can easily sing it with your students. To assist you in singing, the tunes are also included on the CD. Be sure to practice before introducing the songs to your students!

SELF-MONITORING/ DECODING STRATEGIES

Use Picture Clues

Get Your Mouth Ready

Skip and Read Through

Reread

Look Through the Word for Sounds You Know

Look for Chunks

Pause, Think, and Check for Understanding

> # MINI-LESSON COMPONENTS
>
> You will notice that the mini-lessons found in this book contain the following components. Here we explain the purpose of each component.
>
> **Preparation:** Consult this section while creating your lesson plans to find any books or materials you may need to gather in order to do the mini-lesson. When possible, we've provided multiple book titles for the mini-lesson. You can use the additional titles to teach the same mini-lesson at a different grade level, to teach a follow-up lesson, or for guiding readers in small groups.
>
> **Explanation:** The explanation that appears in this section is for you, not for your students. We will give you a glimpse into our thinking by answering the key questions: "What is the point of this mini-lesson?" and "What do I want my students to learn from it?"
>
> **Demonstration:** A few tips for teacher modeling, including language and/or questions to spark readers' thinking, are included in the demonstration portion of the lesson.
>
> **Invitation:** Students need time to apply what they have learned in mini-lessons with a partner, in a small group, or during independent reading. To this end, each mini-lesson concludes with an invitation. We write this invitation in kid-friendly language to help guide your teaching.

COMPREHENSION STRATEGIES: HELPING READERS TO READ AND THINK AT THE SAME TIME

Reading is a meaning-making process. We're guessing that you have met students who are skilled word callers, but when you ask them to have a conversation about what they just finished reading you realize that they are not comprehending the meaning of the text. When it comes to comprehension instruction, the works of Ellin Keane, Stephanie Harvey, Ann Goudvis, and Debbie Miller have steered us in the right direction. Proficient readers use strategies flexibly and interactively. Although we believe it may be helpful for some young readers to have the concept of the strategy introduced in isolation, it is also important that they see how that strategy connects to the others they are using. This understanding comes through teacher modeling when reading aloud and thinking aloud and also by giving descriptive feedback during one-on-one conferences or while guiding readers in small groups. To support you in this teaching, we've put together a collection of mini-lessons that target the comprehension strategies listed on page 14, so that children can meet the standard of comprehending increasingly complex fiction and informational text (NGA Center/CCSSO, 2010). To provide students with a visual reminder of each comprehension strategy, we've included a resource called a Comprehension Strategy Wheel (CD Resource 3.5). We enlarge this wheel and display it near our meeting area so that we can refer to it as we teach the comprehension strategy mini-lessons. You can also display it on your whiteboard using IWB_Comp_Wheel (see CD). You can also make small copies for students to keep in their individual book boxes or to use as you guide readers in small groups. Another collection of resources that you may find helpful when teaching the strategies are the comprehension strategy songs. For each comprehension strategy, you will find a strategy song. We wrote these songs to highlight the key ideas that readers need to remember about the strategy. In the preparation section of the mini-lessons, we've reminded you to locate and/or make copies of the song. We usually begin the mini-lesson by singing the song, and then review the song at the end of the lesson. In addition, we give students their own copy of the song to place in their poetry notebooks. Each song is written to a familiar tune so that you can easily sing it with your students; the tunes are included on the CD.

Proficient readers use strategies flexibly and interactively.

FLUENCY FUN: HELPING READERS READ WITH STYLE

Not only do we want students to love reading, we also want them to be good at it. One of our goals for young readers is for them to be able to read fluently. Fluent readers can focus on the meaning of what they read because they are effortlessly decoding words that they understand. They read connected text at a conversational rate, accurately and effortlessly using the right phrasing and expression while drawing the intended meaning from that text. Children who do not read fluently are at a disadvantage because their comprehension suffers. For them, reading is a labor-intensive process as they sound out one word at a time (Walther & Fuhler, 2010). To help you boost students' fluency in a meaningful and joyful way, we've included a feature in each chapter called Fluency Fun that offers a quick suggestion for working on fluency with your students.

COMPREHENSION STRATEGIES

Activate, Build, and Change Your Schema

Use Your Schema to Make Text-to-Self Connections

Think About Books You've Read to Make Text-to-Text Connections

Use Your Schema and Make Connections to Predict

Make Mental Images as You Read

Use Your Schema and Mental Images to Infer the Author's Meaning or Big Idea

Ask Questions Before, During, and After Reading

Answer Questions to Determine Important Information

Synthesize New Understandings

Pause, Think, and Check for Understanding

VOCABULARY DEVELOPMENT: HELPING READERS EXPAND THEIR VOCABULARY AND UNCOVER WORD MEANINGS

Remember the readers we talked about a moment ago—those who are adept at reading the words but are lacking deep understanding of what the words mean? This is where vocabulary development plays an important role. If you create a classroom environment where you and your students marvel at words, learners will soon be pondering aloud, "I wonder what that word means?" In addition to the types of mini-lessons found in chapters 3–8 that are listed on this page, targeting the keys to vocabulary development and promoting word wonder,

Create a classroom where students marvel at words.

we've included a chart in chapters 2–8 entitled "Read-Alouds With Rich Vocabulary," showcasing picture books with rich vocabulary. These books are ideal for an activity dubbed "Three Read-Aloud Words" by renowned literacy expert Patricia Cunningham (2009b). Cunningham suggests targeting three words from one read-aloud selection each week. She defines read-aloud words as "Goldilocks" words—words that are neither "too easy" nor uncommon, obscure or "too hard," but rather words that are generally known or "just right." Once you've selected the target words, follow the lesson sequence she's created.

1. Read the text aloud for pleasure.
2. Show the target words to your students on index cards, one at a time. Teach your students to pronounce each word, but ask them not to share the meanings. This way you can demonstrate the strategies that readers use to acquire new word meanings during reading. Place the words where your students can see them.

KEYS TO VOCABULARY DEVELOPMENT

Read and Discuss Books That Contain Rich Vocabulary

Predict Word Meanings Based on Picture Clues

Predict Word Meanings Based on Context Clues

Study Compound Words

Learn About Synonyms and Antonyms

Study Common Prefixes, Suffixes, and Root Words

Understand Figurative Language

Understand Multiple-Meaning Words

Understand the Language of Informational Writing

3. Reread the text and invite your listeners to yell "STOP!" when they hear a target word. At this point, stop reading and demonstrate for your readers how you use the context, illustrations, and word parts to figure out and explain the meaning of that particular word. Continue with the two other words.

4. After reading, ask questions to help readers connect the words to their own experience.

5. The next day, reread the text and ask students to retell the text to a partner using the target vocabulary words.

6. Display the words in your classroom next to the cover of the book or poem. Then, challenge students to be on the lookout for these words. Place a tally mark next to each word that a student reads, hears, or notices in print. Your challenge is to also try to use these words in your conversations throughout the week.

> ### ASSESSMENT TIP: ASSESS VOCABULARY KNOWLEDGE
>
> When you are administering an individual reading inventory or a running record, consider jotting a few challenging words from the text at the bottom of your recording sheet. Once the students have finished reading, ask them what each word means and record their answers. This is helpful information to share with parents and to guide your reading conferences or small-group teaching.

To help get you started with this in your classroom, the Read Alouds With Rich Vocabulary chart in each of chapters 2–8 lists three picture books and for each book highlights three "Goldilocks" words along with their kid-friendly definitions. Enjoy adding this vocabulary-building strategy to your weekly classroom routines.

READING RESPONSE: HELPING READERS ORGANIZE AND TRANSFORM THINKING INTO CONVERSATIONS AND WRITING

In a recent report published by the Alliance for Excellent Education (Graham & Hebert, 2010), research confirmed that writing is an effective tool for improving students' reading ability and that writing about the texts they read enhances their comprehension. Asking our youngest readers to put their thinking into pictures or written words "engages students, extends thinking, deepens understanding, and energizes the meaning-making process" (Knipper & Duggan, 2006). When students are invited to respond to their learning, they make connections between new and known understandings, utilize recently acquired vocabulary, and articulate their latest knowledge. In short, they are writing to learn. Writing to learn differs from learning to write in the following ways: writing to learn serves as a catalyst for future

Writing about the texts they're reading enhances students' comprehension.

learning and meaning-making and also provides an opportunity for students to recall, clarify, and question what they've learned (Knipper & Duggan, 2006). To guide you in helping students as they clarify their thinking by writing, we've included reading response ideas in each chapter. To build students' repertoire of reading response options, we will provide one morning message and two mini-lessons in each chapter that follows. If you choose, you can ask students to record their responses in their Read, Think, and Respond Book, described on page 18.

GENRE AWARENESS: HELPING READERS UNDERSTAND DIFFERENT TYPES OF BOOKS

We all know about the importance of eating a balanced diet. The same theory holds true for readers. Readers need a balanced diet of books from a variety of genres and perspectives. As you read aloud, discuss, and study different genres, you are helping students attain the following goals:

- expand their background knowledge about different types of text
- apply their knowledge of different genres to notice the similarities and differences among text types

> ### BOOK ORGANIZATION TIP: ENTER YOUR BOOKS INTO AN ONLINE DATABASE
>
> To keep the books that we use for mini-lessons organized, we enter them into an online database. Our preferred database is LibraryThing.com, where you can tag each book with various categories and genres. LibraryThing also sells an inexpensive barcode reader, so all you have to do is scan the back of the book, and zip! It's in the database.

- understand how authors choose to write different types of text to match their specific purpose
- analyze the structures of various text types and how those structures support the reader
- compare and contrast texts and explain their similarities and differences
- critique texts, state their opinion about each text, and support that opinion with evidence from the text

So, when you are selecting books to read aloud, you want to keep in mind the various genres

Readers need a balanced diet of books from a variety of genres and perspectives.

READ, THINK, AND RESPOND BOOK

On the CD, you will find Resources 1.1–1.7 for students to use as they read, think, and respond. You can choose to organize these pages in the following ways:

- Make a few copies of each page and staple or bind them all together in a booklet for students to use throughout the year. Don't forget to number the pages so that students can locate a particular page! The advantage of having all the pages in one booklet is that if you have students date their responses, you can see the growth over time from their first response to their last.
- Make copies to store in an easy-to-access spot in your classroom.
- If copy paper is scarce in your school, use the files on the enclosed CD to project the documents on an interactive whiteboard, and then teach students how to create their own pages in a spiral notebook.

CD Resource 1.1: Read, Think, Respond Book Cover

Types of Reproducible Pages	Possible Reading Response Ideas
Lined Pages (CD Resource 1.2)	• Write a riddle about your favorite character (page 110) • Write a book blurb (page 126) • Write a book review (page 149) • Compose a poem about the book (page 190)
H-Chart (CD Resource 1.3)	• Compare and contrast adventures and experiences of characters • Compare and contrast the character and the reader (page 102) • Compare and contrast two versions of the same story by different authors or from different cultures (page 148) • Compare and contrast the two key points presented in two informational books on the same topic
Web (CD Resource 1.4)	• Create a character web (page 124) • Create a questioning web • Compile an informational text fact web (page 210)
Story Map Page (CD Resource 1.5)	• Identify and describe characters, setting, and major events in a story
Two-Column Notes (CD Resource 1.6)	• Record schema before reading a nonfiction book and new learning after reading (page 101)
Three-Column Notes (CD Resource 1.7)	• Notice the beginning, middle, and end of a story (page 125) • Ask questions before, during, and after reading (page 172)
Blank Pages	• Create a sticky note parking lot (a place for students to store completed sticky notes) • Create a timeline (pages 156 and 173)

from which you can choose. In each chapter that follows, Part 3 focuses on genre studies. We spotlight the following genres: read-aloud favorites for the beginning of the school year, personal narrative, real and make-believe stories, traditional tales, biographies, poetry, and pairing fiction and nonfiction books. Keep the goals listed above in mind as you read, think, and talk about the books in each genre study.

How to Teach: Children's Literature at the Heart of Powerful Reading Instruction

The more we teach and interact with young learners, the more we realize that effective literacy instruction is all about the books you choose to share with your students. Whether you are selecting a book to spotlight a comprehension strategy or searching your shelves for yet another book about fishing to appeal to a fan of the outdoors, your classroom library is the key to powerful reading instruction.

One of our favorite professional development activities is spending time with our colleagues reading, reviewing, and discussing children's books.

Book enthusiasts, like us, are always searching for books that will spark discussions, open windows to other places and times, and reflect the students in our classroom, because we know that "one of the best measures of how we honor students' cultures and backgrounds is the breadth of literature we read aloud to them and make available in the classroom" (Routman, 2008, p. 10). With these goals in mind, we have scoured the shelves in libraries and at our favorite independent bookstore to find the best books for you to read with your students and add to your own classroom library. In fact, one of our favorite professional development activities is spending time with our colleagues reading, reviewing, and discussing children's books! The results of our book quests are found in the charts in each chapter. In addition to the book lists for each

> **CHILDREN'S LITERATURE IS ESSENTIAL FOR ELLs**
>
> ELLs benefit when well-chosen books are at the heart of your teaching, because literature serves as a springboard for the following authentic learning opportunities:
> - Teaching vocabulary and other nuances of the English language
> - Listening to or reading language patterns that speakers use in different settings
> - Making connections to other cultures
> - Analyzing, discussing, and writing about topics from different cultural points of view
>
> (Richard-Amato, 2003)

genre, we've included lists of picture books to inspire young readers, stories for readers and writers, read-alouds for the winter months, and our favorite biographies, poetry collections, and nonfiction books.

SHARING RICH READ-ALOUD EXPERIENCES

In our classrooms, read-aloud time is a priority. It is the foundation for everything else we do with children. If your school is like ours, you are probably collecting quite a bit of reading-related assessment data. A few years ago, we decided to collect our own classroom-based data to reflect the rich experiences our students were having with books. That was the year we created the read-aloud tally. To create the tally, we make a mark for each time we sit down to read, whether it be a book, a chapter, a part of a book, and so on. As you can see from the photos, the children in Maria's classroom heard 573 read-alouds during the 2008–2009 school year and 630 the following year. Yes, that is about five read-aloud experiences each day. Now, if you're thinking "I don't have time for that many read-alouds," think again. As Regie Routman (2008) reminds us, "Literature is one of the most powerful ways we educators can connect to our students" (p. 10). Along with helping us bond with our students, read-aloud experiences have all of the benefits enumerated on page 21.

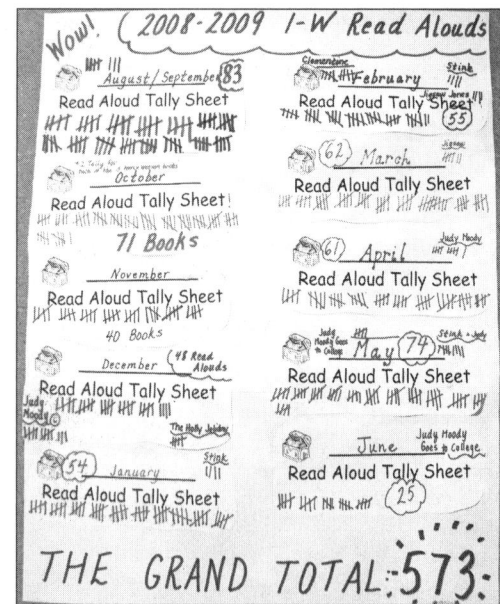
Collect classroom-based data by tallying your read aloud experiences.

Make read-aloud time a priority.

WHY READ ALOUD?

- Fosters a strong sense of community
- Builds a shared textual lineage—a wealth of reading experiences from which to draw when reading, writing, and thinking about other texts and real-world situations
- Demonstrates how books work
- Provides a catalyst for rich discussions
- Models how proficient readers apply strategies, monitor comprehension, and read with fluency and expression
- Offers children opportunities to recognize and identify how characters are feeling—to empathize with others—in order to better understand and express their own feelings
- Helps ELLs hear the nuances of the English language, including intonation, pauses, rhythm, and pronunciation. In addition, they hear how the inflection of our voice, our tone, or our phrasing can change the meaning of a word or phrase.

TIPS FOR DESIGNING A CLASSROOM LIBRARY THAT MEETS THE NEEDS OF ELLs

When you purposefully seek out books about characters from different cultural backgrounds or those written by authors who write books from their own cultural perspective, you are providing all students with a broader worldview and sending the message to ELLs that their experiences are an important part of learning in your classroom.

- Gather fiction and nonfiction books that are culturally relevant to your ELLs.
- Provide a balance between "just right" leveled books and non-leveled, high-interest, more challenging texts so that ELLs can develop and extend their reading skills.
- Include in book baskets books written by authors from different backgrounds. For example, in a poetry basket you might include poetry books written by Pat Mora, Francisco X. Alarcón, Nikki Grimes, Janet Wong, and Joseph Bruchac.

(Celic, 2009)

FACILITATING COMPREHENSION CONVERSATIONS

If you have not read the book *Choice Words* by Peter Johnston (2004), we recommend it as another book to add to your professional reading list. Peter wisely reminds us that the way we converse with students makes a crucial difference. In his words, "Talk is the central tool of [teachers'] trade. With it they mediate children's activity and experience, and help them make sense of learning, literacy, life, and themselves" (p. 4). We define a comprehension conversation as an interactive discussion about a piece of text that is best sparked by posing higher-level questions and inviting students to listen to and respond to their peers' thoughts and ideas. The purpose is to provide students frequent opportunities to develop deeper understanding of texts.

Comprehension conversations can occur during read-aloud and/or while guiding readers independently or in small groups. They can also be used to assess students' comprehension after a running record. For beginning readers, comprehension conversations during read-aloud challenge them to listen to and think about texts more complex than those that they can read independently. To facilitate comprehension conversations, reflect on the type of questions you are posing and the way you respond when students share their thinking. We've spent a lot of time over the past few years noticing and adjusting the language that we use with our students when we are conversing about their thinking. In chapters 3–8, we've included a chart labeled Read-Alouds to Spark Comprehension Conversations, which includes questions to help guide you as you discuss specific books that we have chosen because of their complexity, in the qualitative measures of text complexity outlined by the Common Core State Standards (NGA Center/CCSSO, 2010). In addition, we've carefully crafted the questions to guide readers to integrate multiple comprehension strategies and also engage in the type of thinking necessary to attain the standards put forth in the Common Core. Use these sample texts and questions as a springboard to more comprehension conversations!

How to Teach: Releasing Responsibility

To review, we've outlined the components of powerful reading instruction that we will address in this book, including creating book lovers, self-monitoring/decoding strategy instruction, comprehension strategy instruction, vocabulary development, reading response, and genre awareness. We've spotlighted the importance of children's literature and given you a few tips for collecting and organizing books for your classroom library, reading aloud, and facilitating comprehension conversations. As we continue to map out effective core literacy instruction, let's think about *how* we teach young readers. A time-tested technique for teaching is the gradual release of responsibility approach (Harvey & Goudvis, 2000; Miller, 2002), or optimal learning model (Routman, 2003). When we use the gradual release of responsibility approach during our reading instruction, we provide students with the explicit teaching, modeling, and continuous support they need to learn and apply new reading skills and strategies. As we nudge our readers along on the road toward independence, we carefully plan our instruction to scaffold their learning. Applying the gradual release of responsibility approach to our reading instruction simply makes sense. Therefore, we'll

> ## THE LANGUAGE OF THINKING ALOUD
>
> - That's interesting!
> - I'm noticing . . .
> - I'm thinking . . .
> - I'm wondering . . .
> - What kind of text this is? Have I read something like this before?
> - From reading the title, the back cover blurb, and looking at the illustrations, I predict . . .
> - When I read that, it reminded me of . . .
> - This part makes me feel . . .
> - I'm wondering why [the character] did that.
> - Wait! This isn't making sense. What should I do?
> - Let me rethink this . . .
>
> (Routman, 2003; Johnston, 2004)

quickly discuss the following stages to releasing responsibility:

- Demonstrating by Reading Aloud/Thinking Aloud
- Demonstrating by Reading Aloud/Thinking Together
- Guiding Readers

DEMONSTRATING BY READING ALOUD/ THINKING ALOUD

The first step to releasing responsibility to students is letting students have a peek inside your head to discover how a proficient reader thinks. Observing what you do when you encounter difficulty is a powerful teaching moment. To think aloud while reading, stop periodically to unpack your thought process. It is wise to inform students when you are thinking aloud, or they will immediately want to share their answers to your questions. If you've read the Mercy Watson books by Kate DiCamillo, you've met Officer Tomilello, who always asks himself questions and then answers himself. So we tell our listeners, "We are thinking like Officer Tomilello right now; we will be asking ourselves questions and then answering them. If we need your help, we'll let you know!" Throughout this book, we've included "Foundation Lessons"—lessons in which you will be thinking aloud to demonstrate a specific skill or strategy. Certainly, every read-aloud provides an occasion to do a quick think-aloud. See the sidebar on page 22 for some think-aloud phrases to add to language you already use.

THE LANGUAGE OF THINKING TOGETHER

- What do you already know about this topic/author/type of text?
- What do you notice? Any patterns or things that surprise you?
- What are you thinking right now? Why?
- What do you think might happen next? Why do you think this?
- What are you wondering?
- What do you think the character is thinking right now?
- How do you think [character] feels about that? Have any of you had that sort of feeling?
- What kind of text is this? Have you read any other texts like this? What is a different text on the same theme? Why do you think the author wrote this text?
- How are _____ books different from _____ books?
- Who else do you think might like this book?

THE LANGUAGE OF RESPONDING TO STUDENTS' THINKING

- Interesting! Hmmmm! Wow!
- Let's see if I've got this right.
- Can anyone add to [his or her] thinking?
- Would you agree with that? Why/why not?
- Do you have the same thinking, or is your thinking different? Why?
- Can you say more about that?
- Thanks for straightening me out!
- Wow! I never thought about it like that before!
- How did you know that?
- Are there any other ways to think about that?

(Johnston, 2004)

DEMONSTRATING BY READING ALOUD/THINKING TOGETHER

After you have demonstrated your thought processes by reading aloud and thinking aloud, invite students to apply the reading skill or strategy in guided situations. Reading aloud and thinking together in a shared format is one way to guide readers either in whole-class mini-lessons or in small groups. Again, the depth of your conversation is paramount to making this a productive teaching context. To that end, we've provided more language in the sidebar on page 23.

GUIDING READERS

You'll notice that we use the term "guiding readers" rather than teaching "guided reading." Over the years, with the help of reading experts like Debbie Miller, Sharon Taberski, and Regie Routman, we have broadened our definition of guided reading. We meet with readers in different grouping structures and for different purposes, depending on our students' needs. We know that to cement understanding, students benefit from the challenge of applying newly learned strategies to a new genre or effectively using the strategy with a more challenging text (Harvey, 2002). This is one of the many purposes for guiding readers. Fortunately, we have not been mandated to meet with every group every day, so we scaffold and support our readers in various ways. Our definition is echoed by Regie Routman when she says, "I define guided reading as any learning context in which the teacher guides one or more students through some aspect of the reading process. . . . *The teacher builds on students' strengths and demonstrates whatever is necessary to move the child toward independence.* Independence is the end goal, not meeting with a group" (2008, p. 62). If independence is your end goal, use your formative assessment tools to look at each child to determine what type of support he or she needs to move toward understanding. For one child this might mean meeting one on one for three minutes each day to build her reading skills and confidence. Other children might benefit from working with you and a small group of supportive peers to build conversational skills along with digging deeper into texts. Guiding readers is not a "one size fits all" venture. It evolves all year as your students grow and change. That's what makes it so challenging!

Guiding readers is not a "one size fits all" venture.

When to Teach: Making Every Minute Count

Although we have many school-mandated scheduling requirements, we work around them to design our daily schedule to meet the needs of our readers. As we do this, we think about how we can surround our core literacy instruction to provide young learners with multiple opportunities across our teaching day to increase the amount of time they spend engaged in real reading and writing. The following rich literacy experiences occur in a "deliberate environment that invites, nurtures, and sustains immersion in stories and characters, and says every day of every school year, Welcome to the [reading] zone" (Atwell, 2007, p. 25). To that end, we begin each day with an independent reading time lasting anywhere from 10 to 20 minutes. This gives us the opportunity to work with a few of our striving readers each morning. Most of the time, this means we grab the child's conferring notebook and listen to him or her read while we sort through papers or tackle the other morning jobs. While listening, we can give students descriptive feedback by noticing the strategies they are using or simply chat with them about their favorite part. Just think, if you listen to a child read for even two minutes each day, multiplied by the roughly 175 days in a school year, that adds up to five hours of extra instruction. Certainly, that is making every minute count! In this section, we will unpack three simple, yet powerful practices that surround our core literacy instruction, and then share our thoughts about the cornerstone of reading instruction, the reading workshop.

MORNING MESSAGE, POETRY POWER, AND MORNING READ-ALOUD

We are continually searching for ways to carve out more time for rich literacy instruction. Many of our professional conversations revolve around designing our literacy instruction so that students have, as Debbie Miller states, "That luscious feeling of endless time" (2008, p. 106). With this goal in mind, we believe that literacy instruction has to be a thread that runs throughout the day. Of course, the focus of this book will be on the reading workshop and guiding readers, but that isn't the only time our students are engaged in reading-related thinking. As you can see in the sample daily schedule on page 26, once students have completed their first independent reading time, we continue our day with three powerful practices: the morning message, poetry power, and, of course, our first read-aloud experience of the day. Let's take a quick look at each of these teaching practices.

Morning Message

In our book *Month-by-Month Trait-Based Writing Instruction* (Walther & Phillips, 2009), we demonstrate the advantages of using a morning message as a time-efficient way to teach young writers. Wise teachers know that every minute counts and look for ways to make connections among different literacy strategies. The morning message time offers that opportunity. Over the years, we've expanded our definition of a morning message. A traditional definition of the morning message is a short, focused piece of text that you write to your students or with your students, or you have them write to each other with the focus on

SAMPLE DAILY SCHEDULE					
	MONDAY	TUESDAY	WEDNESDAY	THURSDAY	FRIDAY
8:50–9:10	Independent Reading	Independent Reading	Independent Reading	Independent Reading	Independent Reading
9:10–9:35	Morning Message, Poetry Power, Read-Aloud	Morning Message, Poetry Power, Read-Aloud	Morning Message, Poetry Power, Read-Aloud	Morning Message, Poetry Power, Read-Aloud	Morning Message, Poetry Power, Read-Aloud
9:35–10:05	Journal	Word Study	Journal	Journal	Journal
10:05–10:40	Word Study	Writing Workshop	Word Study	Reading Workshop Mini-Lesson	Reading Workshop Mini-Lesson
10:45–11:20	LUNCH/RECESS	LUNCH/RECESS	LUNCH/RECESS	LUNCH/RECESS	LUNCH/RECESS
11:30–12:10	Reading Workshop Mini-Lesson	Reading Workshop Mini-Lesson	Writing Workshop	Writing Workshop	Writing Workshop
12:10–12:55 Intervention Block	Reading Workshop Read-Aloud/Reading Zone Guiding Readers/ Explore W.O.R.L.D.	Reading Workshop Read-Aloud/Reading Zone Guiding Readers/ Explore W.O.R.L.D.	Reading Workshop Read-Aloud/Reading Zone Guiding Readers/ Explore W.O.R.L.D.	Reading Workshop Read-Aloud/Reading Zone Guiding Readers/ Explore W.O.R.L.D.	Reading Workshop Read-Aloud/Reading Zone Guiding Readers/ Explore W.O.R.L.D.
1:00–1:25	P.E.	Music	Art	Word Study	Music
1:25–1:50	SNACK, Calendar, Thinking Journal, MATH	SNACK, Calendar, Thinking Journal, MATH		P.E.	P.E.
1:55–2:30			SNACK, Calendar, Thinking Journal, MATH	SNACK, Calendar, Thinking Journal, MATH	Catch-Up Time
2:30–2:45	RECESS	RECESS	RECESS	RECESS	RECESS
2:45–3:20	Science/ Social Studies	Science/ Social Studies	Science/ Social Studies	Science/ Social Studies	Catch-up Time

writing instruction. We've found that we can also use morning message time to introduce or review literacy skills, strategies, or concepts. For that reason, view the messages in this book as versatile lessons that you can also use with your striving readers. Although we always begin our day with a whole-class morning message, messages are also quick, engaging, and an ideal way to begin a small-group lesson. They also serve as ready-to-use lessons that paraprofessionals (if you are lucky enough to have them in your building) can do with students to enrich or review skills and content. When you begin thinking this way, the possibilities are endless!

As you will see when you browse through the message ideas in the book, you can use this time to focus on self-monitoring at the word level, demonstrate the use of a reading strategy, highlight a vocabulary word or two, or model a way to respond to a text. But, more important, if you choose to gather

A MORNING MESSAGE . . .

- models writing every day.
- creates opportunities for literacy-related conversations.
- provides time to introduce or review concepts.
- strengthens connections between reading and writing instruction.
- encourages students to notice and name the conventions of language.
- incorporates literacy skills and strategies in an authentic, time-efficient manner.
- differentiates instruction for the diverse group of learners who enter our classrooms each year.

students together on the floor to read, think about, talk about, and interact with the information in the message, it is also a daily time to build a strong literacy community. In the sidebar, you will find the reasons we read, write, or discuss a daily message with our students. Be confident that the short amount of time you spend conversing during message time has long-lasting benefits.

Once the message is complete, we read, sing, or chant a poem.

Poetry Power

Poetry is a powerful teaching partner, and working with poems in the pocket chart or on the interactive whiteboard is a daily opportunity to focus on the skills or concepts that boost students' reading. We typically share three to five different poems each week because, over the years, we've collected or written poems to launch many of our lessons. The morning poem is often a seasonal or holiday-related poem. We use poetry to increase students' reading fluency by reading and rereading the poem, and we then zoom in on letters and sounds, chanting rhyming words, clapping the syllables of words, locating and spelling high-frequency words, and so on, which takes no more than five to seven minutes. To extend this experience, you can reproduce the poems and give each child a copy to keep in a three-ring Poetry Binder. Children often choose to read poems during independent reading. Consider recording your students as they read or sing the poems aloud, and then place the recording in the "Be a Listener" center. For struggling readers or ELLs, send the recording home along with the Poetry Binder for extra reading practice. Poetry Power is followed by the first read-aloud of the day.

Use the morning message to make connections among the different literacy strategies you are teaching.

Each child has his or her own Poetry Binder.

Morning Read-Aloud

We choose to set the stage for the day with a morning read-aloud. This read-aloud should take 5–10 minutes at the most. We might select that read-aloud to extend the learning in our morning message, to build background for a topic of study later in the day, to introduce a genre, or to read for fun! To add to your collection of read-aloud books, we've included a chart in chapters 2–8 of ten recently published (except for a few old favorites) Morning Read-Alouds. For each title you will find a summary and a suggested focus or purpose for reading. We strongly believe in the power of read-aloud to boost readers' skills. This is just one of the three to five read-alouds children will hear during a typical day. We've learned that it is helpful to read books, especially long, thought-provoking picture books, in shorter segments. So, if we have two extra minutes at another time during the day, we'll read a few pages of a book. Then we'll leave our readers "in suspense" until we can finish. Now that we've set the stage for the day, we'll share the nuts and bolts of a powerful reading workshop.

READING WORKSHOP

Although we would love to tell you that we have an uninterrupted 90-minute block of time for reading workshop, our reading workshop time is often broken up because of mandated scheduling demands, as you see on the sample schedule below. So, like you, we create the best schedule we can within the parameters we're given. In a perfect world our reading workshop would look something like this:

SAMPLE READING WORKSHOP SCHEDULE

Part 1:
- Read-Aloud/Whole-Group Mini-Lesson (5–15 minutes)—This is the time when we teach the "Focus" and "Follow-up" mini-lessons found in this book. These mini-lessons are often repeated as we guide readers in small groups. To decide which mini-lessons to teach, you will select from the menu of mini-lessons to find those that match the needs of your students and the standards or goals set out by your school.
- Guided Practice (20 minutes)—Students apply what they've learned from the mini-lesson either by responding in writing or while reading independently, with a partner or a small group.
- Share Time (5–10 minutes)—Students share their new learning with the whole group, in a small group, or with a partner.

Part 2:
- Guiding Readers while students read independently and explore the W.O.R.L.D. (45 minutes)—This is the time during which we confer with students individually or guide readers in small groups. The focus of these interactions is based on the needs of the students and is usually a review, reinforcement, or extension of the whole-group mini-lesson. We use the ABC Guide (page 30) and the Conferring Notebook (Resources 1.10 and 1.11) to guide our planning for these interactions. While we are guiding readers, students are involved in engaging independent activities that we've named "Read" and "Explore the W.O.R.L.D."
- In chapters 3–8, you will find mini-lessons to teach self-monitoring/decoding strategies, comprehension strategies, vocabulary, and reading response. In addition, we've included an ABC Guide to support you as you plan your mini-lessons and the focus of your conferences and guided reading groups.

The ABCs of a Powerful Reading Instruction

How do I pick a teaching focus before I meet with a small group to guide readers? How can I quickly select a learning target for a student during a conference? How do I informally assess to monitor whether my students are making progress toward their goals? We've found that the answer to these three questions is as easy as ABC. Let us explain. To streamline our planning for guided reading and reading conferences, we've categorized reading instruction into two ABC Planning Guides that appear as CD Resources 1.8 and 1.9. ABC Planning Guide 1 focuses on the following elements of reading:

- Building Background Knowledge and Beginning Word Knowledge
- Broadening Reading Interests and Improving Strategic Reading Behaviors
- Retelling Fiction and Recounting Nonfiction to Demonstrate Understanding
- Strengthening Word Knowledge

ABC Planning Guide 2 focuses solely on comprehension strategies. We typically use ABC Planning Guide 1 with our students who are at the beginning stages of reading and need to focus on all elements of the reading process and then transition to ABC Planning Guide 2 with our more advanced readers.

Now, why do we call it an ABC Planning Guide? We call it this because when we are sitting down with a child or working with a small group we wanted a time-saving way to streamline our planning and instruction. So, we categorized our interactions into four types: A for an Assessment opportunity, B for a Book chat, C for a Comprehension conversation, and D for an opportunity to focus on decoding/self-monitoring strategies. To further explain each type of interactions see the overview below.

THE ABC GUIDE: AN OVERVIEW	
Assessment Opportunity	As you confer with a student or meet with a small group, you have the opportunity to collect some informal assessment data. As you can see in the left-hand column of ABC Planning Guide 1, you might choose to assess your students' interests or background knowledge, oral reading and fluency, their ability to retell a fiction book or recount an informational text, or their word knowledge. On ABC Planning Guide 2 in the left-hand column, we've provided questions that you can use to assess your students' application of each comprehension strategy. Consider having advanced readers write one of these questions in a reading response notebook and answering it in writing so that you have a record of their growth as thinkers.
Book Chat	The focus for your interaction may be a book chat about book selection or the content and structure of either a fiction title or an informational text. In Book Chat sections of ABC Planning Guides 1 and 2, we've provided you with specific learning targets for guided reading lessons or conferences of this type.
Comprehension Conversations	Comprehension conversations are key to developing students as readers and thinkers. Again, we've listed learning targets in the Comprehension Conversation section of both guides to streamline your instruction and narrow the focus of individual reading conferences.
Decoding/ Self-Monitoring Strategy Coaching	This section appears only in ABC Planning Guide 1. The focus is on word-level reading instruction. Here we've provided learning targets for readers who are still figuring out how words work and need additional support with phonemic awareness, phonics, building sight vocabulary, cross-checking, self-monitoring, and/or building their meaning vocabulary banks.

We've designed these two planning guides so that you can adapt them to meet your needs. At its simplest, you can use the letters A, B, C, or D to code the type of conference you had with a child. We do this a lot at the beginning of the year when we are walking around with our clipboard taking notes. When we have a quick book chat with a child, we write something like, "B—Moriah likes books about mermaids," or when we notice a child applying a decoding strategy, we'll jot, "D—Kyle reread to figure out known word." Another option is to make one two-sided copy of the two planning guides back-to-back for each of your students and organize them in a three-ring binder. Then, as you confer with a child, you can highlight each learning target they've met and use the guide to help select their next target. For guided reading, you could place a copy in your plan book or in your guided reading area to help you choose a learning target for your small-group interactions. Since ABC Planning Guide 2 is focused on comprehension strategies, you might consider posting the specific strategies on a bulletin board as you introduce and practice them with your students.

CD Resource 1.8

CD Resource 1.9

Read! and Explore the W.O.R.L.D.: Creating and Sustaining Engaging Independent Practice Opportunities

One of our biggest challenges is launching, managing, and sustaining the independent practice portion of our reading workshop. Why? Because we work with young readers who have short attention spans. It would be lovely if our students were able to read independently for 30–45 minutes on the first day of school, wouldn't it? But you know that it takes a lot of teaching, modeling, and practicing to foster the independence needed for young learners to stay focused on independent literacy tasks. We know from the work of Dick Allington that we have to offer students abundant opportunities to engage in independent reading. Of course, when you are working with the youngest readers this can be a challenge. We will begin here by giving you an overview and rationale of how we divide reading workshop time in two parts. Then, in Chapter 2, you will find the specific procedural lesson plans to help you set up the routines that are necessary for you to be able to work with individuals or small groups to customize their learning experiences to meet their specific needs.

Read!

Independent reading is an essential part of the reading workshop, and one that we model, teach, and practice, practice, practice. Dick Allington, the rock star of reading instruction, tells us in his book *What Really Matters for Struggling Readers* (2006) that we must increase the volume of students' reading because "there exists a potent relationship between volume of reading and reading achievement" (p. 44). The term we choose to use for this time of our day is also the title of Nancie Atwell's must-read book *The Reading Zone* (2007). We believe this term can help you communicate to students the magic that occurs when you truly leave the classroom behind and enter the zone that is created when the words of the author connect with the reader, transporting him or her into the world of the book. That is a lofty but worthwhile goal, and difficult to achieve, not only because we are working with students who are reading many short books rather than one long novel, but also because we are competing with the fast-paced, multitasking world in which they live. So, how do we transform our classrooms into places where students are able to read just-right books for longer and longer each day, until a collective groan is heard when that time ends?

On the very first day of school, we begin building excitement about books and reading, and we work until each child has caught the reading bug. Not only do students read independently each morning but they also read during the Reading Zone every day from 3–5 minutes at the beginning of the year to 20–30 minutes or more by the end. Each child's book box is overflowing with books that are "just right" for that particular reader, because "kids not only need to read a lot, but they also need lots of books they can read accurately, fluently, and with comprehension right at their fingertips" (Allington, 2006, p. 85). So, each day, Part 2 or the independent practice portion of our workshop begins with time for students to read and us to confer. That time stretches out as the year progresses. To balance individual reading time with time for them to interact with their peers, we divide our independent practice time into two parts. When we notice students getting wiggly, we play a snippet of the transition song "A Whole New World," which signals it's time to Explore the W.O.R.L.D.

Explore the W.O.R.L.D.

During Explore the W.O.R.L.D. time, students continue their literacy work in small groups that we've created based on their learning needs. Look for a detailed guide to launching Explore the W.O.R.L.D. time on pages 65–70.

Over the years, we've read many different books on literacy centers, and always find the ideas overwhelming and too much extra work for us. So we created a simple structure that you can think about as you set up your classroom. Once you've launched Explore the W.O.R.L.D. time by introducing, practicing, and debriefing about each literacy activity, you are ready to set up the structure that you will use for the rest of the year by doing the following:

> # EXPLORE THE W.O.R.L.D.
>
> W – Be a WRITER
> O – Be an OBSERVER
> R – Be a READER
> L – Be a LISTENER
> D – Be a word DETECTIVE

1. Create five groups of children, one for each color: red, blue, green, yellow, and orange. These groups *are not* our guided reading groups (we do not have set groups for guiding readers); they are just five groups of kids who interact and work well together.

2. Post the groups on colored paper near the Explore the W.O.R.L.D. Wheel (CD Resource 2.5; there's also an interactive whiteboard version you can display—see CD Resource IWB_2.8).

Students may continue reading on their own or with a buddy instead of Exploring the W.O.R.L.D.

3. When children are done reading independently, they refer to the Explore the W.O.R.L.D. Wheel to see whether they are going to Be a Writer, Be an Observer, Be a Reader, Be a Listener, or Be a Word Detective for the remainder of the time, usually about 20–30 minutes. If your classrooms are as crowded as ours, then you probably don't have enough space to have five different center spots. In our classrooms we have a designated reading center, writing center, and listening center. Children who are observing or being word detectives take a plastic basket filled with supplies to an area of the floor and continue their learning there.

4. The next day, and every day after that, you simply turn the wheel to the next color so that each group of students does a new activity (see chart below).

Note that we choose to give students the option to continue reading on their own or with a buddy, and many students make this choice each day!

	Monday	Tuesday	Wednesday	Thursday	Friday
Be a Writer	Red Group	Blue Group	Green Group	Yellow Group	Orange Group
Be an Observer	Orange Group	Red Group	Blue Group	Green Group	Yellow Group
Be a Reader	Yellow Group	Orange Group	Red Group	Blue Group	Green Group
Be a Listener	Green Group	Yellow Group	Orange Group	Red Group	Blue Group
Be a Word Detective	Blue Group	Green Group	Yellow Group	Orange Group	Red Group

How to Assess: Sensible, Reader-Focused Techniques

We believe the purpose of assessment is two-fold. First, assessment helps focus instruction on the individual needs of students. When you can identify what your young readers know and are able to do, you can set goals, design lessons, and give descriptive feedback that will nudge them further. Second, it helps you determine specific learning targets for each student, especially striving readers, and then decide how

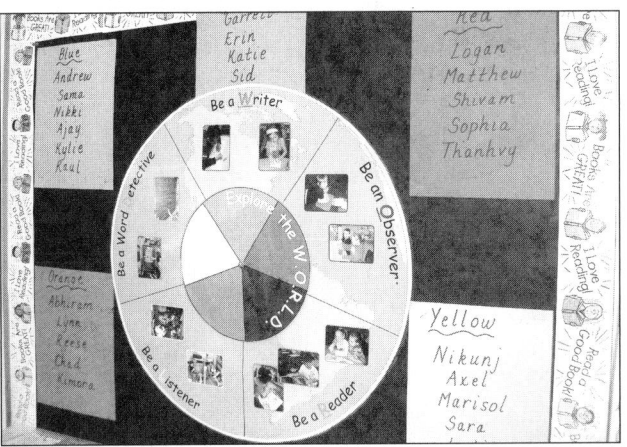

With just a quick turn of the wheel, students know what to do!

much extra support or intervention a child needs in order to meet the learning target. So, in order to align our assessment data with our reading instruction, we use multiple assessment tools and contexts, gather additional, ongoing data in our conferring notebooks, work with students to determine learning targets, collect multifaceted data on our struggling readers, and use that data to determine the most meaningful and effective interventions for each child.

So how do we assess students' reading progress in ways that are both meaningful and manageable? For the most part, we use teacher observation and anecdotal assessment data to drive our instructional decisions. We carefully observe our students as we engage in whole-class conversations, guide readers in small groups, and meet with children individually as they read, think and talk about books. In addition to the important information we gather through observation, we use multiple assessment tools.

USE MULTIPLE ASSESSMENT TOOLS AND CONTEXTS

To get a well-rounded view of each reader, we collect assessment data using the following tools and teaching contexts:

- Reading Interest Surveys: Discovering Children's Preferences
- Reading Coaching Conferences: Observing and Discussing Children's Reading Behaviors
- Word Knowledge Inventories: Pinpointing Children's Word Knowledge

- Reading Assessment Conferences: Determining Children's Instructional Level
- Listening Comprehension Assessments: Understanding Children's Higher-Level Thinking

GATHER ADDITIONAL, ONGOING DATA IN A CONFERRING NOTEBOOK

To ensure that our assessment mirrors our instruction, we use the ABC Guide described on pages 29–30 along with the conferring notebook (CD Resources 1.10 and 1.11) to gather ongoing, additional data on the following aspects of reading.

- Reading Interests
- Background Knowledge
- Oral Reading Ability
- Oral Reading Fluency
- Retelling Fiction
- Recounting Informational Text
- Word Knowledge
- Comprehension

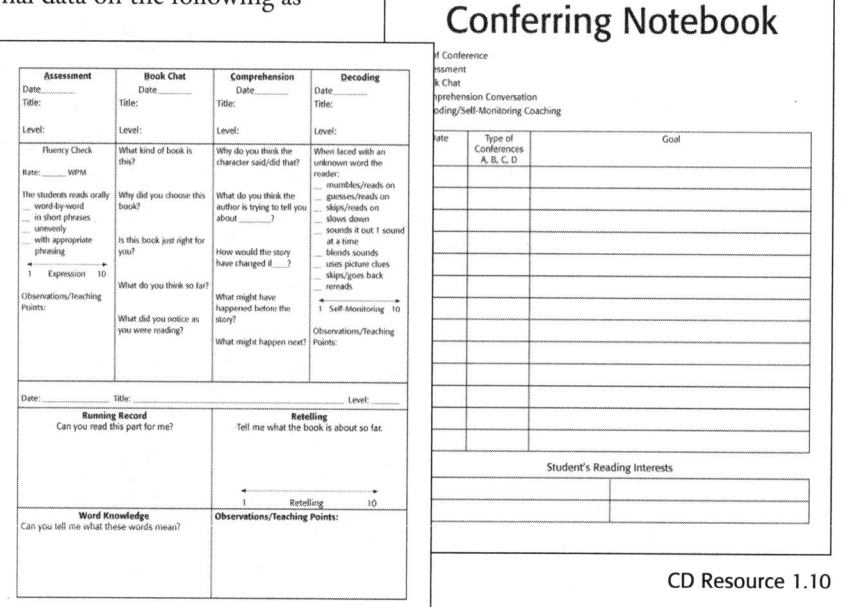

CD Resource 1.11

CD Resource 1.10

It is important to note that at the beginning of the year, when we are getting to know all our readers, we find that it is easier to jot quick notes on a one-page grid with a square labeled for each student, which we keep on a clipboard. Later, we transition to the conferring notebook.

To assemble students' conferring notebooks, staple together one copy of the cover page (CD Resource 1.10) for each child and as many inside pages (CD Resource 1.11) as you think you will need. You may want to make extra copies of the covers to staple on top after you've filled the first one up.

To use the conferring notebook when you are working with a reader:

1. Determine the focus for the conference. Will it be Assessment, Book Chat, Comprehension Conversation, Decoding Strategy Coaching or a quick running record, with a retelling and a check of the child's word knowledge? For some readers you may have a dual focus such as an assessment of their fluency and a comprehension conversation.
2. Record the date, title, and level (if you know it) of the book the child is reading on the inside page.
3. As you confer, note your observations and teaching points.
4. Together, with the child, set a goal and a time for the next conference. Record the goal and the date for the next conference on the front cover of the notebook.

5. We keep our notebooks in a basket organized by conferring dates, so when it's time to confer we can grade that day's notebooks and get started.

DETERMINE LEARNING TARGETS

Along with helping us select learning targets for students, assessment helps guide students as they learn to self-monitor their own reading and thinking. We use the chart below to help us determine learning targets and to guide our students in creating their own learning targets and assessing their own reading progress.

What Readers Do

Readers Read

I can . . .

- read different kinds of books
  - read to laugh
  - read to learn
  - read to ponder
- read a lot of books
- choose books that are just right for me
- read for a long time
- read with style

Readers Think

I can . . .

- read with a purpose in mind
- pause, think, and check for understanding
- read for big ideas
- reread, revise, and refine my thinking as I read
- clarify ideas by writing about my reading

Readers Retell

I can . . .

- retell my favorite parts
- retell using story elements and details
- recount important details from a nonfiction book

Readers Converse

I can . . .

- discuss my reading with others
- ask and answer questions about my reading and the reading of others
- share my opinions about what I've read
- recommend books to my friends

CD Resource 1.12

COLLECT MULTIFACETED DATA ON STRUGGLING READERS

When you have readers who are struggling, consider collecting a multifaceted set of data to guide you as you make decisions on how to best meet their needs. Instead of basing our decisions on a single fluency measure, as some seem to think is a good idea, we analyze four different measures when we meet about our struggling readers. Based on this broader view, we can follow the decision-making process described on page 36.

• Letter Recognition/Sound Knowledge • Phonemic Awareness and/or Phonics Knowledge	• High-Frequency Word Knowledge • Vocabulary Knowledge

• Early Literacy Concepts
• Running Record/Individual Reading Inventory
  • Determine reading level
  • Diagnose reading errors
  • Observe self-monitoring/decoding strategy use
  • Assess comprehension
	Fluency Measure
	• Rate
	• Accuracy
	• Phrasing
	• Expression

Our ultimate goal is to get to know as much about our readers as possible so that we can determine the most appropriate instruction to meet their needs.

USE MULTIFACETED ASSESSMENT DATA TO DETERMINE APPROPRIATE READING INTERVENTION	
Investigate	Investigate students' strengths and struggles to determine possible causes for their reading difficulties. Talk to the student, the student's family, and his or her previous teachers.
Question	What is my primary area of concern? What do I want this reader to do that he/she is not doing right now? How can I build on this reader's strengths to scaffold his or her weaknesses?
Notice and Infer	What patterns do I see as I look at this student's formal and informal assessment data? What do these patterns tell me about this student as a reader?
Develop a Hypothesis	Use what you've learned about this student and what you know about teaching young readers to develop a hypothesis.
Determine a Goal	Although you may have multiple goals for this student, it is helpful to focus on one goal at a time. This is not to say you are not providing powerful instruction in all aspects of reading. Again, use this question to guide your goal setting. What do I want this reader to do that he/she is not doing right now?
Design an Intervention (intense, focused, meaningful instruction)	In many schools, the word *intervention* refers to a packaged or computer program. We strive to create interventions that offer students rich experiences interacting with real books and accomplished adult readers. You'll find some examples in the section titled Sensible Strategies for Struggling Readers in the chapters that follow.
Collect and Analyze Data	What kind of data will I collect to determine if my instruction is working? How will I determine if this intervention is successful?

Final Thoughts

Certainly, powerful reading instruction is a complex, multifaceted, and cyclical process. We begin by getting to know our young readers. Next, we determine what content to teach, and then select the best process or teaching context (whole-group, small-group, or individual conference) for delivering that content. Additionally, you must figure out when to fit all this teaching in during your day, and how to continually assess whether your students are growing as readers so you can determine what they need to know to nudge them forward. We can feel our blood pressure rising even as we write these words. But the payoff is well worth the effort. When we design our own reading instruction, rather than relying on a reading program, we rediscover the joys of teaching young children.

CHAPTER 2: SEPTEMBER

Setting the Stage

As we are writing this book, I (Maria) am working to renew my National Board Certification. While reacquainting myself with the standards, I came across this description of our profession: "Like the conductor of a great orchestra, accomplished early childhood teachers make and execute dozens of complex decisions as they create the symphony that is their work with children" (National Board for Professional Teaching Standards, 2001, p. 2). The complexity of our work as primary teachers is impossible to quantify in test scores and data points. It is the orchestration of a diverse group of young learners into a cohesive community of readers, writers, thinkers, and problem solvers, while at the same time teaching them the skills and strategies necessary to be passionate and proficient readers. We view this chapter as the overture, because the focus for this month is launching the reading workshop along with setting expectations and routines that will serve as a framework for a year's worth of learning. As you know, what we do in the first month of school gives our students an overview of all the learning that is to follow. For you, it is a sampling of all the different types of lessons you will find in this book. You may choose to do some of the lessons in September and decide to share others later in the year. We'll begin each chapter by offering a sampling of reading-related morning messages followed by mini-lessons and other helpful resources from which you can choose as you plan your literacy instruction. Let the decision making begin!

Part 1: Reading-Related Morning Message Ideas and Samples

If you've used a morning message before, then you've already discovered the power it holds for young writers. We shared more than 75 morning message ideas in *Month-by-Month Trait-Based Writing Instruction* (Walther & Phillips, 2009) and in this book would like to add to that bank of messages by shifting the focus from messages for writers to messages that enhance reading instruction. To balance our instruction, we typically do three or four writing-focused messages and one or two reading-related messages each week. In each chapter that follows, you will find messages that you can use to review key concepts from the mini-lessons you've taught. The messages target decoding strategies, comprehension strategies, vocabulary, or reading response ideas. Enjoy mixing and matching the messages to meet the needs of your students.

MORNING MESSAGE IDEA: LAUNCHING READING-RELATED MORNING MESSAGES

Use this message early in the month to introduce the fact that you are going to be using some of the morning message time to help students grow as readers, in addition to the messages that target writing instruction. The focus of this message is on monitoring comprehension by discussing the meaning of some challenging vocabulary words. It also works as a quick, informal assessment to see if any of your students already know the meaning of the targeted words. Read the message aloud. Then, reread the word *avid*. Ask if anyone knows the meaning of that word. If not, provide a kid-friendly definition and then invite students to use it in a sentence. Follow the same procedure for the words *converse, multiple,* and *remarkable*. After reading and discussing the message, ask students, "Do you think today's message helped you more as a reader or as a writer?" To cement their newly learned word knowledge, challenge children to listen for the four new words in the books you read aloud and use them in conversations.

> ### MORNING MESSAGE SAMPLE
>
> Good morning, **avid** readers. Today we are going to **converse** about words. Some words, like **play**, have **multiple** meanings. I love learning about words. Words are **remarkable**!

MORNING MESSAGE IDEA: SELF-MONITORING/DECODING—PICTURE CLUES

Interactive Whiteboard Morning Message 2A

This message is a continuation of the mini-lesson Let's Use Picture Clues to Help Us Read the Words, found on page 56. The purpose of this message is to encourage students to begin using picture clues to figure out words when they are reading. If you have an interactive whiteboard, then access lesson IWB_MM_2A on the CD and invite students to complete each sentence by dragging the appropriate image to it. If you don't have a whiteboard, follow these simple directions. Gather photos, clip art, or real items that your students might have in their desks. Post or place the items where students can see them. Then, write on a chalkboard or chart paper the sentences listed in the sample at right. Invite students to match the picture to the missing word that makes sense in each sentence and write the word on the line using their best developmental spelling.

> **MORNING MESSAGE SAMPLE**
>
> I have a _____ to read.
>
> I need _____ to cut.
>
> I color with my _____.
>
> An _____ helps me fix my work.
>
> *Note you can discuss the reason you used the word <u>an</u> instead of <u>a</u> in this sentence.
>
> It is time to sharpen my _____.

MORNING MESSAGE IDEA: COMPREHENSION—KNOCK, KNOCK! WHO'S THERE?

A concrete way to introduce the concept of a two-way conversation is to teach youngsters the format of knock-knock jokes. (Thanks to Katie Walther for this clever idea!) Prior to this message, begin your morning by sharing a few knock-knock jokes from a book like *Knock, Knock! Who's There?* (Hills, 2000), which would be a great choice for kindergarteners, while *Super Incredible! Knock-Knock Jokes for Kids* (Phillips, 2007) may be better suited for second graders. Once you are confident that students understand the format, you can prewrite or compose in a shared writing format a few jokes of your own. After you've done this a few times in your morning message, consider adding joke writing to your "Be a Writer" menu during Explore the W.O.R.L.D. time.

> **MORNING MESSAGE SAMPLE**
>
> Knock, knock!   Knock, knock!
> Who's there?   Who's there?
> Canoe   Lettuce
> Canoe who?   Lettuce who?
> Canoe count to 100?   Lettuce read a book now!

MORNING MESSAGE IDEA: VOCABULARY BUILDING—LABELING THE PARTS OF A BOOK

Interactive Whiteboard Morning Message 2B

In order to engage in book-related conversations with your students, it is helpful if you have a common language to use when referring to specific parts of a book. If you have an interactive whiteboard, display Message IWB_MM_2B from the CD and discuss the parts of a book. If you don't have a whiteboard, simply place a hardcover picture book in your message spot and make labels with the following parts of a book: front cover, back cover, front flap, back flap, endpapers, copyright page, title page, spine, and gutter. You could also introduce your students to the different types of covers such as wraparound covers, dual-image covers, and single-image covers. For helpful information on the parts of a book, refer to www.picturingbooks.com.

MORNING MESSAGE IDEA: READING RESPONSE—WHAT KINDS OF BOOKS DO YOU PREFER?

After your students have had time to discuss the different types of books available in your classroom, pose the question, "What kinds of books do you prefer?" To sneak a little math practice into your morning message, invite students to make a tally mark under their preference.

Morning Message: What Kinds of Books Do You Prefer?

POETRY POWER: POEMS FOR THE BEGINNING OF THE YEAR

Title	Brief Summary
Good Books, Good Times (Hopkins, 1990)	A collection of 14 poems about books and reading. Some of our favorites include "Good Books, Good Times!" and "Books to the Ceiling."
I Am the Book (Hopkins, 2011)	A collection of 13 poems to celebrate books and reading. Consider using the Hopkins poem "Poetry Time" to launch your own poetry time. The poem "This Book" by Avis Harley is ideal to share when discussing just-right books.

MORNING READ-ALOUDS: PICTURE BOOKS ABOUT READING

Title, Author, and Focus	Brief Summary
A Book (Gerstein, 2009) **Focus:** Reading and Writing	The girl who lives inside this book is the only member of her family without a story, so she travels through various genres in search of one. Ultimately, she decides to write her own.
Born to Read (Sierra, 2008) **Focus:** Reading	Sam begins reading as soon as his eyes open, and he continues reading to learn about his interests and accomplish his goals.
The Day Dirk Yeller Came to Town (Casanova, 2011) **Focus:** Reading	Dirk Yeller arrives in town looking for something "to keep jumping beans from jumpin'!" After a few unsuccessful stops around town, Dirk follows Sam to the library, where he meets Miss Jenny and the world of books.
Hip and Hop Don't Stop (Czekaj, 2010) **Focus:** Fluency; see teaching idea on page 71	Hip, the turtle, raps s-l-o-w while Hop, the rabbit, raps fast, fast, fast. The two rappers live in different parts of Oldskool County and don't socialize until they decide to practice together for a rapping contest.
How Rocket Learned to Read (Hills, 2010) **Focus:** Reading; see vocabulary idea on page 72	A little yellow bird entices Rocket, the dog, to learn about the "wondrous, mighty, gorgeous alphabet" by reading captivating books aloud.
How to Teach a Slug to Read (Pearson, 2011) **Focus:** Reading	This would be the perfect book to read aloud to parents on curriculum night. It highlights the importance of reading aloud nursery rhymes, talking about vocabulary words, rereading, and much more, in a humorous, slug-friendly way.
Read Anything Good Lately? (Allen & Lindaman, 2003) **Focus:** Reading	This book is an alphabetical look at 26 different forms of writing and the various locations in which to read them.
We Are in a Book! (Willems, 2010) **Focus:** Reading	Elephant and Piggie realize that they are in a book and have fun tricking their readers.
The Wonderful Book (Gore, 2010) **Focus:** Reading	The forest animals find an unusual object in the forest—a book. They each use it for a different purpose until a boy comes along and reads it to them.
You're Finally Here! (Watt, 2011) **Focus**: Reading	A rabbit is impatiently waiting inside this picture book for a reader to arrive. Thank goodness "You're finally here!"

Part 2: Launching the Reading Workshop—Menus of Reading Workshop Mini-Lessons and A Guide to Explore the W.O.R.L.D. Time

You'll find that this chapter's menu of mini-lessons follows a different format than do the chapters that follow. The mini-lessons here are separated into five sections so that you can choose the lessons that meet the needs of your students and match your grade-level standards and expectations. The sections include the following menus and tips:

- A Menu of Mini-Lessons for Creating a Class of Book Lovers
- Procedural Mini-Lessons for Reading, Thinking, and Talking in a Whole-Class Setting
- Procedural Mini-Lessons for Establishing Independent Reading Time
- A Menu of Mini-Lessons for Reading Response
- Tips for Launching Explore the W.O.R.L.D. Time

To assist you as you select lessons that will guide your readers toward independence, we've created a suggested sequence of mini-lessons for the first 25 days of school; you'll find the complete list of lessons on the CD. We're hopeful that this planning guide will help you coordinate your instruction for the first month or so of school. Because, like you,

Reading Workshop: The First 25 Days

Day 1	Day 2	Day 3	Day 4	Day 5
Mini-Lesson: We Are Readers **Independent Reading:** Explore Classroom Library Explore the W.O.R.L.D. Be a Writer Whole Class Introduction Practice Debrief	**Mini-Lesson:** Reading Makes Us Feel Good **Independent Reading:** Explore Classroom Library Explore the W.O.R.L.D. Be a Writer Whole Class Practice Debrief	Catch-Up Day	**Mini-Lesson:** We Read to Laugh **Independent Reading:** Let's Read, Think, and Talk About the Pictures Explore the W.O.R.L.D. Be a Writer Doing/Learning Chart Practice Debrief	**Mini-Lesson:** We Read to Learn **Independent Reading:** Let's Read, Think, and Talk About the Pictures Explore the W.O.R.L.D. Be an Observer Whole Class Introduction Practice Debrief

Day 6	Day 7	Day 8	Day 9	Day 10
Mini-Lesson: We Read to Ponder **Independent Reading:** Retell a Folk Tale, a Fairy Tale, or a Nursery Rhyme Explore the W.O.R.L.D. Be an Observer Whole Class Practice Debrief	**Mini-Lesson:** Readers Have Their Favorite Kinds of Books **Independent Reading:** Retell a Folk Tale, a Fairy Tale, or a Nursery Rhyme Explore the W.O.R.L.D. Be an Observer Doing/Learning Chart Practice Debrief	Catch-Up Day	**Mini-Lesson:** Have I Got a Book for You! **Independent Reading:** Let's Use Picture Clues to Help Us Read the Words Explore the W.O.R.L.D. Divide Class in Two Groups Practice Be a Writer and Be an Observer Debrief	**Mini-Lesson:** Have I Got a Book for You! **Independent Reading:** Let's Use Picture Clues to Help Us Read the Words Explore the W.O.R.L.D. Be a Reader Whole Class Introduction Practice Debrief

Day 11	Day 12	Day 13	Day 14	Day 15
Mini-Lesson: Are You Listening? **Independent Reading:** Let's Read the Words Explore the W.O.R.L.D. Be a Reader Whole Class Practice Debrief	**Mini-Lesson:** Are You Listening? **Independent Reading:** What Are You Doing? What Are You Learning? Explore the W.O.R.L.D. Be a Reader Doing/Learning Chart Practice Debrief	Catch-Up Day	**Mini-Lesson:** You Talk While I Listen, I Talk and While You Listen **Independent Reading:** What Do Readers Do? R-E-R-E-A-D, Reread, Reread Explore the W.O.R.L.D. Divide Class in Three Groups Practice Be a Writer, Be an Observer, and Be a Reader Debrief	**Mini-Lesson:** You Talk While I Listen, I Talk and While You Listen **Independent Reading:** What Do Readers Do? R-E-R-E-A-D, Reread, Reread Explore the W.O.R.L.D. Be a Listener Whole Class Introduction Practice Debrief

Day 16	Day 17	Day 18	Day 19	Day 20
Mini-Lesson: Let's Link Our Thinking Together **Independent Reading:** What Do Readers Do? Readers Read Book, After Book, After Book . . . Explore the W.O.R.L.D. Be a Listener Whole Class Practice Debrief	**Mini-Lesson:** Let's Link Our Thinking Together **Independent Reading:** What Do Readers Do? Readers Read Book, After Book, After Book . . . Explore the W.O.R.L.D. Be a Listener Doing/Learning Chart Practice Debrief	Catch-Up Day	**Mini-Lesson:** How to Politely End a Two-Way Conversation **Independent Reading:** What Do Readers Do? Readers Read, Think, and Talk with a Friend Explore the W.O.R.L.D. Divide Class in Four Groups Practice Be a Writer, Be an Observer, Be a Reader, and Be a Listener Debrief	**Mini-Lesson:** How to Politely End a Two-Way Conversation **Independent Reading:** What Do Readers Do? Readers Read, Think, and Talk with a Friend Explore the W.O.R.L.D. Be a Word Detective Whole Class Introduction Practice Debrief

Day 21	Day 22	Day 23	Day 24	Day 25
Mini-Lesson: Get Your Mouth Ready (October Chapter) **Independent Reading:** What Do Readers Do? Readers Read, Think, and Write Explore the W.O.R.L.D. Be a Word Detective Whole Class Practice Debrief	**Mini-Lesson:** Get Your Mouth Ready (October Chapter) **Independent Reading:** What Do Readers Do? Readers Read, Think, and Write Explore the W.O.R.L.D. Be a Word Detective Doing/Learning Chart Practice Debrief	Catch-Up Day	**Mini-Lesson:** Skip and Read Through (October Chapter) **Independent Reading:** Choosing Just-Right Books Explore the W.O.R.L.D. Divide Class into Five Groups Practice Be a Writer, Be an Observer, Be a Reader, Be a Listener, and Be a Word Detective	**Mini-Lesson:** Skip and Read Through (October Chapter) **Independent Reading:** Choosing Just Right Books Explore the W.O.R.L.D. Divide Class into Five Groups Practice Be a Writer, Be an Observer, Be a Reader, Be a Listener, and Be a Word Detective

CD Resource 2.1

we are still teaching in the classroom every day, our plan includes two features absent from many other plans we've read. First, we've included catch-up days to help keep you on track when scheduling disruptions occur. Second, we've allotted two days to teach many of the mini-lessons. This gives you the flexibility to differentiate the lessons based on your grade level or to add or replace our lesson with your favorite reading workshop mini-lessons.

LAUNCHING THE READING WORKSHOP: A MENU OF MINI-LESSONS FOR CREATING A COMMUNITY OF BOOK LOVERS

The mini-lessons that follow demonstrate the different purposes for reading. We've highlighted reading for enjoyment, reading for information, and reading to expand your thinking. As students are reading independently, snap digital pictures or take quick video clips to use later in the month as you demonstrate and practice independent reading.

MINI-LESSON: We Are Readers!

Preparation: Read aloud and discuss a book that highlights the importance of reading. A few books to consider are listed below.

The Incredible Book-Eating Boy (Jeffers, 2007)	The more books Henry eats, the smarter he gets, until he eats too much, gets sick, and decides reading books makes more sense. Notice that Jeffers created the illustrations by painting on recycled book pages!
What Are You Doing? (Amado, 2011)	Chepito, who is hesitant to begin school, greets people around his neighborhood by asking, "What are you doing?" He soon finds that each person is reading for a different purpose. At school, he discovers that reading is fun.

Explanation: We believe that the first lessons you share with students are critical in setting the tone for reading workshop, illuminating the value of reading, and creating a community of enthusiastic learners. Rather than jumping right in with procedures, we begin with conversations about books and readers. To that end, the first series of lessons establishes the fact that your classroom is a place where all students are viewed as readers and that people read for a variety of purposes.

Demonstration: After sharing the book with your students, ask, "When I was reading the book aloud, what did you see or

Record students' ideas about the purposes for reading.

hear me do? What did you notice?" Listen to the responses. Continue the conversation by asking, "What else do readers do? What did you learn in kindergarten or first grade about being a reader?" Record students' responses in a notebook or on sticky notes affixed to a piece of chart paper.

Invitation: "I'm going to tell you the secret to being an even better reader than you are today—READ! It's that simple! So every day we are going to spend time reading. I can't wait to read and learn with you!"

MINI-LESSON: Reading Makes Us Feel Good

Preparation: Read aloud and discuss the book *Reading Makes You Feel Good* (Parr, 2005). Other books you might choose to use for this lesson include the titles listed below.

| *Miss Smith's Incredible Storybook* (Garland, 2003) | Zack and his friends are amazed to find that when Miss Smith reads, the characters come to life. |
| *A Story for Bear* (Haseley, 2002) | This story illuminates the power of reading aloud and the joy it can bring, even to a bear. |

Explanation: We borrowed the title of this mini-lesson from Todd Parr's colorful book *Reading Makes You Feel Good*. The aim of this mini-lesson is to introduce young readers to the different purposes for reading. This mini-lesson is the first in a series. Depending on your grade level, you can extend this series of lessons to include other reading purposes.

Demonstration: Launch the conversation with, "I noticed that in Todd Parr's book the people read books for different reasons or purposes. Let's think about our reasons for reading." Collaborate with your students to create an anchor chart that lists the different purposes for reading.

Invitation: "Today, when you are reading, think about how the book makes you feel." As students are reading, remember to snap a few digital pictures or film a few quick video clips to use in future lessons.

MINI-LESSON: We Read to Laugh!

Preparation: Select a humorous picture book or two to share with your students. Here are a few of our favorite funny books.

Record the reasons your students read.

Let's Do Nothing! (Fucile, 2009)	Frankie and Sal tried very hard to do nothing. Fucile's hilarious illustrations will keep your listeners laughing!
Pigs to the Rescue (Himmelman, 2010)	In the sequel to *Chickens to the Rescue*, Farmer Greenstalk and his family have some problems on the farm. Fortunately (or not!), the pigs are always ready to lend a helping hand. In the end, Lulu the cat spills her milk. Guess who comes to the rescue next!

You might consider displaying a collection of humorous picture books in a basket or on a shelf with a sign posted nearby that says "We Read to Laugh!"

Explanation: As you continue to build your community of readers, this mini-lesson will reinforce the fact that people read with different purposes in mind. Since children generally enjoy books that make them laugh, this seems like a good place to begin.

Demonstration: After enjoying the book together, ask students what they noticed while you were reading aloud. "Did you laugh?" Continue your discussion by talking about why they think the author wrote this book. Ask, "Do you think he/she wrote the book to make you laugh? Do you know any other books that make you laugh? Are there certain authors who always write funny books?"

Invitation: "Readers, today when you select a book to read, think about whether you might want a funny book that will make you laugh."

MINI-LESSON: We Read to Learn

Preparation: Gather a few engaging nonfiction read-aloud titles.

Let's Look at Sharks (Nelson, 2011)	This is one of the titles in the Animal Close-Up Series from Lerner Publications. The books in this series are short, engaging, and filled with nonfiction features.
Polar Bears (Newman, 2011)	The photographs in this well-designed informational book will keep readers engaged as they learn about polar bears.

This might also be a good time to show children the nonfiction section of your classroom library or to gather a set of nonfiction books from your school or local library. If you don't have a separate section, shelf, or basket for nonfiction books, you could enlist the help of your students in gathering the nonfiction books from your collection and organizing them by topic. This would give your readers a chance to familiarize themselves with the books in the room. Again, you might post a sign near your nonfiction books stating "We Read to Learn."

Explanation: Young readers are naturally curious about the world around them. This is just one of the many reasons to include nonfiction books as part of your read-aloud fare.

Demonstration: Before you begin reading, say something like, "You know, I've always been curious about _____. Luckily, I found this book. I can't wait to read it to learn more about _____." During and after reading, pause and point out your new learning by using statements such as "Isn't that amazing!" or "That's new learning for me," or "Wow! I want to remember that fact, so I'll jot it in my notebook."

Invitation: "Readers, we often choose books that help us learn. What are you interested in learning more about? Think about that as you choose a book today."

MINI-LESSON: We Read to Ponder

Preparation: Look for books that offer opportunities for students to infer meaning or see the world from a different perspective. We've listed a few here that are ideal for the beginning of the year. Any of the books listed in the sections titled Read-Alouds That Spark Comprehension Conversations found in chapters 3–8 or the wordless picture books listed on page 55 would also work well for this mini-lesson.

City Dog, Country Frog (Willems, 2010)	It is spring, and City Dog is thrilled to be in the country. There he befriends Country Frog. Each season, City Dog visits Country Frog until winter, when frog disappears. City Dog misses Country Frog but finds a new friend the following spring.
The Sandwich Swap (Al Abdullah & DiPicchio, 2010)	In this story of tolerance and acceptance, Salma and Lily eat different kinds of sandwiches and voice their distaste for each other's food. This attitude snowballs, resulting in a school-wide food fight. In the end, the best friends work together to organize a multicultural feast for all.

Explanation: If our goal is to create a safe, caring, inclusive, and intellectually engaging environment for our young learners, then we need to read aloud and discuss books that challenge their thinking and help them to see the world from different perspectives.

Demonstration: As you read aloud, encourage students to think about the book from a different point of view by using phrases such as "I never thought about it that way."

Invitation: "As you are reading today, think about what the character is thinking and how he or she is feeling. That is called putting yourself in that character's shoes! Ponder what it would feel like to be that character."

MINI-LESSON: Readers Have Their Favorite Kinds of Books

Preparation:

- Prior to this lesson, you might send a note home requesting that students bring their favorite book from home. If you have students in your classroom who don't come from a book-rich household, guide them in finding a favorite from your classroom or school library.
- Copy and display the Interest Inventory (CD Resource 2.2).

Explanation: Some students in your class may already know what kind of books they like to read, while others may simply lack enough exposure to the world of books to have defined their reading interests. This lesson is designed to initiate conversations about reading interests.

Demonstration: If students have brought in their favorite book, provide time for them to share it with their friends. Then, together with your students, categorize the books. Jot the categories in your notebook or create a chart called "Our Favorite Kinds of Books."

Invitation: "Wow! We've talked about a lot of different kinds of books. I'd like you to take a few minutes to think about the kinds of books you want to read this year by filling out this Interest Inventory. I will keep this handy when I'm looking for books to share with you."

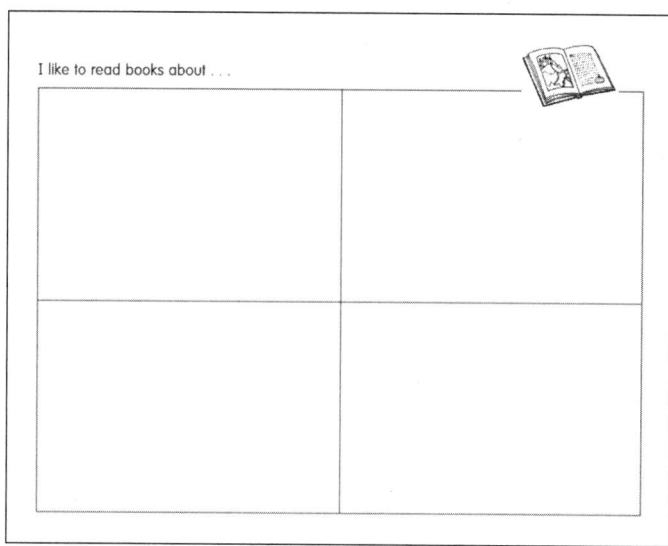

CD Resource 2.2

Completed Interest Inventory

MINI-LESSON: Have I Got a Book for You!

Preparation: Read and discuss a book about a reluctant reader. Some possibilities include:

Miss Brooks Loves Books! (and I Don't) (Bottner, 2010)	The first-grade narrator thinks Miss Brooks's love of books is "vexing" until her mom introduces her to a book about warts—*Shrek*!
Miss Malarkey Leaves No Reader Behind (Finchler & O'Malley, 2006)	Miss Malarkey is determined to find the perfect book to motivate each reader in her class, even the video game fanatic!
Read All About It! (Bush & Bush, 2008)	Tyrone Brown thinks reading is "so last year" until his teacher, Ms. Libro, invites him into the world of books.

Based on your observations, conversations, and students' interest inventories, do the following in the next week or so. Spend a few minutes locating a book for each child, place a sticky note on it, and then either slip it into students' book boxes, hand the book out after reading it aloud, or place books on students' desks before they arrive.

Explanation: One of your most important jobs is to help students locate books they want to read, and you can begin putting books in their hands in various ways. This is an ongoing task to keep up during the year. To help keep you on track, place a class list on a clipboard near your conferring area to note the date that you give each child a book. Set a goal to find one book per child per month. If this seems a bit daunting right now, start with one book per child per quarter.

Demonstration: If you've selected a book for each child and placed it in his or her book box, then this demonstration may sound something like, "Girls and boys, I've been working hard

Children will read their special books again and again!

Select a special book for each child and place it in his or her book box.

the last few weeks doing one of my most important jobs—finding books for you to read. In your book box you will find a book or books that I selected especially with you in mind. I can't wait to hear what you think about your new books. Let's read!"

Invitation: "Readers, as we get to know each other and each other's reading interests, you can also recommend books for your friends. We'll create a space in our classroom for you to do that!"

LAUNCHING THE READING WORKSHOP: PROCEDURAL MINI-LESSONS FOR READING, THINKING, AND TALKING IN A WHOLE-CLASS SETTING

In Chapter 1, we underscored the importance of multiple daily read-aloud experiences and conversations that surround those experiences. In our classroom we have a meeting place for our students on the carpet. After the first day or two of school, to make transitions run smoothly, we assign learners a designated spot on the floor, called their "place for learning." To do this, we simply make a chart listing the students' names in order on a grid; see below. Depending on how much space you have and the number of students in your class, you might have children sitting in five rows of five or six students. In addition, we strategically pair them up with a "think and share" partner. By thoughtfully pairing students with a supportive peer, we offer assistance to our struggling learners and our ELLs. We have never had to put tape or any other kind of marking on the floor. Once students know which child they sit behind and next to, they move in and out of these spots with ease. Of course, to build community and give children a chance to interact with different classmates, the places for learning change at least one time per month. You may encounter students who find it challenging to sit in their own space. For these learners, we've found that having them sit in a small chair (from a preschool kitchen play set, often found at garage sales) or on a carpet square helps them to better define the boundaries of their personal space. To facilitate whole-group conversations, we often move from our Places for Learning into a circle (or oval, in our small rooms!) so we can see one another as we converse.

The following mini-lessons are designed to teach students how to have meaningful conversations before, during, and after read-alouds.

Places for Learning

← Coathooks

Sama	Reese	Ajay	Stefan	Nikunj	
	Lynn	Sara	Marisol	Shivam	Logan
	Kylie	Katie	Sophia	Ben	Axel
Ryan	Justin	Garrett	Abhiram	Nikki	Kimora
Sid	Chad	Erin	Thanhvy	Andrew	Matthew

Dr. Walther

A FEW OF OUR FAVORITE PICTURE BOOKS FOR BUILDING A COMMUNITY OF RESPECTFUL LEARNERS

Title, Author, and Focus	Brief Summary
Enemy Pie (Munson, 2000) **Focus**: Resolving Conflicts	The narrator's summer is nearly ruined when Jeremy Ross moves in, but his father has a solution to his problem. He tells his son to invite Jeremy over and "be nice" while he prepares the "enemy pie."
Odd Velvet (Whitcomb, 1998) **Focus**: Accepting Differences	Velvet, who begins the school year without a new dress and without friends, is slowly appreciated for her uniqueness.
One (Otoshi, 2008) **Focus**: Bullying	This is an amazing book about bullying! When you begin reading, it might appear to be yet another book about colors until you realize that the quiet color blue and his buddies are being bullied by the "hothead" color red. Fortunately, "one" shows up and teaches the colors to stand up for themselves.
One Smart Cookie: Bite-Size Lessons for the School Year and Beyond (Rosenthal, 2010) **Focus**: Character Education, Vocabulary	Rosenthal's latest addition to his "Cookie" series is ideal for reading at the beginning of the year to help illustrate words such as *prompt*, *organized*, and *prepared*. We would suggest reading one or two pages a day, and then using the words throughout the day to reinforce their meaning.
Two of a Kind (Robbins, 2009) **Focus**: Healthy Friendships	If you are looking for a book to spark a conversation about kindness and true friendship, this is the one. Kayla and Melanie are two of a kind. When they "befriend" Anna, she discovers that being friends with them means making choices that cause her stomach to hurt and her true friendship with Julisa to suffer.
What If? (Seeger, 2010) **Focus**: Friendship, Considering the Feelings of Others	Laura Vaccaro Seeger uses only six words in varying combinations to tell a tale three different ways. This book will spark a conversation about friendship and consideration for the feelings of others. It is also ideal for pointing out the difference between predicting and inferring.

MINI-LESSON: Are You Listening?

Preparation: Read and discuss a book about listening, such as *Listen Buddy* (Lester, 1995).

Explanation: Each moment you spend at the beginning of the year modeling, practicing, and celebrating the art of good listening will pay off as you read aloud and have conversations during the school year.

Demonstration: Begin your after-reading conversation by asking, "What was the problem Buddy was having in the story? Let's think for a moment about what it means to be a good listener. What are some things good

listeners do? Let's write down some of your ideas." Record students' ideas on a chart like the one shown here. You'll notice that when others are talking, I ask you to put your hands down, look at them, and listen. This is to make sure you are concentrating on what they are saying instead of about what you want to say next."

Invitation: "Remember that everyone in our classroom is a teacher with unique ideas to share. Listen carefully when others are talking—that's what learners do!"

MINI-LESSON: You Talk While I Listen; I Talk While You Listen

Preparation: Prior to this lesson you may want to assign students a think-and-share partner (see page 49 for explanation). We realize it is the very beginning of the year, so do your best with this task. You will want to change these partners often as the year progresses, to give students a chance to share their thinking with many different classmates.

Explanation: When you invite your young listeners to think and share, they need to know exactly what you mean. In this lesson, you can introduce students to their think-and-share partner and to the nature of a two-way conversation. We suggest revisiting this lesson each time you change think-and-share partners.

Demonstration: Begin the lesson by saying, "Today you are going to meet your think-and-share partner and get to know him or her. I'm going show you what I mean." Invite a student to join you in front of the class. Pose a question such as, "What are your favorite things to do at recess?" Then, demonstrate how you think and share with that student. Continue with a few more questions, modeling "you talk while I listen, then I talk while you listen." Next, invite students do the same by posing additional questions to spark a conversation.

How many sisters and brothers do you have?

Teach students how to "think and share" with a partner.

What kinds of books do you like to read?

What kinds of games do you like to play?

To challenge students to listen carefully to their partner, ask them to share their partner's answer rather than their own.

After students have observed you and your partner and have had an opportunity to try it with their partner, brainstorm what they noticed and/or learned and list it on a chart.

Invitation: "Listeners, when I'm reading aloud, I'm going to pause to give you a chance to think and share with your partner. Now you know what that looks like and sounds like, we can do it more often. I can't wait to hear all of your original ideas!"

Students share their thinking with their partner.

MINI-LESSON: Let's Link Our Thinking

Preparation: Grab a handful of paper clips or another item in your classroom that easily links together. Select a favorite read-aloud book from your collection. You might also consider prerecording on video a brief conversation and an in-depth conversation to show and discuss with students, noting the differences between the two.

Explanation: Have you ever noticed that young children have difficulty carrying on a conversation? Yes, children can *tell* you all about the adventures they had the night before. But when it comes to building on the thinking of others, asking questions, or responding to a statement made by another child, they benefit from repeated demonstration and practice. So, the purpose of this mini-lesson is to begin to show them how to build on the thinking of others. Of course, it will be helpful if you revisit the concepts covered in this lesson throughout the year. You could also enlist the help of upper-grade buddies to practice having conversations.

Demonstration: After completing a read-aloud, begin your demonstration by saying, "Today I want to show you how you can work with a friend to link your thinking together, just like I can link these paper clips together to make a chain. Let's take a look at some different questions and phrases you can use to link your conversation together." Create a chart like the one found on page 53 to display some helpful phrases that extend a conversation.

Continue the demonstration by saying, "I'm going to start a conversation with my friend _____ (select a child to help you demonstrate) about the book we just finished reading." Demonstrate a conversation. Each time a statement or question links to the one before it, add a paper clip to your chain. If the child shares an idea that doesn't link to the previous idea, scaffold the conversation by looking back at the chart. Your conversation might sound something like this.

   T: I liked the book _____.
         What did you think about the book?
   S: I like it too.
   T: What was your favorite part?
   S: My favorite part was _____. (You may have to prompt the child to ask, "What was your favorite part?")
   T: My favorite part was _____ because _____. Did you notice how the author _____?

> I can LINK my THINKING to my friends' THINKING by saying/asking...
> What do you think?
> Why do you think that?
> Tell me more about your thinking.
> Did you notice . . . ?
> I have the same thinking because...
> My thinking is different because...

Make a list of phrases and questions students can use to link their conversations together.

Invitation: "When you have conversations with your friends, challenge yourself to link your thinking to their thinking. Notice how much more you learn from your friends when you do this."

MINI-LESSON: How to Politely End a Conversation

Preparation: Begin an anchor chart like the one pictured here with some possible phrases students could use as they end a conversation. Leave space for children to add their own ideas.

Explanation: This mini-lesson continues the work you've been doing with students on conversational norms. Conversational norms are an essential part of the "Learning and Innovation Skills" found in *A Framework for 21st Century Learning* (Partnership for 21st Century Skills, 2009). In order for learners to

> WAYS to POLITELY END a CONVERSATION...
> * Nice talking with you!
> * I learned something new today!
> * Thanks! You really made me think!
> * Thanks for being such a good listener!
> * It's O.K. that we don't agree
> * Wow! I never thought about it like that!
> * You really challenged me think in a different way!

Create a chart of possible phrases students could use to end a conversation.

clearly communicate and collaborate with others, they need practice in the following agreed-upon discussion norms. Setting these norms early in the year will pay off in the long run as children converse with each other.

Demonstration: "Imagine if you were talking on the phone with your friend and you hung up without saying good-bye. How would your friend feel?" Listen to students' responses. Continue the discussion with, "What do you do before you hang up the phone or when are leaving a friend's house?" Listen to responses.

"Yes! That's right, you say good-bye. Well, the same is true in our classroom. When you are having a conversation with your friend, it is polite to end it with a quick phrase. Let's look at the chart to see some ideas to get you started."

Invitation: "Thinkers, I'll give you a signal to draw your conversation to a close that will remind you that it is time to end with a phrase from the chart."

LAUNCHING THE READING WORKSHOP: PROCEDURAL MINI-LESSONS FOR ESTABLISHING INDEPENDENT READING

Before you get started with the following mini-lessons, you have a few book management options to consider. In order to read independently, students need a supply of books that are appealing, engaging, and challenging, yet comprehensible to them as readers. There are a number of ways to organize your classroom library to ensure that students have ready access to books. Here are two suggestions to spark your thinking.

Whole-Class Book Bins

Before the school year begins, create four or five whole-group book bins. This idea comes from Debbie Miller's book *Reading With Meaning* (2002). We follow Debbie's suggestions by creating a large bin for each group or table, containing a balanced diet of books which, depending on your grade level, could include the following types of books: alphabet books, repetitive pattern books, laminated poems, song picture books, folktales/fairy tales, books you've read aloud, nonfiction books, beginning-of-the-year books, and wordless books.

You may want to create a system for rotating the bins around the room each day and also for keeping them fresh by regularly adding new books. There is nothing more thrilling to children than finding in their bin the book you read aloud the day before!

Individual Book Boxes

Once students are comfortable using the whole-class book bins, we transition to individual book boxes. We purchased our book boxes from a teacher supply

---

Where and when do students get new books for their book boxes?

Leveled books from small-group guided reading lessons are placed in their book box.

Books from Reading Boost Bag (page 75) are placed in book box.

Books from Take-Home Book Club (page 151) are placed in book box.

We support children as they shop for books during reading conferences.

We use one small-group guided reading time every few weeks to "shop" for books together.

Once children become adept at selecting just-right books, we do a "one-book swap" prior to each Reading Zone time. They take one book out of their book box and replace it with a new book from the classroom or school library.

catalog, but many teachers choose to make their own using decorated cereal boxes or plastic zipper bags. This container is essential for housing each student's collection of just-right books. We usually begin this just about the time we do the "Have I Got a Book for You" mini-lesson found on page 48. To keep a fresh supply of books in students' book boxes, consider what works for us; see the box on page 54.

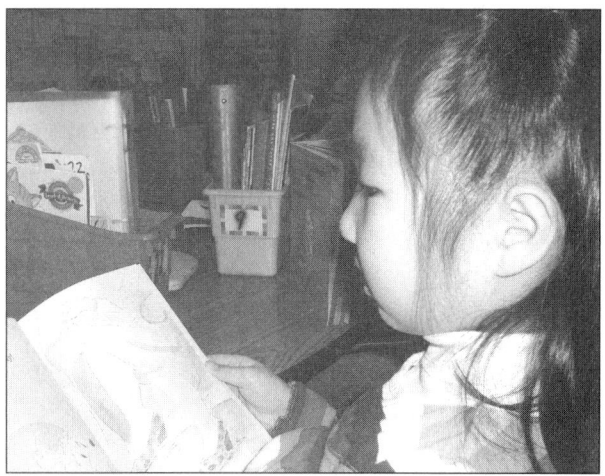

A book box is essential for housing each student's collection of just-right books.

MINI-LESSON: Let's Read, Think, and Talk About the Pictures

Preparation: Gather 12–15 wordless picture books, enough for students to share one with a partner. For additional lists of wordless books, see *Month-by-Month Trait-Based Writing Instruction* (Walther & Phillips, 2009), page 63, and *Literature Is Back!* (Fuhler & Walther, 2007), page 52.

Chalk (Thomson, 2010)	When a group of children find a bag of magical chalk, they draw some amazing adventures.
The Lion and the Mouse (Pinkney, 2009)	Take your time as you read the pictures and discuss Pinkney's stunning, wordless rendition of Aesop's fable.
Mirror (Baker, 2010)	Your students will spend hours poring over Baker's signature collages and the unique design of this wordless book. See the similarities, differences, and connections between two boys' daily life, one in urban Australia and the other in rural Morocco.
Shadow (Lee, 2010)	A cluttered attic and a little girl with a vivid imagination make this wordless picture book a visual treat.

Explanation: Depending on your grade level or your students' previous reading experience, you may decide to skip this lesson.

Demonstration: To effectively "read" a wordless picture book with the class, begin by going on a picture walk through the entire book. Encourage students to look and ponder. If time and attention spans permit, go through the book a second time, pausing to discuss students' thinking. If this is too much for one mini-lesson, stop after the pondering picture walk and reread and discuss the book the next day.

Invitation: "Girls and boys, now it is your turn to read, think, and talk with a partner about the pictures in a wordless picture book. Remember to take a pondering picture walk first, then

reread, think, and talk about what you notice and what you are thinking."

MINI-LESSON: Let's Retell a Folktale, Fairy Tale, or Nursery Rhyme

Preparation: Depending on your grade level and students' interests and reading abilities, you can gather a collection of familiar folktales, fairy tales, or nursery rhymes. See suggestions on pages 149–150. Collect enough books so that students can read a book with a partner following your demonstration.

Explanation: Familiar tales offer emerging readers the opportunity to mimic the act of reading by retelling the story using their schema for the tale.

Young readers enjoy retelling familiar traditional tales.

Demonstration: Determine if most of your children know the tale by asking, "How many of you know the story of Goldilocks and the Three Bears [or other familiar tale]?" Try to select a story that is familiar to most of your students. Then, invite readers to join you in retelling the story. Say, "Today we are going to retell this story together. Let's begin." Ask different students to tell parts of the story as you show the illustrations.

Invitation: "Today you are going to pick a familiar tale from our library to read and retell with our partner."

MINI-LESSON: Let's Use the Picture Clues to Help Us Read the Words

Preparation: Gather books with a strong picture to match with the text. Copy and display the song "Picture Clues" (CD Resource 2.3) and the Decoding Strategy Wheel (CD Resource 2.4). Select and cover with a sticky note a key word on each page.

Explanation: Picture clues are helpful for beginning readers. Proficient readers integrate the use of picture clues with the other decoding strategies found on the Decoding Strategy Wheel. If you have

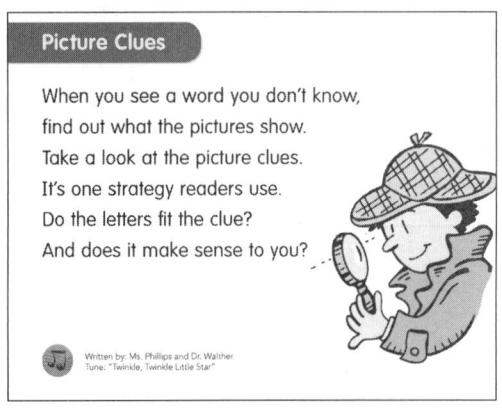

CD Resource 2.3 and IWB_Song_2.3

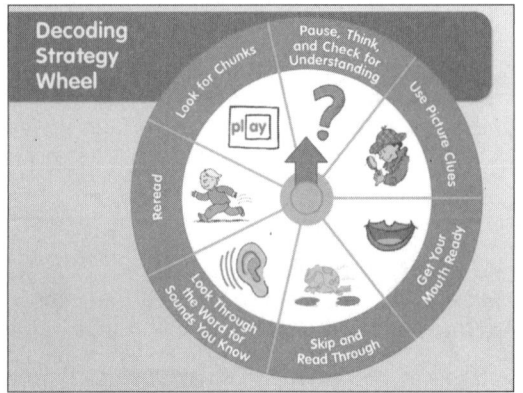

CD Resource 2.4 and IWB_Decoding_Wheel

determined that most of your readers are successfully using the picture clue strategy, save this mini-lesson to teach with the small group of students who need it.

Demonstration: Before reading the book, read the title and invite students to look at and discuss the illustrations on the book cover. Read the text together and guide readers to identify the covered key vocabulary words in the text by using the corresponding picture clue. Reveal the word and point out how the picture clue helped to identify the key word. To recap the learning, sing the strategy song "Picture Clues" and point out the strategy symbol on the Decoding Strategy Wheel; if you have an interactive whiteboard, display IWB_Song_2.3 and press the musical note to play the tune. Discuss the importance of using strategies to figure out unknown words.

Invitation: "Let's review the different ways you can read a book. You can read, think, and talk about the pictures, retell a familiar tale, and use the picture clues to help you read the words."

MINI-LESSON: Let's Read the Words

Preparation: Gather a collection of repetitive, predictable pattern books. We've listed a few of our favorites in the box below. For your demonstration, it is helpful if you have a Big Book or enlarged version of the text.

Explanation: Picture books with repetitive words, phrases, or questions that invite children to join in are helpful for your emerging readers and ELLs. Many of these titles have illustrations that support the reader as he or she tackles the words. Titles such as those listed here also promote reading enjoyment, and you will notice that children return to them time and again, even after they've learned to read.

Demonstration: Read aloud a predictable book. While reading, invite students to join in. Discuss how the word patterns and the picture clues support you as a reader.

Invitation: "I have a basket of some old favorite books here. Let's work with a partner to use the pattern to read the words in the book."

MINI-LESSON: Independent Reading— What Are You Doing? What Are You Learning?

Preparation: Think about how you want to organize your students for independent reading. A strategy that works well for us is separating the class into two groups, according to students' class numbers (each student is assigned a number,

---

PREDICTABLE PATTERN BOOKS

Bear Snores On (Wilson, 2002)

I Went Walking (Williams, 1989)

Jump, Frog, Jump! (Kalan, 1981)

The Napping House (Wood, 1984)

Not a Box (Portis, 2006)

Silly Sally (Wood, 1992)

starting with 1, in alphabetical order of their last names). One group consists of students with odd class numbers; in the other group are students with even class numbers. Then, each day, we alternate between even-numbered students reading in a "pillow place" and odd-numbered students reading in a "desk place" and vice versa. To keep track, we move a clothespin back and forth between the words *odd* and *even*—simple! To use this strategy, you will need about 12–15 pillows. (We suggest finding someone who can make pillowcases with zippers, or request that parents donate them, so you can easily wash them when the lice invade your room!) When it is time for the Reading Zone, quickly spread the pillows around the room. (Eventually, this becomes a student's job.) Move the clothespin and the kids know where to go. If you have students in your classroom who need to be in a certain spot each day, designate a certain color pillow and spot for those children.

Explanation: As we mentioned earlier, extended time for independent reading is a critical component to powerful reading instruction. All of the lessons we've done up to now have included invitations for students to read and enjoy books with partners or in small groups. The purpose of this mini-lesson is to help students make the transition from partner reading to independent reading.

Demonstration: If you are familiar with *The Daily Five: Fostering Literacy Independence in the Elementary Grades* (Boushey & Moser, 2006) then you know about the importance of setting up predictable routines for independent reading. We use many of the ideas in their book combined with those we've learned from Debbie Miller (2002) and Nancie Atwell (2007) as we introduce, model, and practice independent reading. During our demonstration, we explicitly show children what we expect during this time. Then provide a brief time to practice. You always want to leave your students wanting more time. After they've had a few minutes to practice, debrief, and problem solve, assure students that they will have more time to read tomorrow!

Invitation: "Readers, it is time for the Reading Zone. It is the most important time of our day. Remember, the more you read, the better you get!"

INDEPENDENT READING

We Are Readers!	
What are you doing?	**What are you learning?**
Picking a just-right place	The more we read, the better we get.
Choosing a just-right book	Books can teach us many things.
Staying in one place	We love to read!
Starting right away	
Reading with a whisper voice	
Reading the whole time	

MINI-LESSON: Independent Reading—Choosing Just-Right Books

Preparation: At this point you should have collected some formal and informal assessment data about your students to help you determine their independent reading level. When helping children choose books for independent reading, you want to make sure that they can read them with at least 97 percent accuracy (Allington, 2006). Copy and display the strategy song "Just Right Books" (CD Resource 2.5).

CD Resource 2.5 and IWB_Song_2.5

Explanation: Why is it important to help children learn how to choose just-right books? It . . .

- fosters students' reading success because enjoyment of texts is a critical factor in becoming a passionate, lifelong reader.
- improves comprehension because children can read and think at the same time.
- develops reading skills. Research shows that if a child reads a steady diet of books that are too hard, his or her reading actually gets worse.
- builds competence. Although reading lots of easy books is helpful for building confidence and fluency, once students are competent readers, reading easy books is not enough for continued growth.
- challenges readers to apply previously learned strategies as they read various genres.

Common Core State Standards (NGA/CCSSO, 2010) offer three factors to measure text complexity. It is helpful to keep these in mind as you teach students how to choose books that are just right for them.

- Qualitative—What does the reader need to know in order to be able to read this text?
- Quantitative—What is the measured readability of this text according to measures of text complexity (guided reading levels, lexile levels, and so on)?
- Matching the reader to the text and task—Is the reader ready for this type of text?

Demonstration: Read aloud *You'll Soon Grow Into Them, Titch* (Hutchins, 1983). Ask, "How many of you went shopping for clothes before school started? What do you do when you shop for clothes?" (Responses may include: look for clothes I like, try them on, and so on.) Continue, "Yes, you're right. This year we are going to learn how to shop for books. Books are like clothes—some are a little too small, and although you may love to read them over and over, they are not as helpful to you as those that are just right. Some books are too big, but if you read lots and lots of just-right books, you will soon grow into

Guide children as they learn how to choose just-right books.

them. Other books fit just right, like the clothes that Titch finally bought at the store."

- Select three books from your personal collection: one book with very few words (maybe a picture book that you read as a child), one book that you would enjoy reading (a favorite professional book or summer read), and one book that is very difficult (science text or technical book). Read aloud a little bit from each book, starting with the easiest. While reading aloud, describe how you feel about the book (too small, too big, and just right).

> ### HOW TO SUPPORT RELUCTANT AND UNMOTIVATED READERS DURING INDEPENDENT READING
>
> You may have a few students who struggle with sustaining attention during independent reading, even though you have worked very hard to build their stamina. We've developed some helpful strategies for these students.
> - Find books that match their interests. Beginning-reader graphic novels, like the ones listed on page 129, and accessible series books like Mo Willems's Elephant and Piggie books are excellent resources.
> - Before you begin conferring with individuals, gather these students together and "feed" them books, handing them another book as soon as they finish reading one. Since the books they are reading are usually short, the habit of reading one book after another has to be fostered. Left to their own devices, these students will find many ways to avoid reading. We've found that if you take a week or so to show these students how to take out their books, put them in a stack, start with the book on top, read that one, then the next and so on, they begin to gain confidence and to understand exactly what they should be doing.
> - Provide books on CD or MP3 for their listening pleasure.

- Explain that when choosing a just-right book it is important to look at the pictures, think about the topic, and think about other books by the same author.
- Say, "If I can read most of the words on the page, it appeals to me, and it makes sense, then I am ready to make my decision."
- It is also important to demonstrate abandoning a book by reading a page or two and explaining, "I just didn't like it as much as I thought I would, so I will put it back and choose another book."

Sing the Just-Right-Books song. If you have an interactive whiteboard, display IWB_Song_2.5 and press the musical note to play the tune.

Invitation: "Readers, today try to find a just-right book to read during independent reading."

LAUNCHING THE READING WORKSHOP: A MENU OF MINI-LESSONS FOR READING RESPONSE

Often when we think of reading response, we associate it solely with written response. Equally essential is a child's ability to respond independently, orally, and by conversing with his or her friends. Think about how you respond to your own reading. One response may be simply to reread a favorite part. Another response might be to read another book by the same author or about the same topic. Many of us belong to book clubs because we want to talk about books once we are finished reading them to see what others think about them. Hearing the opinions and ideas of others often changes the way we think about a book. Finally, many of us respond to a book by jotting a quote or memorable phrase in a notebook. With this in mind, we developed the next few mini-lessons to introduce the idea that readers interact with the text.

MINI-LESSON: What Do Readers Do? R-E-R-E-A-D, Reread, Reread

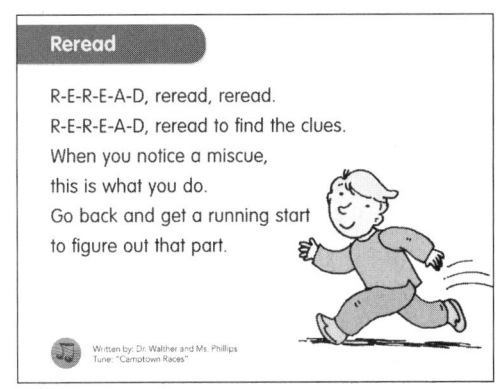

CD Resource 2.6 and IWB_Song_2.6

Preparation: Select a book that offers opportunities to reread for various reasons. For the demonstration, we read *George and Martha Encore* (Marshall, 1973).

Copy and display the strategy song "Reread" (CD Resource 2.6) and the Decoding Strategy Wheel (CD Resource 2.4).

Explanation: How many times have you finished a good book and heard a chorus of "Read it again!"? Readers reread for a variety of purposes. They reread at the word level to figure out an unknown word using context clues. They reread at the text level to clear up any confusions in their understanding of the text. Many readers reread to enjoy a book another time or notice things they missed on the first reading.

Demonstration: Begin by reading and singing the "Reread" song. Then, do a demonstration similar to the one below. If you have an interactive whiteboard, display IWB_Song_2.6 and press the musical note to play the tune.

George and Martha Encore Reread Demonstration	
p. 4 Read the word *recital* with a hard c, so it sounds like re-kite-al.	Wait! I've never heard the word "re-kite-al" before. Let me **reread** that sentence to see if I can figure out that word. Oh, I see here that Martha is inviting George to her dance _____. Hmmm! Oh, I know sometimes the letter c makes the /s/ sound, let me try that.
The French Lesson (pp. 16–20)	This chapter made me laugh so hard, I'm going to **reread** it because I love it so much!
pp. 34–35 When you read the first sentence, leave out the words *refused to*.	This part isn't making sense. I thought I read, "Martha put on her suntan lotion." How did she get a sunburn? I need to **reread** to figure it out. Oh! I left out the words refused to and it changed the whole meaning of the sentence. Good thing that I went back to **reread**!
p. 40 Read it as if Martha is happy.	Let me **reread** this page again. I don't think I read it the way James Marshall wanted it to sound. It says here that "Martha was so discouraged." I don't think he wanted me to read that in a cheery voice.

Invitation: "In your reading today, after you are done reading, reread the book. Let's talk later about what you discovered when it's time to share. Happy reading!"

MINI-LESSON: What Do Readers Do? Read Book After Book, After Book . . .

Preparation: Collect a stack of books you've read that are similar in some way. Perhaps you enjoy reading mysteries and have read a lot of books in that genre or you have a preferred author and have all of his or her books. If you prefer to use children's books for your demonstration, then select books that are connected in some way. The books might have similar characters, settings, themes, topics, or organizational structures/patterns, or might come from the same series or author.

> R-E-R-E-A-D Reread, Reread...
> We reread to...
> * Make sense of the words (Logan)
> * Look for chunks (Reese)
> * Check if the word is right (Andrew)
> * Help us learn (Erin)
> * Figure out the word we skipped (Nikunj)
> * Understand the whole story (Lynn)
> * Get better at reading the words (Justin)
> * Help us use our sounds better (Nikki)
> * Read with style (Dr. W.)
> * BE AN EVEN BETTER READER (Sophia)

Record all the reasons students reread

Explanation: The point you are trying to make is that when you are a reader, one book leads to another. In the March 2011 issue of *Book Links* magazine, Sylvia Vardell shared an idea that caught our eyes. To celebrate National Poetry Month she created a Poetry Tag, consisting of a chain of poems that she linked together based on a word, an image, a topic, a poetic device, and so on. After reading the article, we began using her idea with our students to play Book Tag. For a quick example, see the Beginning-of-the-Year Book Tag, right.

Demonstration: Using the "book tag" idea, show how some of the books you've been reading to children are connected and how one book led to another book. Then, share with your students how you go about choosing books to read. You might say something like, "When I'm deciding what book I want to read next,

> ### BEGINNING-OF-THE-YEAR BOOK TAG
>
> 1. *Book! Book! Book!* (Bruss, 2001)
> 2. *Wild About Books* (Sierra, 2004)
>   Connection to previous book: Animals get hooked on reading.
> 3. *The Gruffalo* (Donaldson, 1999)
>   Connection to previous book: Both authors use a rhyming sentence pattern.
> 4. *When a Monster Was Born* (Taylor, 2006)
>   Connection to previous book: The illustrations of the gruffalo and the monster look alike.
> 5. *If You Take a Mouse to School* (Numeroff, 2002)
>   Connection to the previous book: Both are circular stories.
> 6. *Library Mouse* (Kirk, 2007)
>   Connection to previous book: The main character in both books is a mouse.

I think to myself, 'If I enjoyed reading this book by [author's name] then I think I will probably like his or her next book.'" Continue this conversation by asking a few children what topics they enjoy reading about. Say, "[Name], I noticed that you really love dinosaur books, so I'm guessing I'm going to have to help you find a lot of books about dinosaurs for you to read!"

Invitation: "Readers, remember that one book leads to another and another. See if you can make a Book Tag today and bring it with you when it is time to share!"

MINI-LESSON: What Do Readers Do? Read, Think, and Talk With a Friend

Preparation: Gather enough books so that each set of partners has one book to share. Prior to the lesson you will want to think about how you want to organize students into reading partners or triads. One clever way to get students to quickly find a partner is by gathering various colored pairs of baby socks. Then, simply toss a sock to each child and invite him/her to find his or her matching sock partner. To strategically preassign reading partners, consider your readers' strengths and weaknesses. We've had more success when we pair our struggling readers with students who are average rather than with our advanced readers. Depending on the student, some advanced readers lack the patience to guide and help a reader who struggles. Also, if you pair your advanced readers together, you can quickly differentiate your reading instruction by providing them with more-complex texts and tasks. If you happen to have assistance in your room during this time, you might consider pairing striving readers together and having them work with an adult. There are so many options! Of course, you will have to observe the interactions between the pairs or triads and adjust them as the year progresses.

Explanation: Your goal for this mini-lesson is to create and review the partner reading guidelines, model what reading with a partner looks and sounds like, and provide

---

Partner Reading Tips!

1. Sit side by side. Share the book.
2. Decide how you are going to read the book.
   - Tag-team reading—One partner reads a page/part, then the other reads a page/part.
   - Together reading—Read together so it sounds like one voice.
   - Tell-something reading—One partner reads a page and tells something about it, then the other reads a page and tells something about it.
3. Listen carefully when your partner is reading and talking.
4. If you or your partner gets stuck on a word:
   - Count to three to give him or her time to figure it out.
   - Say, "Try this!" (point to the strategy on the Decoding Strategy Wheel)
   - If your partner is still stuck, show (don't tell) how you would figure it out.
5. When partner reading time is over, thank your partner for reading with you.

CD Resource 2.7

children with time to practice. Certainly, you will have to repeat this demonstration for a number of days until you feel the children are comfortable, and also throughout the year when you observe that your students need a review or when you switch their strategically paired partners. In addition, you will want to review this mini-lesson as students learn the self-monitoring/decoding strategies, so that children can use these prompts when their partner gets stuck on a word.

Students read, think, and talk together.

Demonstration: Invite a pair of students to the front of the classroom. Prompt them as they model how readers read, think, and talk with a friend using the tips found on page 63.

Invitation: "Readers, it is time to share a book with your reading partner. Begin by deciding how you will read the book. Happy reading!"

MINI-LESSON: What Do Readers Do? Read, Think, and Write

Preparation: Assemble "Read, Think, and Respond" book (CD Resources 1.1 – 1.7). Copy and display Resource 1.1, Lined Page. Select a short, engaging read-aloud.

Explanation: When you invite students to respond to their reading, they make connections between new and known understandings, utilize recently acquired vocabulary, and articulate their latest understandings. In short, they are writing to reflect and learn. For their first written response, we choose to have students write about their favorite part. If your students are more advanced, we suggest selecting one of the other response options found in chapters 3–8.

Demonstration: After reading the book aloud,

Young learners write about their reading.

discuss your favorite part. Demonstrate how to write the words: My favorite part was _____ because _____. Use evidence from the book to support your choice.

Invitation: "Today after you read a book, I want you to get out your Read, Think, and Respond books and write about your favorite part."

LAUNCHING THE READING WORKSHOP: A GUIDE FOR EXPLORE THE W.O.R.L.D. TIME

Because each of the mini-lessons for Explore the W.O.R.L.D. time will follow a similar format, we will share some tips and ideas here, then follow it with specific materials needed for each area and a sample doing/learning chart to complete during the debriefing sessions.

Whole-Class Introduction

Introduce one independent literacy activity at a time. Briefly share your expectations, the purpose for the activity, and what children will be doing and learning while they are engaged in that particular activity; create an anchor chart summarizing this information that students can refer to when working independently to help keep them focused.

- Begin each introduction with a mini-lesson to demonstrate the procedures specific to that activity, such as proper use, care, cleanup, and storage of materials. Remember that mini-lessons to teach cooperation, sharing of materials, and turn taking are also essential!

Provide ample time for students to practice. While they are practicing you may choose to individually assess a student or two and, in between, walk around to observe, reteach, and model how to work independently and how to be a respectful, thoughtful, and kind learner. We snap pictures of students engaged in activities that we then post on our anchor charts as a visual reminder of what students should be doing during Explore the W.O.R.L.D. time.

- At the end of each Explore the W.O.R.L.D time, debrief by asking the following questions: "What problems did you come across today?" followed by "How did you solve that problem?" and "How else could you solve that problem?" and "What did you learn today about Explore the W.O.R.L.D. time?" (Johnston, 2004, p. 32). Jot down students' thinking during these

Explore the W.O.R.L.D. Wheel

debriefing session to add to the doing/anchor chart.

- Continue in this fashion until all five Explore the W.O.R.L.D. activities have been introduced. As indicated on the First 25 Days Plan on page 42, we introduce one activity at a time, providing time for modeling, practicing, and debriefing before we move on to another. Once all five literacy activities are introduced, divide the class into five groups that work well together. One of the benefits of preassigning Explore the W.O.R.L.D. groups for ELLs is that we can ensure that each group has students with a variety of ethnic and cultural backgrounds and mixed language abilities (Richard-Amato, 2003). In addition, we can plan to have our struggling readers grouped with supportive peers.

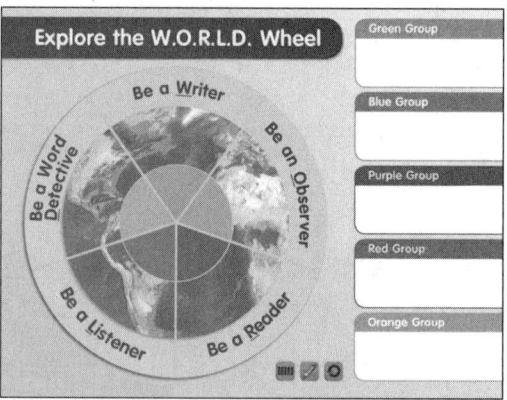

CD Resource 2.8 and IWB_WORLD_Wheel

Be a Writer

Preparation: Begin a "Be a Writer" menu, as shown below, that you will add to as the year progresses. We match our Be a Writer activities to the mini-lessons and genres that we are studying during writing workshop and that appear in *Month-by-Month Trait-Based Writing Instruction* (Walther & Phillips, 2009). To begin the year, make an assortment of "little books" in various sizes (see suggested sizes below) and with varying number of pages and place five books in each child's two-pocket Explore the W.O.R.L.D. folder. Organize your writing center so there is space for children to work. If you are short on space, provide clipboards for students to take to a quiet writing spot.

- 5½ by 8½ inches (a half sheet of copy paper portrait, staple some on top and some on side)
- 4½ by 11 inches (a half sheet of copy paper landscape, staple some on top and some on side)
- 4¼ by 5½ inches (a quarter sheet of copy paper)

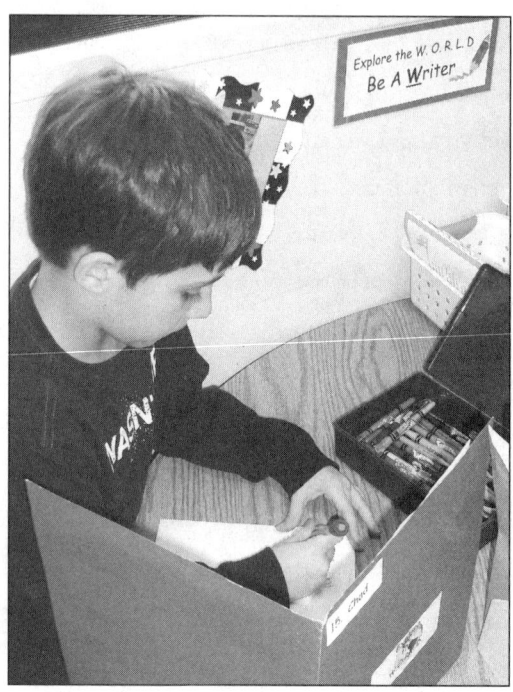

Explore the W. O. R. L. D. Time: Be a Writer

BE A WRITER

Write little books

Write riddle books

Write stories

Write jokes

Write biographies

Write nonfiction books

SAMPLE ANCHOR CHART

Explore the W.O.R.L.D. Time—Be a <u>W</u>riter	
What are you doing?	**What are you learning?**
Finding a good writing spot for me	How to be an even better writer
Thinking about what I want to write	How to stretch out words for writing
Writing the whole time	How to experiment with new writing ideas
Concentrating on my writing	How to tell about my experiences with pictures and words
Rereading and revising	
Sharing the writing tools	How to record ideas and thinking I want to remember
Using a whisper voice	

Be an Observer

Preparation: If you are like us, you occasionally run out of time for your science and social studies lessons. To solve this problem, we created this center to enhance our instruction and provide time for students to observe and explore content-related books and materials. Observers are always excited to share their new learning, and we're amazed at how much they discover on their own when given time to observe, think, and learn together. We've provided a few ideas to get you started, but it is best if you match the materials in this center to what you are studying in your classroom. Students can record their observations on individual recording sheets, on sticky notes to add to a chart posted nearby titled "What I Noticed/What I Learned," or in a

Explore the W. O. R. L. D. Time: Be an Observer

SAMPLE ANCHOR CHART

Explore the W.O.R.L.D. Time—Be an <u>O</u>bserver	
What are you doing?	**What are you learning?**
Using my senses to learn	How to add details to my illustrations
Writing or drawing to record my observations and my new learning	How to ask questions about things in my world
	How to make connections
Sharing my new learning	How to talk with my friends about what I'm learning

"Be an Observer" notebook that they use only in this center. You'll find the Be an Observer response sheet we use in Resource 2.9 on the CD.

Be an Observer Ideas	
September	A basket of wordless books, art prints, view masters
October	Geography—maps, globes, atlases
November	Air and Weather Unit—air experiments, weather log
December	Solar System Unit—planet posters, space books
January	A basket of traditional tales
February	History—president posters, biographies
March	A basket of poetry books, sticky notes for noticing craft techniques
April	Rock Unit—rocks/gems, magnifying glasses, rock identification posters, books
May	Insect Unit—caterpillars, bug books, insect diagrams

Be a Reader

Preparation:

- Gather books, books, and more books! Your classroom library should be well stocked with a variety of genres including poetry, picture books, informational books, graphic novels, chapter books, popular series books, and so on. Select books to meet your students' interests and reading abilities and change them regularly to keep things fresh.
- Organize your books in a way that makes sense to you and your students. Some teachers prefer to let children assist in book organization.

SAMPLE ANCHOR CHART

Explore the W.O.R.L.D. Time—Be a Reader	
What are you doing?	**What are you learning?**
Finding a good reading spot for me	How to be an even better reader
Reading the whole time	What kinds of books I like to read
Reading on my own or with a friend	What kinds of books my friends like to read
Taking turns with the books	Facts from nonfiction books
Using a whisper voice to talk about books	Ideas for my own writing
Recommending books to my friends	
Helping a friend use the reading strategies	
Taking care of the books	
Putting books back in their place	

- Create a comfortable reading area with pillows, beanbag chairs, a special carpet, and, if allowed, a lamp or two for atmosphere.
- Make a "book hospital" basket where children can place torn or damaged books.
- Set aside time to teach mini-lessons on the care and keeping of books.

Be a Listener

Preparation: Gather or create the following items:

- A listening center. We recently purchased a unit that plays CDs, MP3s, and cassette tapes. It is handy because we can transfer our old cassette tapes to MP3 files, and then burn them onto CDs (in our free time!).
- Books with accompanying cassettes, CDs, or MP3 files. Consider recording your own books—that way you can add teaching points along the way!

Set aside a bit of time to teach the following mini-lessons:

- How to work together to choose a book
- How to insert, play, rewind (if needed), and put away a tape, CD, or MP3 file
- How to adjust the volume
- What to do if the listening center is not working

Explore the W. O. R. L. D. Time: Be a Reader

Explore the W. O. R. L. D. Time: Be a Listener

SAMPLE ANCHOR CHART

Explore the W.O.R.L.D. Time—Be a Listener	
What are you doing?	**What are you learning?**
Picking out a tape or CD	How to be an even better reader
Passing out the books to my friends	How to read with style
Listening carefully to the book	
Talking about the book with my friends	

SAMPLE ANCHOR CHART

Explore the W.O.R.L.D. Time—Be a Word <u>D</u>etective	
What are you doing?	**What are you learning?**
Word study activities	How to play and work with my friends
[Record specific activities such as the following:]	How to talk with my friends about what I'm learning
Making words	How words work
Sorting words	How to sort words
Playing word games	How to read words
Reading the room to search for certain kinds of words	How to spell words
	How to make words

Be a Word Detective

Preparation:

Gather word study activities such as:

- alphabet books
- word study games
- word sorts

MINI-LESSONS FOR VOCABULARY DEVELOPMENT

As we think about teaching vocabulary to young readers, we want to make sure that our word-focused instruction matches their learning needs.

Explore the W. O. R. L. D. Time: Be a Word Detective

Keep the following tips in mind as you use the lessons in this book to enhance your vocabulary instruction.

- Read aloud, read together, and provide time for students to read independently. Remember, most new words are learned through reading!
- Engage in real, concrete experiences with your students to help them learn new words.
- Display photographs, illustrations, or the real objects when discussing words.
- Use a variety of graphic organizers and word sorts to get students actively engaged with thinking about and categorizing words.
- Teach strategies for learning new words, such as using word parts, context, and other tools like word banks, word charts, and the dictionary.

- Invite students to sketch or draw the definitions of words to strengthen their understanding.
- Provide multiple opportunities for students to apply newly acquired word knowledge in speaking and writing.
- Promote word wonder!

You'll notice that we didn't include any vocabulary-related mini-lessons in this chapter. Our reasoning was that, because it takes so much time to launch the reading workshop, we figured, if you are like us, you would have more than enough to teach! We did, however, include the "Read-Alouds With Rich Vocabulary" chart on page 72 so that you could begin this weekly vocabulary routine, and then, as time permits, weave in the vocabulary-related mini-lessons in October and beyond. Specific mini-lessons on vocabulary development will appear in this section in chapters 3–8.

FLUENCY FUN! SLOW OR FAST?

To introduce the concept of fluency, read aloud two poems from Jack Prelutsky's book *Something Big Has Been Here* (1990). Begin by reading aloud the poem "Slow Sloth's Slow Song" (p. 65) and then invite your students to join in. Follow this slow poem with "Twaddletalk Tuck" (p. 64), which simply begs to be read quickly. Discuss the difference between the two readings and how Prelutsky's use of punctuation marks helps the reader understand how to read each poem. If you have multiple copies of the poem, invite students to read the poems with a partner. After reading " Slow Sloth's Slow Song," young learners might be interested in discovering more about sloths. If so, read aloud the nonfiction title *Let's Look at Sloths* (Piehl, 2011). As a follow-up to this lesson, read either *Hip and Hop Don't Stop* (Czekaj, 2010), which appears in the chart on page 41, or *Wolf!* (Bloom, 1999), in which the wolf learns to read with style!

READ-ALOUDS WITH RICH VOCABULARY		
Title and Author	**Brief Summary**	**Words to Highlight and Kid-Friendly Definition**
Bink and Gollie (DiCamillo & McGhee, 2010)	Three stories about two girls, Bink and Gollie, who have unique personalities but are still "marvelous companions." In the first tale, they make a compromise over a pair of, in Gollie's opinion, outrageous socks. The second tale finds Gollie on a journey to the Andes Mountains. The book ends with a story about Bink's new goldfish.	**compromise:** an agreement in which both sides give up something **journey:** a long trip **companion:** someone who spends time with you
How Rocket Learned to Read (Hills, 2010)	A little yellow bird entices Rocket, the dog, to learn about the "wondrous, mighty, gorgeous alphabet" by reading captivating books aloud.	**disturbed:** bothered, interrupted, or upset **mighty:** showing great power or strength **captivated:** extremely interested in or drawn to something; fascinated
Amos & Boris (Steig, 1971)	When Amos the mouse rolls off his boat into the sea, Boris, a whale, saves him and brings him back to his home. Later, Amos saves Boris's life. Draw readers' attention to the story's similarities to Aesop's fable "The Lion and the Mouse."	**immense:** very big, huge **desperately:** in urgent or critical need; needing action right away **admiration:** a feeling of respect and approval

Part 3: Genre Study—Read-Aloud Favorites for the Beginning of the School Year

To launch your first genre study, consider sharing with students the definition of genre—a category of literature (or music or art) that has a similar form, style, or subject matter. Understanding the differences among genres is important because genre influences the way a reader engages with and interprets a text. To collect information about the various genres as you read them, consider making an anchor chart similar to the one below so that you can add what you and your students discover as you read books from the different genres.

Genre	Definition	Purpose	Clues
Beginning-of-the-Year Books	A beginning-of-the-year book tells about the experiences of children on the first days of school.	To help children feel comfortable about going to school	• Takes place in a school, a classroom, or on the playground • The characters are children, teachers, principals, or other people you find in a school • Includes the feelings/emotions of the characters

Genre	Definition	Purpose	Clues
Personal Narratives	A personal narrative is a story about something that happened to the writer and how he or she feels about it.	To share a story from the author's point of view.	• Main character is the writer or narrator. • Written in first-person point of view • Describes an event or experience • Contains personal comments and observations
Real and Make-Believe Stories	A story is something that has happened. It can be real or make-believe.	To help readers make sense of their world	• Main character could be the writer or another person or creature. • Author uses his or her imagination to create the tale. • Written in either first person or third person • Narrates a chain of related events • Contains a beginning, a middle, and an end • Contains characters, setting, action, problem, events, and solution • Uses sensory details to describe things
Traditional Tales	Traditional tales are stories that were originally told, then eventually written down. Traditional tales have been passed down from generation to generation. They include folktales, fairy tales, and fables.	To help the reader better understand different cultures To help readers understand other stories that are based on or have similar elements as the traditional tales	• Some have a moral or lesson. • Some have magic. • Some have heroes and villains. • Some explain why things in the world are the way they are. • Some have talking animals.
Biographies	A biography is a piece of writing that tells facts and interesting details about a real person.	To better understand the person and the effect he or she had on events and/or history	• Written in third person • Tells about a real person • Describes the person's life, actions, and relationships with others • Includes interesting, sometimes lesser-known details about the person
Poetry	A poem is a short piece of writing that comes from the writer's imagination.	To convey the poet's ideas and feelings to help us see that world in a different way or use our imagination	• Plays with the sound of words and the rhythmic language patterns • Uses vivid language to create sensory images • Condenses ideas into a shorter format than prose • Presented in various shapes, sizes, and formats
Nonfiction	A nonfiction piece tells the reader true facts about people, animals, places, or events.	To inform, explain something to, or persuade the reader	• Gives information • Factually accurate • Sometimes written in narrative format • May use visual features to communicate information

Adapted from *Month-by-Month Trait-Based Writing Instruction* (Walther & Phillips, 2009)

To begin your work with genres, we selected one with which students are familiar. We are sure you have your own collection of books that you share at the beginning of the year because you know that it is a good idea to have a stack of short, engaging books handy to read when you and your students need a break. Reading aloud helps children calm down and settle in to the routines of a busy classroom. Just as we are working on building learners' stamina for independent reading, it is equally important to lengthen the time that they are able to sit and focus on a read-aloud. With this goal in mind we read aloud a lot in the first weeks of school. We read short books and longer books. If we notice the kids losing interest, we will stop the book, take a quick "brain break," and then continue where we left off by asking, "Who can tell me what has happened so far in this book?" This offers listeners an opportunity to retell and summarize the book.

GENRE STUDY: BEGINNING-OF-THE-YEAR BOOKS

Title and Author	Brief Summary
Bedhead (Palatini, 2000)	It wouldn't be a school picture day without reading this uproarious book about a boy who wakes up with bedhead.
Bein' With You This Way (Nikola-Lisa, 1994)	Celebrate the diversity of the students in your class by sharing this rap-like, cumulative chant.
Carmen Learns English (Cox, 2010)	Carmen tells her little sister Lupita about her first day of school in the United States and the kind teacher who helped her learn to speak English and deal with bullies.
Dear Teacher (Husband, 2010)	When Michael gets a letter from the principal inviting him back to school, he writes a series of imaginative responses explaining why he will not be able to attend. Original, funny, and boy-friendly, this book is worth adding to your beginning-of-the-year collection.
Miss Fox's Class Shapes Up (Spinelli, 2011)	When Miss Fox discovers that her students are tired, not eating right, and out of shape, she teaches them sensible ways to shape up.
The Gingerbread Man Loose in School (Murray, 2011)	In this clever version of the familiar tale, the Gingerbread Man is running around the school looking for the children who went out for recess.
My Name is Yoon (Recorvits, 2003)	This affecting picture book depicts a Korean girl's adjustment to her new school and new country.
Pete the Cat: Rocking in My School Shoes (Litwin, 2011)	Download the free "Pete the Cat" song and enjoy singing it with your students as you follow Pete and his rocking shoes to the library, lunchroom, playground, and more.
Substitute Creacher (Gall, 2011)	Ms. Jenkins' students are in for a surprise and a few cautionary tales when they arrive at school and meet their substitute "creacher." Pair this with *Miss Nelson Is Missing* (Allard, 1977).
Suki's Kimono (Uegaki, 2003)	With spunk and self-confidence, Suki chooses to wear her beloved kimono to school.

Meeting the Needs of ALL Learners

Every time we learn about strategies for diverse learners, we turn to one other and say, "Wouldn't that idea be helpful for all of our kids?" Dedicated teachers like you are responsive to their students' individual needs and, therefore, modify and adapt their teaching practices every day. With that said, in each chapter we will share two ideas, one aimed at struggling readers and the other to target talented readers, knowing that you certainly could use each idea with your whole class, if you wish. Obviously, with the move toward Response to Intervention, we dedicate the majority of our professional development time to discussing strategies for students who struggle. And with time in such short supply, learners who exceed our expectations often don't get as much attention. Our goal is to help our talented readers become "self-extending" readers, who are able to use strategies not only to understand the meaning and message of the text but also to extend their knowledge of the reading process. In other words, self-extending readers independently and confidently activate and bring together their knowledge of how our language works, their background knowledge, and their literary experiences. They use these sources of information flexibly in a "smoothly orchestrated system" (Fountas & Pinnell, 1999, p. 5). We've noticed that many of our "advanced" readers are adept at reading the words but fall short of meeting the criteria for self-extending readers. So we want to nudge them further until they can seamlessly integrate different sources of information when processing a text. We felt it was important to take time out to think about our talented readers and share with you a few sensible ideas that will help them when they encounter many different types of complex texts. The goal is for them to problem-solve and transfer what they've learned about reading across texts, genres, and content areas.

SENSIBLE STRATEGIES FOR STRUGGLING READERS: THE READING BOOST BAG

When it comes to interventions for our struggling readers, we are adamant about the importance of reading real books and having authentic conversations about those books with real people, not learning from a scripted program or a computer program. Our classroom data have confirmed what Dick Allington has been saying for years—when you increase the amount of time students spend reading, they progress as readers because "there exists a potent relationship between volume of reading and reading achievement" (Allington, 2006, p. 44). To this end, the in-class intervention that we've created for our struggling readers and dubbed the Reading Boost Bag does just that. If we are doing this intervention ourselves, we begin the Reading Boost Bag very early in the year with just one or two students. If you are lucky enough to have a paraprofessional or assistant, you could add more readers. Please note that this intervention works best with students who have supportive families. If the students you are targeting do not get support at home, then it is helpful to pair the student with an upper-grade buddy for ten minutes a few days a week to practice reading.

Here's how it works. We label a plastic zipper bag with the student's name and "Reading Boost Bag." In the bag, we place a letter to parents with the directions (see CD Resource 2.10) along with a set of five sight words for students to practice (see the lists and corresponding flashcards in CD Resources 2.11–2.16). The sight word lists also contain a record-keeping sheet that facilitates communication between parents and the teacher. Then, we choose one or two selections from our leveled book library that the child can read. We preview the book with the child and send it home the sight words. Then, we follow the directions that we created to guide our paraprofessionals (see CD Resource 2.17).

TARGETING TALENTED READERS: MY READING AUTOBIOGRAPHY

You may have a few students in your classroom who are already self-motivated, voracious readers. They are able to read *and* comprehend a variety of books. Of course, they need your guidance in selecting appropriate books from various genres and opportunities to confer with you to discuss their reading and thinking. Students such as these enjoy having a special place to record the books they are reading, their reaction or response to the book, and the books they would like to read in the future. We like to call this notebook a reading autobiography

---

MY READING AUTOBIOGRAPHY

1. Choose a just-right book.
2. Write the date and the title of the book at the top of the page.
3. Carefully read the book.
4. If the book is a chapter book, PAUSE after each chapter, THINK, and RESPOND with a quick thought or idea.
5. If the book is not a chapter book, PAUSE at the end, THINK, and RESPOND by writing a quick thought or idea.

Here are some ideas to help spark your thinking. Please choose a different idea each time you write.

- This chapter/book was about . . .
- This chapter/book made me think of . . .
- I predict . . .
- I wonder . . .
- I noticed . . .
- What if . . .
- My favorite part was _____ because . . .
- My favorite character was _____ because . . .
- I felt _____ when _____ happened because . . .
- A different ending would be . . .
- Dear [teacher's name] (write me a letter about your book)

6. When you are finished, place your reading autobiography in the basket.
7. Confer with your teacher about the book.
8. Happy reading!

CD Resource 2.18

because, when read as a whole at the end of the year, it can answer the questions, "Who am I as a reader?" "What do the books I have read mean to me?" and "What are my future plans as a reader?" To help students create their reading autobiography, provide them with a composition notebook or spiral notebook. Invite each student to decorate the cover to reflect his or her reading personality. Then, with tab dividers, divide the pages into three sections labeled with the titles "Me" (just a few pages at the beginning), "My Reading" (most of the pages), and "My 'Someday' Books" (just a few pages at the end). In the Me section, ask students to write about their reading interests. Save a page or two for them to revisit this and reflect at the end of the year. In the My Reading section, place the note found on page 76 to guide their reading and response. Please keep in mind that we've listed a lot of response choices. For young readers, it is best to begin with two or three, and then add to the list as you introduce and demonstrate different types of responses during whole-group mini-lessons or while guiding readers in small groups. Finally, in the My "Someday" Books section, students record books they want to read in the future.

Final Thoughts

Wow! There is so much to do in September. Between setting up routines and getting to know your students as learners, it is a wonder we have any energy left at all! We know as we begin to turn the corner to October that the cooler breezes usher in a sense of calm. Students are beginning to gain independence with your classroom's carefully orchestrated routines, and you notice amazing things happening even when you are not directing them anymore. As a part of this community of learners, you will continue to stand back, listen, notice, and ask questions to discover as much as you can about each of your students.

CHAPTER 3: OCTOBER

Making Meaningful Connections

Well-written stories, like the ones that we've featured in this book, are an unmatched resource for young readers and writers. Certainly, the power of a story cannot be overemphasized. A carefully crafted narrative draws the reader in as it provides opportunities to discuss key ideas and details of a text, identify author's craft and text structures, and compare and contrast characters, plots, and ideas presented in increasingly complex tales (CCSS, 2010). Although this resource is focused on reading instruction, we'd be remiss if we didn't highlight the possibilities that these books and mini-lessons hold for our budding writers. To that end, we've identified picture books that we've found to be successful mentor texts for a particular craft technique in the charts with a focus on "Read Like a Writer," along with a few tips to launch a writing-related conversation. The morning messages that follow target the remaining decoding strategies and introduce students to the concept of comprehension. Happy reading and writing!

Part 1: Reading-Related Morning Message Ideas and Samples

Now that the routines are falling into place, we hope that you are also discovering the power of weaving reading-related morning messages into your daily routine. As you plan your literacy lessons for this month, you can choose from the morning messages found in this chapter if your students need reinforcement of the Skip and Read Through strategy or to introduce the concept of comprehension. In addition, there is an interactive whiteboard message targeting compound words and a reading-response message idea where you can model different types of reading responses.

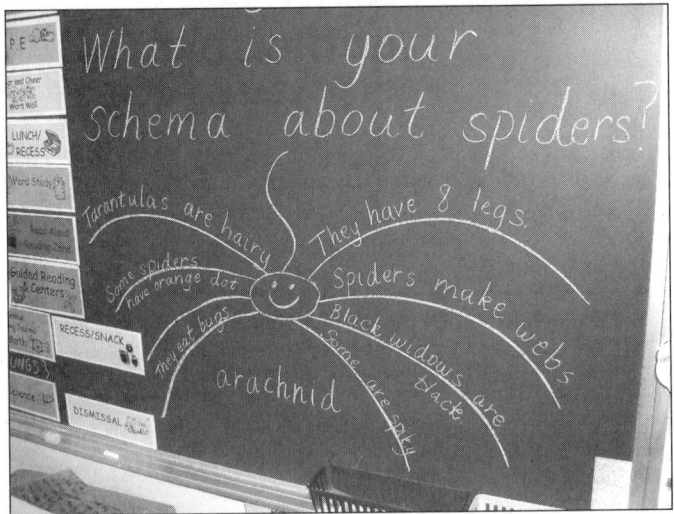

The morning message strengthens connections between reading and writing.

MORNING MESSAGE IDEA: SELF-MONITORING/DECODING—SKIP AND READ THROUGH

After teaching the mini-lesson on page 86, use a message like the one here to reinforce the decoding strategy of Skip and Read Through. To create this message, choose sentences from a book that you are planning to read aloud. The following sentences come from *This School Year Will Be the Best* (Winters, 2010), an excellent beginning-of-the-year book that lends itself to a discussion of students' hopes, wishes, and goals for the year.

MORNING MESSAGE SAMPLE

Skip and Read Through

Can you use the context of the sentence to figure out the missing word?

This year I'll _____ the ball into the right goal. (kick)

We'll take a field _____ to someplace really cool. (trip)

I hope I'll _____ friends in my new school. (make)

MORNING MESSAGE IDEA: COMPREHENSION—CAN YOU COMPREHEND THIS SENTENCE?

This message will assist you in introducing the concept of comprehension. You will demonstrate for students that simply being able to read words without understanding what they mean is not real reading. To begin, write a sentence similar to this one: "The educator lectured the pupils regarding the effectiveness of making superior choices." Read the sentence aloud to your students. Pause. Ask if anyone understood the meaning of the sentence. If not, work through the sentence word by word, replacing the difficult vocabulary words with kid-friendly terms. Then, read the kid-friendly sentence and discuss the big idea—comprehension is much more than simply reading the words!

MORNING MESSAGE IDEA: VOCABULARY BUILDING—COMPOUND WORDS

Interactive Whiteboard Morning Message 3

Morning message moments like this one develop your students' vocabulary skills and expose readers to the wondrous world of words and how they work. In this message, you introduce compound words. If you have an interactive whiteboard, display IWB_MM_ 3. Otherwise, write ten familiar words, five multisyllabic words, and five compound words. Read the message with your students and ask the children to look carefully at each word and its parts. Explain that when two words are combined to make a longer word, these words are called compound words. Invite students to locate and circle the compound words. Wrap up the message by reminding students that they can recognize compound words by identifying the two words that comprise it, and longer words by using chunks.

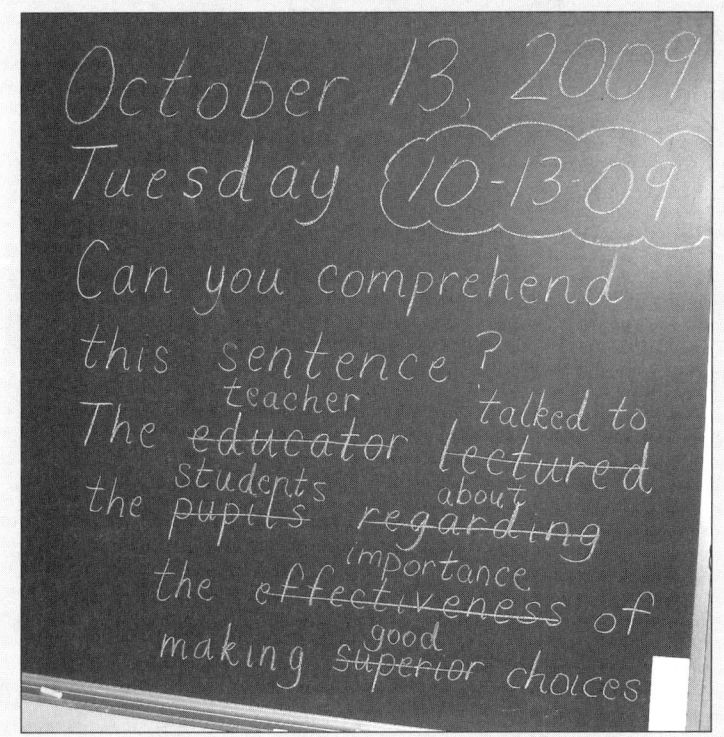

MORNING MESSAGE SAMPLE

MORNING MESSAGE SAMPLE

Look through our spectacular school words and notice the word parts. Can you circle the compound words?

chalkboard	pencil	hallway	library	classroom
playground	desks	pocket chart	bookmark	eraser

MORNING MESSAGE IDEA: READING RESPONSE—THINKING ABOUT BOOKS

The morning message provides a perfect opportunity for modeling the different types of responses that students may have as they think about the books they read. Oftentimes, we will flip the order of our morning routine and read the story before the message so that we can follow up with one of the ideas found in the box below. Once students are familiar with the different responses, they can use them as they think about the books they've read in small groups, as Sara did in the sample pictured above.

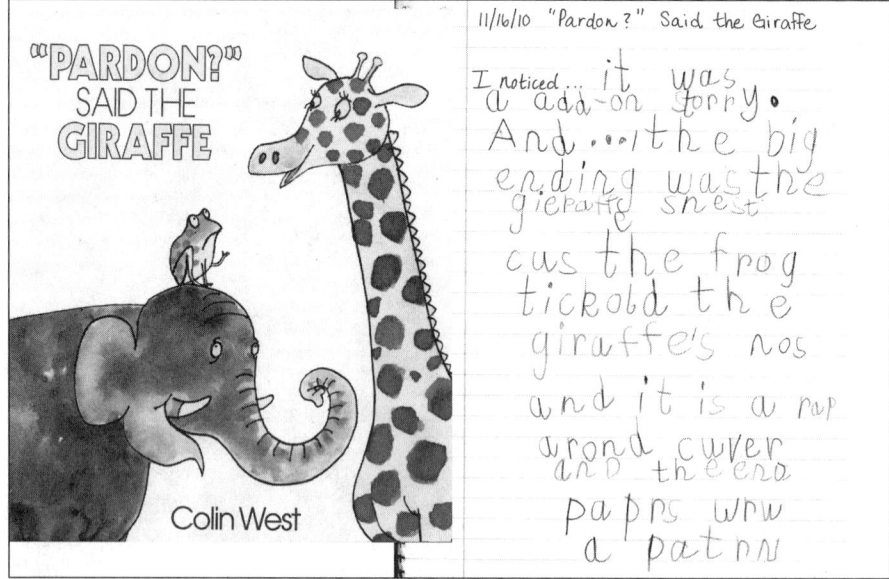

I noticed it was an add-on story. And . . . the big ending was the giraffe sneezed because the frog tickled the giraffe's nose and it is a wrap-around cover and the end papers were a pattern.

MORNING MESSAGE IDEAS FOR THINKING ABOUT BOOKS

My favorite character was . . .

I think the main character feels _____ because . . .

The setting reminds me of . . .

The part I liked best was _____ because . . .

I was surprised that . . .

I wonder why the author . . .

I noticed that the author . . .

I wish that the author . . .

A different ending would be . . .

This book made me think about . . .

I think the big idea was . . .

MORNING MESSAGE SAMPLE

Thinking About *Memoirs of a Goldfish*
What was your favorite part?

82 / MONTH-BY-MONTH READING INSTRUCTION FOR THE DIFFERENTIATED CLASSROOM

POETRY POWER: POEMS FOR OCTOBER	
Title	**Brief Summary**
Come to My Party and Other Shape Poems (Roemer, 2004)	Divided into sections by season, Roemer's anthology of colorful concrete poems touch on such familiar topics as bugs, the beach, and snow, so your students can make connections.
Here's a Little Poem: A Very First Book of Poetry (Yolen & Peters, 2007)	This anthology contains 61 large-print, brightly illustrated poems that are ideal for the youngest readers.

MORNING READ-ALOUDS: STORIES, STORIES, AND MORE STORIES	
Title, Author, and Focus	**Brief Summary**
Bats at the Ballgame (Lies, 2010) **Focus:** Read Like a Writer	During this nighttime baseball game, the bats swoop and slide around the field as the fans hang upside down enjoying "Cricket Jack" and "moth dogs." The detailed pictures of this magical game take the reader from dusk to dawn. There is much for students to notice in the author's clever rhymes and shadowy illustrations.
The Best Story (Spinelli, 2008) **Focus:** Writing Stories/Ideas	This story is told from the point of view of a young writer who wants to win a writing contest. Each of her family members gives her advice, so she adds action, humor, and even romance to her story, but it just isn't right. Fortunately, when her wise mother encourages her to write from her heart, she finally writes what she believes is "The Best Story." Read this book to launch a discussion about where writers get ideas.
Blackout (Rocco, 2011) **Focus:** Making Connections	When a power outage hits the city on a hot, noisy, busy night, a family discovers the joys of relaxing and having fun together. Notice that the author chose to use a graphic novel style for telling this story.
Diary of a Baby Wombat (French, 2010) **Focus:** Writing	In the sequel to *Diary of a Wombat*, we meet a baby wombat who is trying to find a larger home for the wombat family.
Eeeek, Mouse! (Monks, 2009) **Focus:** Read Like a Writer	In the sequel to *Aaarrgghh! Spider!* (Monks, 2004), Minnie thinks that mice are cute with their "twitchy noses," but her dad and the family cat disagree. Dad develops a "cunning" plan to trap the mouse family, but, luckily for the mice, Minnie has a cunning rescue plan of her own. Notice all of the details in the illustrations!
Even Monsters Need Haircuts (McElligott, 2010) **Focus:** Read Like a Writer	Once a month, during a full moon, a young boy sneaks into his father's barbershop to give haircuts to the scariest of customers. A creepy array of monsters visits the barbershop during the night, but everyone is nervous when a "human" enters asking for "a little off the top." The clever and detailed illustrations add much humor to this peculiar personal narrative.
Memoirs of a Goldfish (Scillian, 2010) **Focus:** Writing/Elaboration	Read the comical story of a goldfish's life as he goes from a lonely swimmer in his own bowl to a frustrated fish in an overcrowded bowl. Will he ever get back to his own bowl? This is an ideal book for showing writers how to elaborate and add details to their writing.

continued MORNING READ-ALOUDS: STORIES, STORIES, AND MORE STORIES

Title, Author, and Focus	Brief Summary
Once Upon a Baby Brother (Sullivan, 2010) **Focus:** Writing Stories/Ideas	Lizzie loves to entertain people with her stories, but when her brother Marvin is born, everyone is too busy to listen. Luckily, Miss Pennyroyal, Lizzie's second-grade teacher, enjoys stories too. Lizzie learns to write stories about interesting characters in school, but when her brother goes away to visit "Gramma," Lizzie can't think of an interesting character for her comic book. Will Marvin save the day?
A Pet for Petunia (Schmid, 2011) **Focus:** Making Connections	Petunia "wants, wants, wants! a REAL pet skunk"—until she meets one and gets sprayed. But soon Petunia is longing for another pet—a porcupine! Children who long for a pet of their own can easily connect with Petunia's story.
Where's My Mummy? (Crimi, 2008) **Focus:** Read Like a Writer	Students will undoubtedly make connections when they read this ghoulish version of P. D. Eastman's *Are You My Mother?* In this story, Little Baby Mummy does not want to go to bed. Instead, he runs through the woods playing "hide and shriek," but his mother is nowhere to be found. Little Baby Mummy is not scared by the frightful events until something surprising startles him. The bold illustrations, wonderful word choices, and clever use of onomatopoeia will entice and inspire young readers and writers.

Part 2: A Menu of Reading Workshop Mini-Lessons

As readers, what do you want your students to know and be able to do? How do you take them from where they are now and nudge them forward? These are the questions we ask ourselves each day as we interact with, observe, and assess our young readers. Based on the answers to these questions, we select the best mini-lessons to meet their needs and decide whether to teach particular lessons to the whole class or in a small group. In this chapter, we've included mini-lessons that draw students' attention to the importance of self-monitoring as they read and integrating the decoding strategies they are learning to tackle unfa-

Select mini-lessons to meet your readers needs.

miliar words. In addition, you'll find lessons about the importance of accessing background knowledge or schema in order to make meaningful connections to the texts they are reading. It makes sense that the genre study for this chapter is personal narrative. Stories written from the first-person point of view are ideal for launching discussions about making meaningful connections to the text.

MINI-LESSONS FOR SELF-MONITORING/DECODING STRATEGY INSTRUCTION

As teachers of beginning readers, we have the awesome responsibility of helping children learn how to read the words on the page or screen with accuracy and fluency so that they can understand the author's message. With that aim in mind, we integrate the teaching of decoding or self-monitoring strategies throughout our month-by-month plan. The mini-lessons you will find in this section may be appropriate for your readers at this point, or they may be better taught at a later date. Each mini-lesson is designed either as a whole-group strategy lesson or a small-group lesson to guide readers.

MINI-LESSON: Get Your Mouth Ready

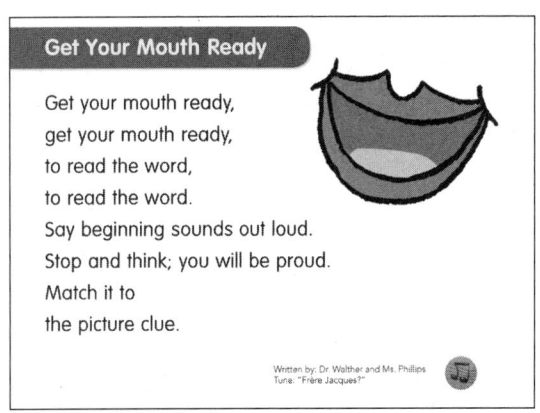

CD Resource 3.1 and IWB_Song_3.1

Preparation: Copy and display the strategy song "Get Your Mouth Ready" (CD Resource 3.1) and the Decoding Strategy Wheel (CD Resource 2.4). To demonstrate this strategy, we use an activity created by Patricia Cunningham (2009a) called "Guess the Covered Word." To prepare, select three or four sentences from a book you are planning to read aloud. Write each sentence, with one word covered by a dark-colored sticky note or piece of black construction paper, on sentence strips or an interactive whiteboard document. For beginning readers, cover the word at the end of the sentence and use words that begin with single consonants. For more experienced learners, cover a word in the middle of a sentence and use words that begin with digraphs and blends.

Explanation: When beginning readers come to a word they don't know, they may stop and do nothing; they may look at us for help or just mumble through it and keep going. The decoding strategy Get Your Mouth Ready is just one of many strategies that readers should have in their repertoire. They quickly learn that if they say the first sound of an unfamiliar word, and then continue reading the rest of the sentence, the word often pops into their head.

Demonstration:
- Read the first sentence, skipping over the covered word.
- Invite students to brainstorm three guesses that might make sense.
- Record students' guesses where children can read them.

- Uncover the first letter(s) in the word. Cross out any guesses that do not contain the beginning letter.
- Ask students to make a few more quick guesses that make sense and begin with the correct letter.
- Record their new guesses.
- Uncover the whole word to check if students' guesses were on target.
- Continue with the next sentence.

Once you've modeled this strategy, read and enjoy the book. Then, teach students the strategy song "Get Your Mouth Ready." If you have an interactive whiteboard, display IWB_Song_3.1 and press the musical note to play the tune. Highlight the strategy on the Decoding Strategy Wheel.

Invitation: "Readers, when you come to a word you don't know, get your mouth ready by saying the first sound. Notice what happens when you use this strategy."

MINI-LESSON: Skip and Read Through

Preparation: Copy and display the strategy song "Skip and Read Through" (CD Resource 3.2) and the Decoding Strategy Wheel (CD Resource 2.4).

Explanation: The aim of this lesson is to teach young readers the importance of integrating the use of picture clues and context clues along with thinking about the meaning of the sentence to figure out an unknown word.

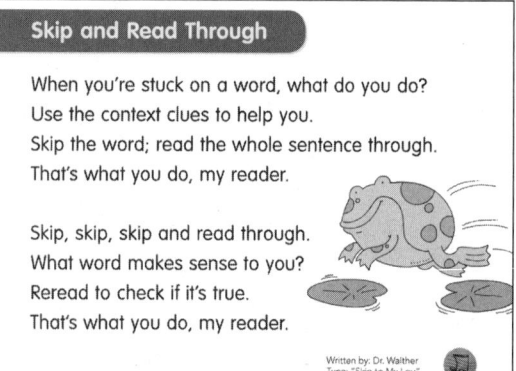

CD Resource 3.2 and IWB_Song_3.2

Demonstration:

- Display a sentence with a word covered in the middle of it.
- Model reading the sentence, skipping over the covered word.
- Invite students to brainstorm guesses based on context clues found in the remainder of the sentence or possibly the next sentence.
- Uncover the letters up to the first vowel.
- Cross-check student guesses using the beginning letter sounds.
- Draw a line through any incorrect guesses.
- Brainstorm new guesses and then uncover the rest of the word.

Then teach students the Skip and Read Through Strategy Song. If you have an interactive whiteboard, display IWB_Song_3.2 and press the musical note to play the tune.

Invitation: "Readers, now you know another strategy to use if you come across an unfamiliar word—skip it and continue reading the sentence. Sometimes the words that follow can help you figure out the tricky word. Don't forget to go back and reread the whole sentence once you've figured it out!"

MINI-LESSON: Look Through the Word for Sounds You Know

Preparation:

- Copy and display the strategy song "Look Through the Word for Sounds You Know." (CD Resource 3.3)
- Choose a book in which the illustrations support the text but decoding strategies are required to figure out many of the words. We have found this lesson to be successful with the book *My Friends* (Gomi, 1995).
- Select three to five words from the read-aloud text that have the same prefixes or beginning letters. If you're using *My Friends*, consider choosing the following words from the text: *monkey*, *march*, and *explore*. Write these words on individual cards or on interactive whiteboard document.
- Display the words with only the prefix or onset showing.

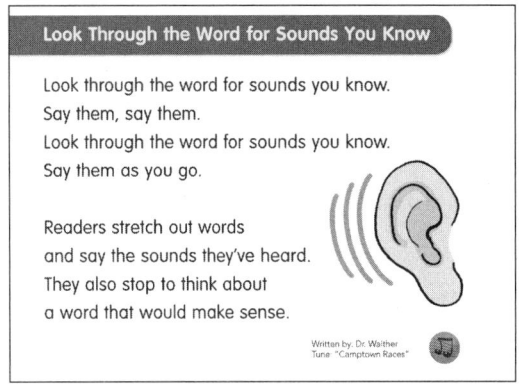

CD Resource 3.3 and IWB_Song_3.3

Explanation: Do you have readers who look at the beginning sound of a word, incorrectly guess a word that begins with that particular sound, and then keep reading? If so, this mini-lesson is helpful in demonstrating the importance of looking at letters and sounds through to the end of the word. Attending to *all* of the sounds, in conjunction with cross-checking using picture and context clues, will help students become more accurate in word decoding and reduce the likelihood of word calling.

Demonstration:

- Display a chosen word from the text. Expose the beginning sounds and cover the remaining letters. Invite the students to guess what the word may be and jot their ideas on a chart.

    mo/nkey (possible guesses include *money*, *Monday*, and *month*)

    ma/rch (possible guesses include *Mars*, *marshmallow*, *marker*, and *marble*)

    ex/plore (possible guesses include *exit*, *exciting*, and *extinct*)

- After the students' initial guesses, slowly reveal the next letter or two and have them guess again. Repeat this process until the entire word is revealed. Continue this activity with the remaining words from the text.
- Refer to the chart of incorrect guesses and share with the children that when readers read a word incorrectly, that mistake is called a miscue. Discuss how looking through the entire word helps readers avoid miscues and enables them to make sense of the sentence.
- Read the book aloud. When you get to the chosen words, say, "When we first saw this word we thought it might have been ____, but we looked through the entire word for letter sounds we know, and now we can see that the word makes sense with the picture clues and the rest of the story."

- Review the strategy by introducing and singing the strategy song "Look Through the Word for Sounds You Know" and point out the strategy on the Decoding Strategy Wheel. If you have an interactive whiteboard, display IWB_Song_3.3 and press the musical note to play the tune.

Invitation: "Readers, when you come to a word that you don't know, take a moment to tackle that word by looking through the entire word for sounds you *do* know. Put the sounds together and ask yourself if it makes sense with the picture clues and what you have already read."

MINI-LESSON: Look for Chunks—Foundation Lesson
Interactive Whiteboard Lesson 3

Preparation:

- Display the strategy song "Look for Chunks" (CD Resource 3.4) and the Decoding Strategy Wheel (CD Resource 2.4).
- Write several multisyllabic words on individual cards, such as *misunderstanding, thundering, fantastic, sportsmanship, interesting, transporter, grandmother, candlestick, mathematics, vocabulary, refreshment,* and *lumberjack*, or display IWB_Lesson_3.

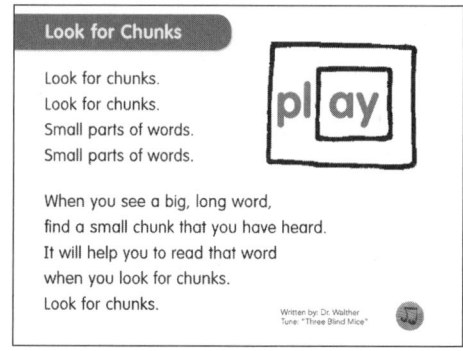

CD Resource 3.4 and IWB_Song_3.4

- Gather markers or highlighters in order to mark identified chunks.
- Choose a big book with a selection of multisyllabic words for shared reading.

Explanation: This strategy is useful for readers who have a working knowledge of phonics and spelling patterns. While identifying word chunks or familiar word parts helps students tackle larger words, the strategy does not always enable readers to decode tricky words.

Demonstration:

- Begin the demonstration by saying, "Sometimes when I am reading I notice a really big word. Instead of trying to read it sound by sound, I look for familiar chunks or patterns that I know."
- Model this decoding strategy for each of the words, breaking down each word into its familiar chunks and highlighting each part.
- Read aloud a Big Book and model the decoding strategy with participation from the students.
- Review the concept of the strategy by introducing and singing the strategy song "Look for Chunks" and by locating it on the Decoding Strategy Wheel. If you have an interactive whiteboard, display IWB_Song_3.4 and press the musical note to play the tune.

Invitation: "Word detectives, when you come across a big word, take a moment to tackle that word by looking for familiar chunks or spelling patterns that you already know. Put those chunks together and ask yourself if it makes sense with what you have already read."

MINI-LESSON: Word Family Chunks—Follow-Up Lesson

Preparation: Select a word family that appears frequently in a book the students will be reading.

Explanation: Focusing on word families will be a valuable review for some of your learners and a direct teaching lesson for struggling readers. For another lesson on word families, see Working With Word Families Mini-Lesson on page 64 in *Month-by-Month Trait-Based Writing Instruction* (Walther & Phillips, 2009).

Demonstration: Write /-ay/ on a chart for easy viewing. Teach the students that chunking words into onsets and rimes will help them figure out new words. Write the words *say*, *stray*, and *away* on the chart. Ask students to repeat them after you. Break the words into onsets and rimes, /s/ /-ay/ = say, /str/ /-ay/ = stray, and /a/ /-way/ = away, highlighting the fact that they all belong to the /-ay/ family. Brainstorm more words to add to this extensive family. Post the list for easy reference.

Invitation: "Readers, recognizing word families in your reading will help you because if you know how to read the word *day*, then you will be able to read the words *say, way, today,* and many more words. We will continue to learn about other helpful word families this year." (Adapted from *Teaching Struggling Readers With Poetry,* Walther & Fuhler, 2010, p. 86.)

MINI-LESSONS FOR COMPREHENSION STRATEGY INSTRUCTION

Young readers need decoding skills to attack unknown words, but, from the beginning of the year, we emphasize that reading is more than merely saying the words on the page. Rather, reading is thinking—not only thinking about what each individual word says, but also about the author's message. We guide our students to use their schema, or background knowledge, and make the meaningful connections that will help them ponder the author's purpose and the story's big idea. Readers who use their schema and connect to books on a personal level are better at comprehending what they read. The following lessons will help learners inch toward that ultimate goal.

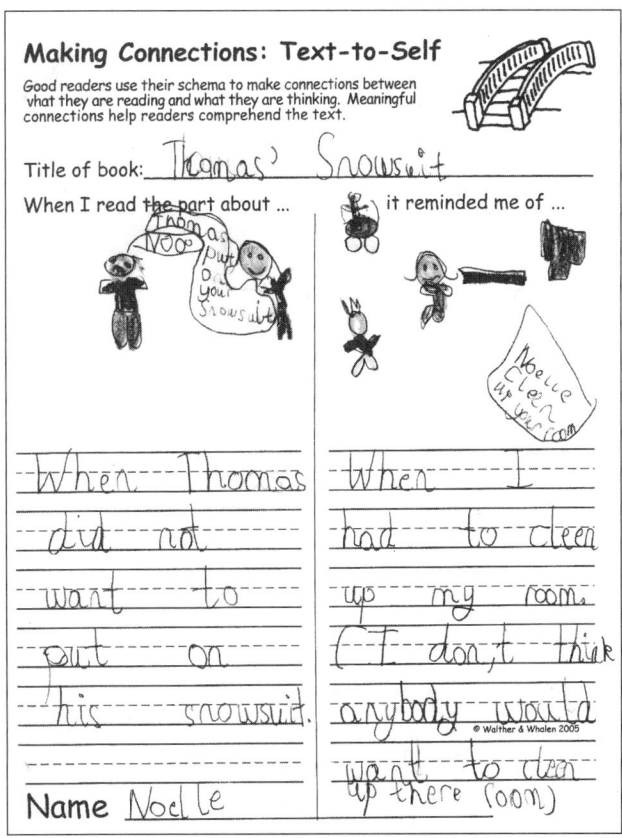

Noelle's Connection to *Thomas' Snowsuit*: When Thomas did not want to put on his snowsuit. [It reminded me of . . .] When I had to clean up my room. (I don't think anybody would want to clean up their room.)

MINI-LESSON: The ABCs of Schema—Foundation Lesson

Preparation:

- The morning message on page 81 introduces the concept of comprehension. To provide students with a visual tool for thinking about the comprehension strategies, you could copy or post the Comprehension Strategy Wheel (CD Resource 3.5; see image on page 93). In addition, copy and display the strategy song "Comprehension" (CD Resource 3.6).

CD Resource 3.6 and IWB_Song_3.6

- Copy and display the strategy song "Schema." (CD Resource 3.7)

- Create a visual representation of your "mental files" for demonstration with the class. To create the visual, staple three different-colored file folders to a large piece of chart paper. Label the first folder "Activate Our Schema," the second "Build New Learning," and the third "Change Misunderstandings." See photo on page 91.

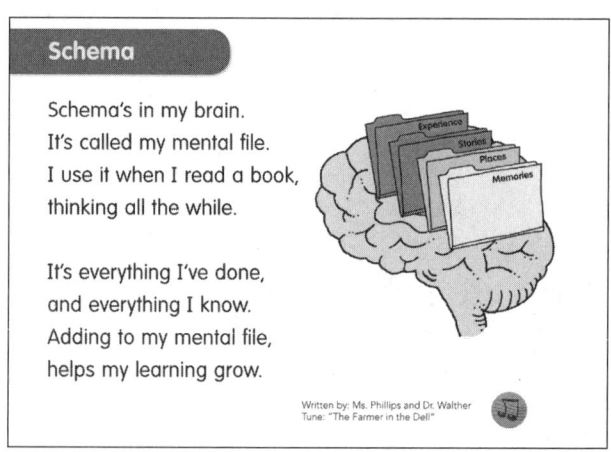

CD Resource 3.7 and IWB_Song_3.7

- Cut copy paper or white drawing paper in strips to collect children's thinking (a less expensive option than using sentence strips).

- Choose a nonfiction text about a familiar topic and pose a question to activate students' schema about that particular topic. For example, if the book is about sharks, the question might be, "What information is already in your mental file about sharks?"

Explanation: This lesson will help your students become aware that their existing knowledge, or schema, can help them to understand what they read. Readers' schema consists of everything they've experienced. They draw upon that background knowledge to help them make connections, learn, and comprehend a variety of texts. Each time we read, we are adding new schema to our "mental files," confirming what we believe to be true, and sometimes discovering that what we thought was true was actually a misconception.

Demonstration:

- Introduce the strategy with the strategy song "Schema" (CD Resource 3.7). If you have an interactive whiteboard, display IWB_Song_3.7 and press the musical note to play the tune.

- Begin with, "Our brain is like a file cabinet. We have a lot of information about different topics stored in our brains." Show the students a file folder or your classroom file cabinet. "The information in your brain is your background knowledge (or schema) about a topic. Everyone's schema about a topic is different, depending on your experiences or what you have read or learned about the topic."

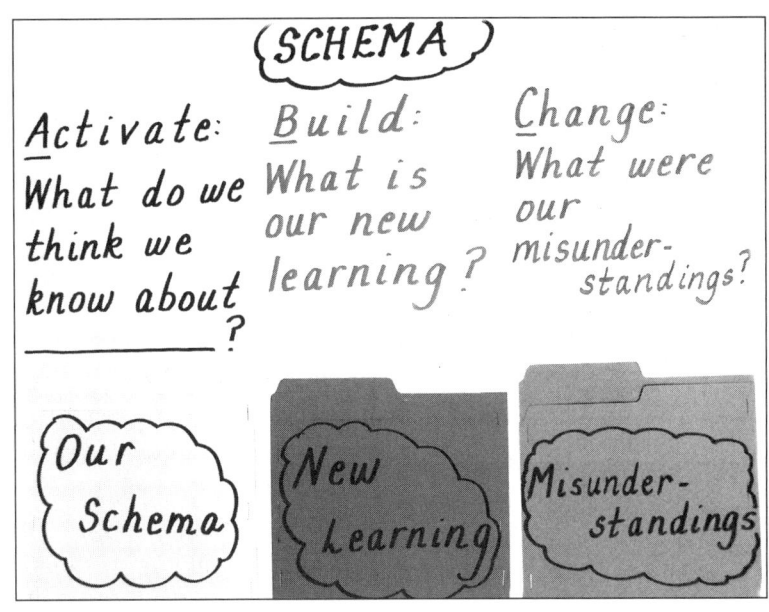

ABC Schema Chart

- Activate—Display the Activate Our Schema "mental file" and pose a schema-activating question to the class. For example, "What information is already in our mental file about [a particular topic]?" Record students' responses on strips of paper and place them inside the Activate Our Schema file folder.
- Build—Read a nonfiction book that answers the schema-activating question. After reading, reexamine the schema strips and discuss which ones will help us read and understand this piece of text and which ideas we should save for another time.
- Discuss which schema cards were confirmed by the information in the text and put them back into the Activate Our Schema file.
- Brainstorm any new facts from the text and place them in the Build New Learning "mental file."
- Change Our Misunderstanding—Note if there were any misconceptions or misunderstandings. We typically model a misconception, or a change in thinking, with our own misunderstanding first. If you come across a student's misconception about the topic, be careful not to devalue his or her idea. Say to the students, "Our schema is changing all the time as we learn and experience new things. What we once thought was true may turn out to be a misunderstanding. When we come across information that is different from our schema, we need to ponder the new learning and read other materials to confirm or revise our thinking." To help demonstrate the value of every student's thinking, do not throw away the misunderstanding. Instead, place the strip in the file labeled "Change Our Misunderstandings" and point out to students that misunderstandings give us ideas to research and ponder.
- Finally, discuss how your schema changed when you read the book. Discuss how readers are constantly changing their schema as they read.

Invitation: "When you begin to read today, open your mental files and think about what you already know about the topic or the story. As you read, think about your schema and pay attention to see if your schema is confirmed, if you have a misunderstanding and have to revise your schema, or if you learn anything new."

HANDS-ON, MULTISENSORY ACTIVITIES FOR BUILDING BACKGROUND

- Photos
- Illustrations
- Video Clips
- Language Experience Approach—This approach builds on children's background knowledge to help them connect the spoken word with the written word. It leads to the understanding that what they think and say can be written down. To apply it in your classroom, record a child's experiences in his or her own words and provide time for the student to illustrate the page. Over the next few days, reread the text with the child until he or she associates the written words with the spoken ones. To build shared background knowledge, you can also write whole-class language experience stories after field trips and other experiences.
- Realia—Realia are actual items or objects that you bring into the classroom to illustrate a vocabulary word or concept. It helps make the abstract concepts and words more concrete and is especially important for ELLs.

MINI-LESSON:
Making Connections: Read-Aloud/Think-Aloud—Foundation Lesson

Preparation:

- Copy and display the strategy song "Making Connections" (CD Resource 3.8). If you have an interactive whiteboard, display IWB_Song_3.8 and press the musical note to play the tune.

- Choose a picture book to read aloud/think aloud that lends itself to making personal connections. Some of your connections can be superficial, but make sure that most have to do with the author's theme or idea. Create a chart to record your connections. Have sticky notes handy to record your thinking as you read. Some obvious choices are books that will resonate with you as a teacher, such as *Miss Malarkey Won't Be in Today* (Finchler, 1998); *Mrs. Spitzer's Garden* (Pattou, 2001); or *First Day Jitters* (Danneberg, 2000). If you have a crazy dog at home, try *Bad Dog, Marley* (Grogan, 2007).

Making Connections

Make connections when you read and you will understand what the author's telling you—let your schema lend a hand!

Text-to-self and text-to-text, text-to-world connections—think and read is what you do. That's how you make connections!

Written by: Dr. Walther
Tune: "Yankee Doodle"

CD Resource 3.8 and IWB_Song_3.8

Explanation: As you read aloud and think aloud, you are offering students a glimpse into the mind of a proficient reader who makes connections to better understand the text.

Demonstration:

- Begin by reviewing the strategy of schema on the Comprehension Strategy Wheel (CD Resource 3.5).
- Model your thinking during a read-aloud and record your connections on sticky notes as you move through the story without labeling them as connections. For example, when reading *Mrs. Spitzer's Garden* (Pattou, 2001), you might say the following:

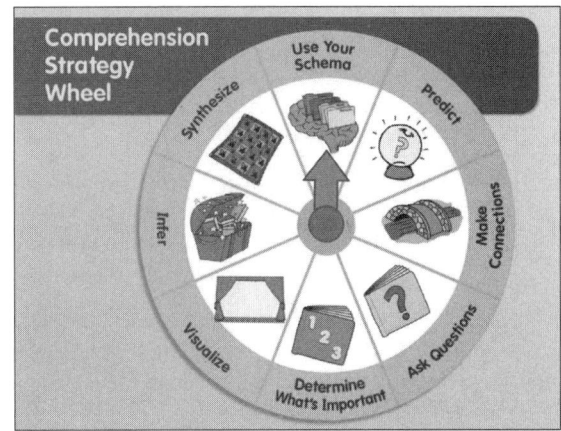

CD Resource 3.5 and IWB_Comp_Wheel

Mrs. Spitzer is a teacher.	Hey! I'm a teacher, too. I bet knowing something about being a teacher is going to help me understand this story.
Inside Room 108 . . .	Mrs. Spitzer has a lot of the same things in her classroom as we do. It looks as if she's getting ready for her kids to arrive, just like I do.

- After reading, invite students to share what they noticed about your thinking. If your students do not recognize any of the connections that you made during the read-aloud, scaffold their thinking by clearly explaining how your ideas are connected to the story.
- Label this strategy by introducing and singing the strategy song "Making Connections." If you have an interactive whiteboard, display IWB_Song_3.8 and press the musical note to play the tune.

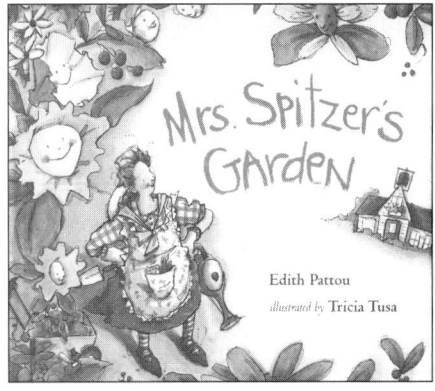

Invitation: "When you are reading today, think about the connections you are making. How does making those connections help you as a reader?"

MINI-LESSON: Text-to-Self Connections—Read-Aloud/Think-Together Follow-Up Lesson

Preparation: Choose a picture book to read aloud that your students can make personal connections with, and create a chart to record the students' text-to-self connections. Have sticky notes handy to record their thinking as you read. Tried-and-true classics for this lesson include *The Art Lesson* (dePaola, 1989), *Best Friends* (Kellogg, 1986), *Ira Sleeps Over* (Waber, 1972/2000), and *There's a Nightmare in My Closet*

(Mayer, 1968). Some more recently published books that would work well with this lesson include the following titles.

Title and Author	Brief Summary
Freckleface Strawberry (Moore, 2007)	The main character is a typical seven-year-old girl with one exception: she has "red hair and something worse…freckles!" After many failed (and humorous) attempts to get rid of her freckles, she decides to accept them because she realizes, "Who cares about having a million freckles when you have a million friends?"
Sloppy Joe (Keane, 2009)	As the title suggests, this is a story of a messy boy, told from his perspective. An ideal pairing with Jane O'Connor's *Fancy Nancy*!

Explanation: To gradually release the responsibility to students, we shift from Read-Aloud/Think-Aloud demonstrations to Read-Aloud/Think-Together conversations. In this case, the focus is on inviting children to make personal connections to the text.

Demonstration: Read aloud the story and invite students to share their connections. Record their connections on sticky notes. Save the chart for Making Meaningful Connections—Follow-Up Lesson described below.

Invitation: "When you are reading today, notice if you make any connections. Remember them so that you can share them with your partner. If you need to jot them on a sticky note to help you remember, take one with you."

MINI-LESSON: Making Meaningful Connections—Follow-Up Lesson

Preparation: Post the chart you created in the lesson on page 93 and get ready to reread the book from that lesson.

Explanation: If you've taught lessons on making connections, you know that once children begin, they will make *a lot* of connections. You'll hear things like, "My dog is named George too!" or "I have a blue shirt like the one that boy is wearing." It is important to guide readers to understand that not all personal connections lead to deeper understanding. That is the point we begin to make in this mini-lesson, but you will continue to make it each time children share the sometimes voluminous number of connections they've made!

Demonstration:

- Begin the lesson by saying, "Let's take a look at the connections we made yesterday as I reread the same story."
- Reread the story aloud, pausing at the places where a connection has been made. Reread the connection from the chart. Ask the children to evaluate the connection to determine if it was useful in understand-

ing the story. Nonverbal responses might include thumbs-up/-down, one finger/two fingers, or yes/no cards. Continue in this fashion until students get wiggly.
- To honor the students' thinking, we place unhelpful connections on a separate chart labeled "What We Noticed." It is best to emphasize that the children's connections, although true, did not aid in their understanding of this particular story.
- Finally, ask the students if they can explain how to figure out when a connection is meaningful. Tell the students, "If you connect to just one thing that is only mentioned one time in the story, it is a small connection. But if you connect to something mentioned many times in a story, like the main idea, that is a bigger, more useful connection because it helps you better understand the story."

Invitation: "When you are reading today, see if you make any connections. Be sure that the connections you make are meaningful and connect to the author's message or big idea. The small connections that you make only once probably won't be as helpful to you. Jot down your connections on the sticky notes to be saved in your Read, Think, and Respond books."

MINI-LESSON: Using Your Schema to Make Text-to-Self Connections

Preparation: Choose a picture book with which your students can make personal connections. Some books that would work well with this lesson include the following titles.

Title and Author	Brief Summary
When Sophie Gets Angry—Really, Really Angry . . . (Bang, 1999)	Sophie becomes angry when her sister takes away her stuffed gorilla. When Sophie's mom tells her it is her sister's turn to play with it, she races out of the house in a rage, but finally calms down. Notice how the colors change with Sophie's emotions. Most children will be able to share a meaningful connection about a time when they've been angry.
A Couple of Boys Have the Best Week Ever (Frazee, 2008)	James and Eamon stay with Bill and Pam, Eamon's grandparents, so they can attend nature camp. Listeners who have stayed with their grandparents or gone to camp with be able to make meaningful connections.

Explanation: Proficient readers naturally use the strategies they need to help them better understand what they read. They don't stop their reading and say, "Right now I'm going to make a connection." We want children to understand that reading is a thinking process and that the strategies offer different ways of thinking about the text. Also, we encourage readers to use strategies flexibly, as needed. To underscore this point, we've included lessons in each chapter designed to demonstrate the integration of strategies. The aim of this lesson is to show young readers how they can make meaningful text-to-self connections by thinking about different elements of the story they are reading.

Demonstration: To introduce readers to the elements of a story so that they can make connections, we use a "secret formula" created by talented children's author Candace Fleming. When she helps students create a story, she teaches them about a strategy she calls C.L.A.P.S. The clever acronym serves as a graphic organizer for students by reminding them that a story must include Characters, Location, Action, Problem, and Solution. For more information and lessons on using C.L.A.P.S., see *Literature Is Back: Using the Best Books for Teaching Readers and Writers Across Genres* (Fuhler & Walther, 2007). We also use this acronym during reading workshop because it not only helps children identify the characters and setting, it also points out a common story structure found in many children's books.

Main characters in stories often make three different attempts to solve a problem. Typically, the first two attempts fail, while the final attempt solves the problem. As students begin to notice this story structure, you can extend those conversations to help students activate their story structure schema and make connections with other stories with similar structures. You can also guide students to make connections by creating a chart with them containing their thinking along with the questions shown below.

Character	What do I already know about this type of character (hero, villain, and so on)? Do I know someone like him/her? How can thinking about this help me better understand the text?
Location/Setting	Have I been to a place like this before? What was it like there? What did I see, hear, taste, or touch? How did it make me feel?
Action	What is this character doing or trying to do? Have I ever had an experience similar to this? How can thinking about this help me better understand the text?
Problem	The problem/goal in this story is _____. I've had that problem before and it made me feel _____. I wonder if the character feels the same way? How can thinking about this help me better understand the text?
Solution	I've had that problem before and I solved it by _____. I wonder if the character will do the same thing? How can thinking about this help me better understand the text?

Invitation: "We've learned that readers use the strategies they need to help them better understand. Activating your schema and making connections makes sense when you're reading about something that is familiar to you. Other strategies may be more helpful in books with new learning. As you read today, think about the strategies that are the most helpful to you."

READ-ALOUDS THAT SPARK COMPREHENSION CONVERSATIONS

Title, Author, Focus, and Brief Summary	A Few Questions to Spark Your Conversation
The Can Man (Williams, 2010) **Focus:** Connecting With the Main Character **Summary:** Tim's parents can't afford to buy him a new skateboard for his birthday, so he is looking for ways to earn money. Along comes Mr. Peters, a homeless man known as "The Can Man," who gives Tim an idea. But Tim soon discovers that he has taken away Mr. Peters's only source of income. Pair this with *Fly Away Home* (Bunting, 1991). 	How do you think Tim was feeling at the redemption center? Have you ever felt that way? Why do you think Tim gave the money to Mr. Peters? What would you have done in that situation? How would the story have changed if Tim chose to keep the can money for himself? What do you think Laura E. Williams is trying to tell us? Why is she telling us this? What is the big idea of this story?
The Name Jar (Choi, 2001) **Focus**: Connecting With the Main Character **Summary**: Unhei has just moved to America from Korea. On her first day of school, the children on the bus cannot pronounce her name correctly, so she decides not to introduce herself to her classmates until she picks a new name. After thinking carefully about choosing a new name, Unhei is ready to introduce herself . . . as Unhei. Pair this with *My Name is Yoon* (Recorvits, 2003).	How do you think Unhei is feeling on the bus? Have you ever been in a similar situation? Why didn't Unhei want to introduce herself to the class? How do you think she was feeling? What do you think about the children collecting names in a jar for Unhei? Why do you think Joey is at Mr. Kim's store? What do you think the author is trying to tell us? What is the big idea of this story?
Yasmin's Hammer (Malaspina, 2010) **Focus:** Connecting With the Main Character **Summary**: In Dhaka, Bangladesh, Yasmin and her sister work all day at chipping bricks into smaller pieces. Yasmin dreams of going to school and learning to read in the hope of creating a different life for herself. One night, Yasmin devises a plan that makes her dreams come true.	How do you think Yasmin feels about her duty to help her family and her desire to go to school? Why is Amma worried about Mita's thumb injury? What is Yasmin's plan? How do you think Yasmin feels when she gets to the bookstore? How will Yasmin's first book change her life and that of her family?

MINI-LESSONS FOR VOCABULARY DEVELOPMENT: STUDYING COMPOUND WORDS

Once students understand the basics of compound words and recognize that a compound word is a word made up of two smaller words, the next step is learning how to use this knowledge to decode and comprehend those large and sometimes intimidating words. We guide readers as they begin to notice how the individual words can affect the meaning of the larger word. It is important to show readers that the meanings of the two words may remain the same within the compound word (*snowball*), change slightly (*watermelon*), or change completely (*butterfly*). If readers are aware of how the separate parts within compound words help create the meaning of the entire word, they will be able to better decode and comprehend these larger words.

> ### FLUENCY FUN! SEESAW READER'S THEATER
>
> Select a book or poem with a "seesaw" structure, like *Tough Boris* (Fox, 1994). In this book, the refrain is "He was tough. All pirates are tough. He was massive. All pirates are massive." Other books with seesaw structures include the following titles:
>
> *First the Egg* (Seeger, 2007)
> *Fortunately* (Charlip, 1964)
>
> As always, read the book for pleasure. Later, return to it for a repeated reading or two. Once students are familiar with the pattern, divide the class in half. Project the lines from the book on an interactive whiteboard or using a document camera to give students an opportunity to practice. Perform the book by having each group take turns reading their part of the seesaw pattern, alternating back and forth.

MINI-LESSON: Introducing Compound Words—Foundation Lesson

Preparation: Create a list of 12 or more compound words to use as a resource during brainstorming and gather enough index cards, one for each word. Organize your students into pairs or triads and provide each set of students with a compound word and a large piece of paper folded on each side so it opens in the middle. See figure on page 99.

Explanation: Recognizing and understanding compound words helps readers decode and comprehend. The students should realize that the meanings of the individual words that make up a compound word may or may not be helpful to understanding its meaning.

Demonstration: Begin by having the students brainstorm a list of 12 or more compound words. Write them on index cards and place them in a pocket chart. Allow each set of students to choose one compound word from the pocket chart to write and illustrate. The partners write and illustrate each smaller word contained in the compound word on the outer flaps of the paper. Then, the students work together to write and illustrate the whole compound word behind the paper flaps. After they complete their work, invite students to share their word and whether the meaning of the two words changes or stays the same. Then, post their work on a bulletin board for future reference.

Invitation: "When you are working with your friends, read each word in your compound word. Talk with your partner about the meaning of each word and if the meaning changes in the compound word. How will your illustrations show the changes?"

MINI-LESSON: Compound Word Webs— Follow-Up Lesson

Preparation: Select a compound word in which the first word has many possible second words that complete it. Some possibilities include the following words.

down	downstairs, downtown, downhill, downstream, downhearted, downfall, downwind
hand	handcuff, handmade, handout, handrail, handshake, handsome, handwriting
out	outburst, outdoors, outfield, outfit, outhouse, outside, outsmart, outspoken
some	somebody, someday, somehow, someone, something, somewhere, sometimes

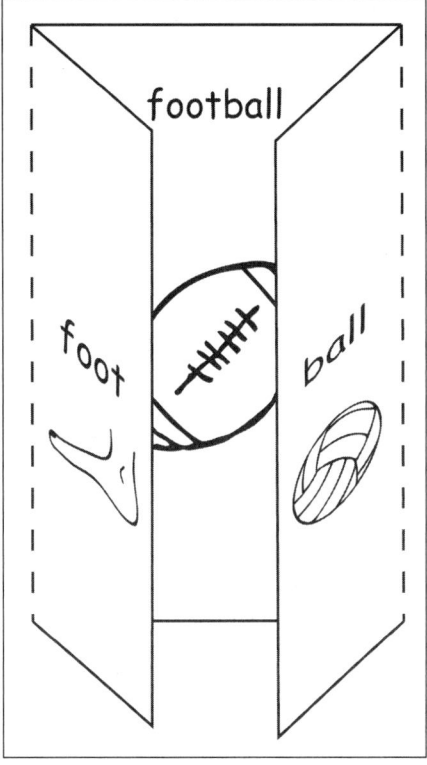

Compound Word Activity

Explanation: Creating compound word webs will extend the learning you began in the foundation lesson. As you add a word to the chart, discuss whether the meanings of the two separate words help the reader understand the meaning of the compound word.

Demonstration: Create a web by writing the first word in the center. For example, put the word *sun* in the center. Invite students to share a second word that would make a compound word, and then write it on a spoke. For instance, you might write *light* on one spoke, *shine* on another, *burn* on the third, *rise* on the fourth, and so on. To offer further support to ELLs, add small illustrations or act out the words as they are added.

Invitation: "Wow! We've discovered that there are a lot of different compound words. Remember to think about what they mean when you come across them in your reading."

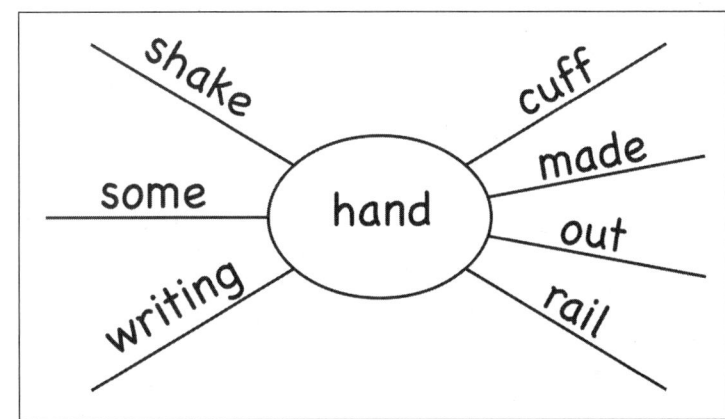

Compound Word Web

CHAPTER 3: OCTOBER—MAKING MEANINGFUL CONNECTIONS / 99

READ-ALOUDS WITH RICH VOCABULARY		
Title and Author	**Brief Summary**	**Words to Highlight and Kid-Friendly Definition**
Bridget's Beret (Lichtenheld, 2010)	Bridget was "drawn to drawing" and always wore her beret as she created her masterpieces. One day, her beret blows away and with it, she believes, her ability to draw. After a futile search for her beret, Bridget's little sister Jessie asks her to make a sign for her lemonade stand. Grumpily, Bridget agrees and, before she knows it, she has decorated the neighborhood with her paintings.	**inspired**: when you really want to do something and feel brave enough to do it **permanent**: describes something that is supposed to last for a very long time **sulked**: showed you were angry or upset by being quiet or staying away from other people
Tiger and Turtle (Rumford, 2010)	In this story inspired by an Indian tale, Tiger and Turtle quarrel over a tiny purple flower. Be sure to read aloud the Author's Note at the beginning of the book. Also, notice how the most suspenseful moments are resolved with a page turn.	**aloft**: high above the ground **waded**: walked in water or in something else **plummeted**: fell down really fast
The Very Best Pumpkin (Moulton, 2010)	Peter lives with his grandparents on a farm where they grow the most wonderful pumpkins of every shape and size. While Peter is busy tending to his very special pumpkin, a new family moves in next door. One day, the little neighbor girl comes to the farm in search of the perfect pumpkin. Will Peter show her where to find his perfect pumpkin?	**clambered**: made a hard climb **dandy**: something that is very good **gingerly**: very carefully

MINI-LESSONS FOR READING RESPONSE

As we discussed in Chapter 1, reading response helps readers organize and transform their thinking into conversations and writing. Young students need ample time to reflect upon and respond to their reading in both spoken and written words. Written response prompts students to apply the strategies they have learned and solidify their thinking. We use these responses as one method of formative assessment to determine how our students are developing as readers and thinkers. In this chapter and those that follow, we have included mini-lessons to teach different types of written reading responses. Depending on the needs of your learners and your curriculum expectations, you can teach the different responses to your whole class or to students in small groups. Of course, readers' responses will be much richer if you teach, model, and practice each type of response a few times before you expect them to complete a response on their own. To that end, beginning in October, you might think about teaching one kind of response for a week or two before moving on to the next. It is important to note here that we certainly do not expect students to respond to everything they read. When teaching a type of response, begin by modeling how you would go about it after a read-aloud. Then, gradually release the responsibility to students by inviting them to respond to a book you've read aloud, circulating among students to offer feedback. Later, you can invite students to respond in the same way to a book they've read in a small group or independently. Once you are confident children understand the thinking that goes into this type of response, you could add it to a "response menu." Then, when you want children to respond to their reading, they can choose from a growing menu of response options. The first two types of responses to add to the menu are two-column notes to record a reader's schema before reading a text and his or her new learning upon completion of reading. The second option is having readers think about a specific character by using an H-chart to compare themselves to that character.

MINI-LESSON: My Schema/My New Learning

Preparation:

- Choose appropriate independent reading material for your students.
- Prepare Read, Think, and Respond Book Page Two-Column Notes (CD Resource 1.6) for each student.

Explanation: This lesson will provide students with an opportunity to demonstrate their understanding of schema as a comprehension strategy. The students will be encouraged to think about the text and show how their schema changes while they are reading.

CD Resource 1.6

Demonstration:

- Prior to reading, invite students to label the first column "My Schema" and the second column "My New Learning." Then, make a list of everything they think they know about the topic in the "My Schema" column.
- Provide the students with time to read the text independently or with a partner.
- After reading, have students list their new learning in the second column.
- Share and discuss how their schema has changed and how activating their schema helps them as readers.

Invitation: "As a reader, you need to always be thinking about the text. Before you read, think about what you already

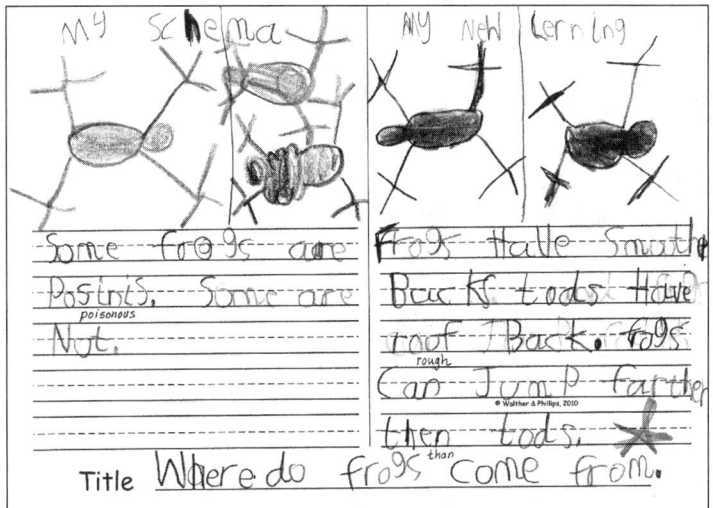

My Schema: Some frogs are poisonous. Some are not. My New Learning: Frogs have smooth backs. Toads have rough backs. Frogs can jump farther than toads.

CHAPTER 3: OCTOBER—MAKING MEANINGFUL CONNECTIONS / **101**

know about the topic. As you read, think about your schema and if the text is confirming what you know, if you have any misconceptions, and if you are learning anything new. This will help your schema grow!"

MINI-LESSON: The Character and Me

Preparation:

- Prepare a Read, Think, and Respond Book Page H-Chart (CD Resource 1.3) for each student and a large copy to use for demonstration purposes.
- Gather texts that have characters with whom your students can connect. If you think this may be a bit too challenging for your learners, another option is to pair them with a fellow student and compare themselves to that peer.
- For your demonstration, select a book with a character with whom you can connect. We use *Ms. McCaw Learns to Draw* (Zemach, 2008), which is about a teacher who sees the talent hidden inside a struggling learner named Dudley. In fact, any picture books that feature main characters who are teachers work well for this lesson.

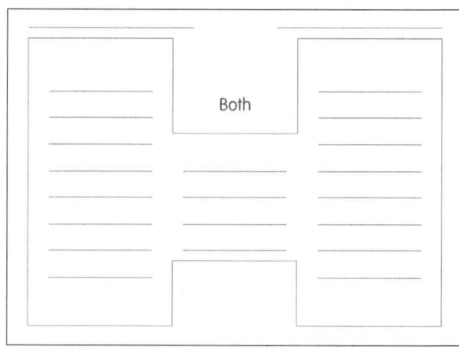

CD Resource 1.3

Explanation: One way that students make connections is by thinking about the characters in the books they've read or heard. Making connections such as these strengthens their comprehension and also helps them as they create their own characters in their writing.

Demonstration: Read the text aloud. Afterward, complete the H-Chart, comparing and contrasting yourself to the main character in the book you selected. To extend this lesson, you might choose to use the comparing-characters morning message found on page 74 in *Month-by-Month Trait-Based Writing Instruction* (Walther & Phillips, 2009), where we work with students to compare their favorite characters using an H-Chart.

Invitation: "Now it is your turn to make connections with a character. Select a character with whom you have the most in common. Think about how you are different from that character and how you are the same."

Part 3: Genre Study—Personal Narratives

Earlier in the chapter we explained our rationale behind choosing personal narratives for this month's genre study. Well-crafted personal narratives are texts with human characters (rather than animals) to which students can connect. In addition, if you are familiar with our writing book, you'll see a genre exploration of personal narratives at the end of the September chapter. In our classrooms, the personal narrative genre exploration spills into October and occurs at the same time we are studying schema and making connections in the reading workshop. With more and more to teach, we are constantly looking for ways to streamline our instruction and dig deeper. Linking the reading workshop and writing workshop is one way we've found to work smarter and help our students see the natural connections between the two interrelated processes. As you read the personal narratives in the chart below, continue the anchor charts that you began in Chapter 2 to record the definition of a personal narrative, the purpose, and the clues that signal the reader that the particular text is a personal narrative. In addition, you can notice other techniques writers use as they craft personal narratives. These conversations will strengthen children's understandings of this genre from both a reader's and a writer's point of view.

GENRE STUDY: PERSONAL NARRATIVE	
Title and Author	**Brief Summary**
Alexander and the Terrible, Horrible, No Good, Very Bad Day (Viorst, 1972)	A classic narrative about a really bad day. After reading this story, your students might enjoy the other books about Alexander.
Everything but the Horse (Hobbie, 2010)	In this memoir, Holly has a hard time adjusting when her family moves from a busy town to the quiet country. In no time at all, Holly falls in love with country life, raising animals and dreaming of having a horse of her own.
Fancy Nancy: Bonjour, Butterfly (O'Connor, 2008)	Nancy's narrative illuminates the characteristics of the genre as she tells the story of missing her friend's butterfly birthday party.
Fred Stays With Me! (Coffelt, 2007)	This simple story is told through the voice of a young girl who must travel back and forth between her parents' houses due to their divorce. Throughout the many changes one thing remains constant: her dog, Fred.
Grandma's Smile (Siegel, 2010)	In this first-person narrative, a six-year-old boy receives a phone call from his grandmother, who says she has lost her smile. The boy describes his journey (and frustrations with the air travel industry) to visit his grandmother and help her find her missing smile.
Jamaica Louise James (Hest, 1996)	Eight-year-old Jamaica Louise James tells the story of her "cool idea" to decorate the dreary subway station where her grandmother works. She hangs her colorful artwork on the walls, transforming the subway station from dingy to dreamy. Jamaica's grandmother is delighted with the gallery of artwork, as are many of the smiling subway passengers.
Pennies for Elephants (Judge, 2009)	In 1914, the children of Boston were given a challenge: collect $6,000 to purchase three trained elephants for the zoo. Told from young Dorothy's point of view, Judge's book recounts how children from all over New England raised enough money.
Recess at 20 Below (Aillaud, 2005)	Experience recess in Alaska from the perspective of a young student.
Saturdays and Teacakes (Laminack, 2004)	Every Saturday a young boy pedals his bicycle to visit his grandmother. Set in rural Alabama in 1964, the story features detailed watercolor illustrations, which capture the mood of this beautifully crafted descriptive memoir.
Sloppy Joe (Keane, 2009)	As the title suggests, this is a story of a messy boy, told from his perspective. Pair with *Fancy Nancy* for a stark contrast in characters!

Meeting the Needs of ALL Learners

When we think about ways to increase the intensity of instruction for our readers who need more support, we always begin by pondering ideas that will help them connect with books so that they will choose to spend more time reading. With that goal in mind, we introduce series books very early in the year. We're hopeful that someday soon we'll get to thank Mo Willems for writing the Elephant and Piggie series, because those books have helped many a struggling reader in our classes. For your talented readers, digging in a bit deeper and studying a series from both a reader's and writer's perspective offers abundant opportunities for discussion and written responses.

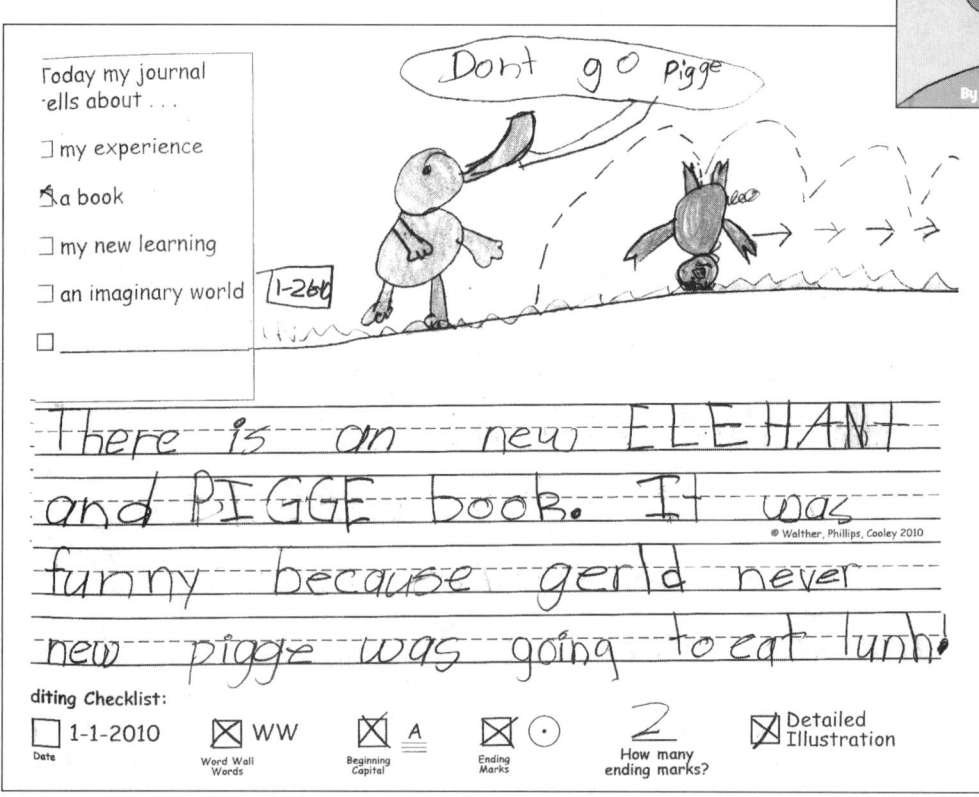

Avinash is excited about a new Elephant and Piggie book. He writes, "There is a new Elephant and Piggie Book. It was funny because Gerald never knew Piggie was going to eat lunch!"

SENSIBLE STRATEGIES FOR STRUGGLING READERS: ENTICING STRIVING AND RELUCTANT READERS WITH SERIES BOOKS

Like adult readers, early readers are often attracted to books in a series. How do these books support striving and reluctant readers? You'll notice as you read the books in a series that oftentimes the same characters appear in each book. As students become familiar with these characters, their personalities, and their actions, they can predict what might happen. Also, the plot structures among the books are often similar, offering additional support to struggling readers. Familiarity with the author's writing style and vocabulary also helps those readers who have challenges with word recognition. Finally, students welcome the challenge of reading all of the books in a series. Sometimes all it takes is reading or book-talking the first title and you've got them hooked. In the chart below, we've listed our favorite series books. Have fun sharing them with your young readers!

Author	First Book in Series *Denotes chapter book
David Adler	*Cam Jansen and the Mystery of the Stolen Diamonds **and** *Bones and the Big Yellow Mystery
Harry Allard	Miss Nelson Is Missing
Tedd Arnold	Hi! Fly Guy
Annie Barrows	*Ivy and Bean
Tomie dePaola	Strega Nona
Kate DiCamillo	*Mercy Watson to the Rescue
Steven Kellogg	Pinkerton, Behave!
Helen Lester	Tacky the Penguin
Lenore Look	*Ruby Lu, Brave and True **and** *Alvin Ho: Allergic to Girls, School, and Other Scary Things
Lois Lowry	*Gooney Bird Greene
James Marshall	George and Martha
Mercer Mayer	There's a Nightmare in my Closet
Megan McDonald	*Judy Moody **and** *Stink: The Incredible Shrinking Kid
Jane O'Connor	Fancy Nancy
Mary Pope Osborne	*Dinosaurs Before Dark
Peggy Parish	*Key to the Treasure
Barbara Park	*Junie B. Jones and the Stupid Smelly Bus
Sara Pennypacker	*Clementine
James Preller	*Jigsaw Jones: The Case of Hermie the Missing Hamster
Cynthia Rylant	*Henry and Mudge: The First Book of Their Adventures **and** *Poppleton **and** *Mr. Putter and Tabby Bake the Cake
Judy Schachner	Skippyjon Jones
Margorie Weinman Sharmat	*Nate the Great
Jackie Urbanovic	Duck at the Door
Judith Viorst	Alexander and the Terrible, Horrible, No Good, Very Bad Day
Mo Willems	Elephant and Piggie: Today I Will Fly!

TARGETING TALENTED READERS: STUDYING SERIES BOOKS

Are your readers hooked on Henry and Mudge books? Do they fight over your copies of The Magic Tree House titles? If so, why not capitalize on this excitement and form a book club study group? To begin, gather enough of the first book in the series so that all members of the group can read and discuss the book. Provide students with a small notebook to gather their thoughts. Prompt them with questions to help them learn more about the series.

- Tell about the main character(s). What does he/she enjoy doing? What adjectives would you use to describe the character(s)?
- Where/when is the book set? Do you think the setting will stay the same or change?
- What do you notice about the book? From what point of view is it written?

Provide time for them to independently read the book. Together with the students, set daily reading goals. Once they've finished reading, gather together to discuss their findings. Then, each child selects another book in the series that piques his or her interest. Continue reading, sharing, and trading books as long as children remain interested. You'll be amazed how much you learn about the series from your enthusiastic and insightful readers!

Readers study their favorite series books.

Final Thoughts

Building and activating background knowledge and making connections is essential for readers, but it is also vitally important to the work we do with our learners. Just as we strive to help students build a store of knowledge to access as they read, think, and learn, we need to collect the same kind of knowledge about our students. The more we know about students' backgrounds, interests, strengths, struggles, and educational needs, the better we are able to determine what they know, set new learning goals, and design instruction that will move them forward. Additionally, the connections that we make with our students and the connections we help them build with each other are fundamental to guiding students as they learn how to interact and work effectively with others in school and beyond. After all, our goal as educators is to help children become critical thinkers who can effectively communicate their knowledge as they grow to become the citizens of the future.

CHAPTER 4: NOVEMBER & DECEMBER

Predicting in Real and Make-Believe Stories

In the past few months, you've set the stage for learning, spent a bit of time discussing the role background knowledge plays in the life of a reader, and discovered, along with your students, the power of a good story. Now it is time to dig a bit deeper into stories and invite students to use their schema and connections to think ahead to predict what might happen. As you read aloud and discuss the real and make-believe stories found in the Morning Read-Alouds chart, you can build students' knowledge of story elements. In this chapter, we define real stories as realistic fiction or those stories that could happen in real life. Make-believe stories are fantasy or imaginary tales. Understanding the ingredients that meld together to create a memorable tale will help readers make logical predictions based on their growing story sense. In this chapter, we share read-aloud experiences and mini-lessons that will expand students' understanding of the mechanics of a story and show them how to think ahead as they are reading by making predictions. In addition, we offer a genre study to help learners distinguish between real and make-believe stories. Don't blink! It will be the end of December before you know it!

Part 1: Reading-Related Morning Message Ideas and Samples

Messages, messages, and more messages! How do you fit them all in? That is a question we are often asked. The simple answer is, "We don't!" It is our aim to help you create a bank of messages from which you can draw to match the specific needs of your literacy learners. When we're standing in front of our chalkboards getting ready for the day, we look at our lesson plans and decide which message will jump-start the upcoming learning or review an important concept that we introduced earlier in the week. We also think about what we've noticed as we conferred with our readers and writers. Did we discover that a child still couldn't figure out what to do when she came to a word she didn't know? If so, she probably isn't the only one—time for a decoding strategy review. Are students still a little shaky on the difference between a real story and a make-believe story? To clear up the confusion, we'll reinforce that concept in a quick, engaging message. We encourage you to select the messages based on your students' needs, rather than where they appear in the book and, as always, celebrate what you *are* doing with your learners instead of focusing on all you wish you *could be* doing!

MORNING MESSAGE IDEA: SELF-MONITORING/DECODING—LOOK FOR CHUNKS

To reinforce the decoding strategy mini-lesson found on page 88, select a book or poem that has a few multisyllabic words. For this message, we chose *Love That Kitty: The Story of a Boy Who Wanted to Be a Cat* (Jarka, 2010). Prior to reading the book aloud, write the long or difficult words on cards or on an interactive whiteboard document. We selected the following: *ordinary, unsuspecting, nocturnal, invisible,* and *decided.*

> **MORNING MESSAGE SAMPLE**
>
> Look for Chunks
>
> Can you chunk these words?
>
> ordinary
>
> unsuspecting
>
> nocturnal
>
> invisible
>
> decided

After enjoying the book, display the first word. Remind students that you don't want them to shout out the whole word. Instead, invite them to point out a letter or word chunk that they recognize. Underline or highlight the identified chunk. Continue in this fashion until you can blend the chunks together to read the whole word. Repeat the same process with the remaining words.

MORNING MESSAGE IDEA: COMPREHENSION—PREDICT THE TITLE

We read about this idea in the book *Primary Literacy Centers: Making Reading and Writing STICK!* (Nations & Alonso, 2001) and have been using it ever since. This message not only builds anticipation for an upcoming read-aloud, but it also helps children improve their title-writing skills. To prepare for this message, select a picture book that you are planning to read later in the day or week. Obviously, it is helpful if students haven't seen the book before. We have had success with the following titles:

Agatha's Feather Bed: Not Just Another Wild Goose Story (Deedy, 1991)—page 118

Badger's Fancy Meal (Kasza, 2007)—page 117

The Wolf's Chicken Stew (Kasza, 1987)–page 117

Cover the title of the book and the spine, if needed. (Yes, children will peek at the spine if you don't cover it.) Place the book where all students can see it. Invite them to look closely at the cover illustration and predict the title based on their observations. Learners can write their prediction on a sticky note and place it near the book as seen in the photo. Before reading the book, share and discuss students' predictions and the ideas that led to each prediction. At this point, you have two options. One option is to reveal the title (we usually do a drum roll by patting our legs) and compare it with the students' prediction. Another alternative is to read the book aloud and then ask students if they would like to revise their prediction based on the reading. If so, students can write their new title on the back of the sticky note or simply share their titles aloud. Once revisions are made, unveil the title and discuss.

MORNING MESSAGE IDEA: VOCABULARY BUILDING—USING ADJECTIVES TO DESCRIBE OUR FAVORITE CHARACTERS

After reading a book or a series of books that featured a distinctive character, invite students to brainstorm a list of adjectives to describe that person. Post the adjectives on a chart in your reading center or create a separate space to put all the adjective charts you make throughout the year. Another option is to have students record the adjectives in their writing workshop folder or writer's notebook to use as they create their own characters.

MORNING MESSAGE IDEA: READING RESPONSE—CAN YOU GUESS THE CHARACTER?

Interactive Whiteboard Morning Message 4

As you read aloud the books in a series, listed on page 103, and children become familiar with specific characters and their individual traits, you can teach them how to write riddles about their favorite characters. Begin writing the riddle with a broad clue, and then continue writing clues to narrow the possibilities. Talk with your students about the importance of listening carefully to all of the clues, and then pondering, as our colleague Rose Jacob suggests, before jumping to conclusions. This is a helpful lesson for your listeners who tend to blurt out answers before taking the time to think! If you have an interactive whiteboard, display IWB_MM_4, which presents the two riddles shown below. For advanced readers, you can demonstrate how students can write riddles about their favorite tales. Read aloud *Spot the Plot: A Riddle Book of Book Riddles* (Lewis, 2009) to spark some ideas.

MORNING MESSAGE SAMPLE

The character is a girl.
She is a pig.
She has a friend named Gerald.
Her friend is an elephant.
Who is the character? (Piggie)

The character is a boy.
He has a pet.
The pet can say the boy's name.
The pet is a fly.
Who is the character? (Buzz)

POETRY POWER: POEMS FOR NOVEMBER AND DECEMBER	
Title	**Brief Summary**
It's Thanksgiving! (Prelutsky, 1982/2007)	This collection includes 12 grin-inducing poems about turkey day. For December, read, chant, and enjoy a few poems from Prelutsky's *It's Christmas!* (1981/2008) or *It's Snowing! It's Snowing!* (1984/2006).
Winter Poems (Rogasky, 1994)	A short anthology of poems that celebrate winter.

MORNING READ-ALOUDS: REAL AND MAKE-BELIEVE STORIES	
Title, Author, and Focus	**Brief Summary**
The Gingerbread Girl (Ernst, 2006) **Focus**: Traditional Tales/Make-Believe	The "younger, wiser" sister of the Gingerbread Boy also escapes from the farm family and outruns a pig, an artist, a cow and her calf, a dog walker, and some children at recess before outsmarting the fox.
Gracias/Thanks (Mora, 2009) **Focus**: Thanksgiving/Real	A young boy gives thanks for his family, friends, and the creatures he finds in the world around him. Written in both English and Spanish.
Hershel and the Hanukkah Goblins (Kimmell, 1989) **Focus**: Hanukkah, Make-Believe	Hershel of Ostropol waits in the crumbling old synagogue at the top of the hill and waits for the Hanukkah goblins to appear so that he can outwit them and light the candles on the menorah.
Mrs. Muddle's Holidays (Nielsen, 2008) **Focus**: Unique Celebrations/Real	Mrs. Muddle moves into Katie's neighborhood and shows the people of Maple Street how to celebrate holidays such as "Earthworm Appreciation Day" and "First Robin of Spring Day."
Tacky's Christmas (Lester, 2010) **Focus**: Christmas, Series Book/Make-Believe	When Christmas comes to Nice Icy Land, Tacky and his companions prepare and exchange gifts. Tacky's odd gift saves the day when the hunters from the first book return.
Three Hens and a Peacock (Laminack, 2011) **Focus**: Predicting/Make-Believe	When a peacock arrives at the Tuckers' farm, he makes himself useful by standing on the roadside attracting visitors to the farm. All is well until he overhears the hens complaining about him. But when the birds switch roles, they discover that the peacock's job is tougher than it looks.
Too Many Tamales (Soto, 1993) **Focus**: Christmas, Predicting/Real	While helping to make tamales, Maria puts on her mother's wedding ring, then forgets about it. Later, when it is time to eat the tamales, she realizes the ring is lost. Will Maria find the ring?
Turkey Trouble (Silvano, 2009) **Focus**: Thanksgiving/Make-Believe	Turkey is sure that Farmer Jake is planning to eat him for Thanksgiving dinner, so he sets out to find the perfect disguise by dressing up as a variety of farm animals.
Under the Ramadan Moon (Whitman, 2008) **Focus**: Ramadan/Real	A story about the Muslim observance of Ramadan, this picture book describes a family's activities during the monthlong observance. Notice the repetition of the line "under the moon."
Winter Trees (Gerber, 2008) **Focus**: Winter, Nature/Real	A boy and his dog crunch through the snow to discover six different kinds of trees in the winter.

Part 2: A Menu of Reading Workshop Mini-Lessons

When we are having conversations about our readers, one topic seems to surface frequently. How do we help readers to self-monitor as they read, notice when they make a miscue, and reread to fix it up? We will continue to address that ongoing goal in this chapter with a few more mini-lesson ideas. You'll also find lessons about the importance of making predictions. To build on students' knowledge of story, the genre study for this chapter is differentiating between real and make-believe stories.

MINI-LESSONS FOR SELF-MONITORING/DECODING STRATEGY INSTRUCTION

In the last two chapters, the decoding strategy lessons were focused on introducing, reinforcing, and practicing the individual decoding strategies. We continue to coach young readers as we sit beside them or guide them in small groups. To help make the use of strategies a natural part of a readers' thinking processes, we provide descriptive feedback to readers (see sidebar). Proficient readers do not use each strategy in isolation—they integrate the strategies. Therefore, the lessons that follow demonstrate the integration of decoding strategies.

MINI-LESSON: Pause, Think, and Check for Understanding—Foundation Lesson

Preparation: Preread a picture book and select a handful of words that you can strategically miscue and replace with a similar-looking word while you are reading the book aloud. The George and

---

DECODING STRATEGY PROMPTS

- Did that sound like the way we talk?
- Can you say it another way?
- Is there another word that might work here?
- What could you try?
- (if a child hesitates or stops) What did you notice?
- What can you do to help yourself here?
- Look at the picture clue. How can the picture clue help you?
- Get your mouth ready. Look at the beginning letter(s). What sound(s) do they make?
- Look through the word for sounds you know. What sound do you hear at the beginning? In the middle? At the end? Does that sound right?
- I heard you read _____. Do we say it that way? Try that again and think about what would sound right. Does that make sense?
- Do you know another word that looks like that? Do you know a word that starts with those letters? Do you know a word that ends with those letters?
- Are there any letter/word chunks that you know?

Adapted from Fountas & Pinnell (1996), Hoyt (2000)

CD Resource 4.1

Martha books by James Marshall work well for this type of lesson. For the demonstration, we used the first book in the series, *George and Martha* (Marshall, 1972). You may want to do a few of the pages for the today's lesson and save the rest for a follow-up lesson. Display the Decoding Strategy Wheel (CD Resource 2.4).

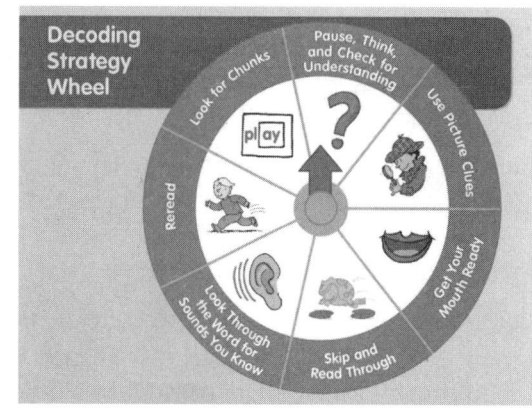

CD Resource 2.4 and IWB_Decoding_Wheel

Explanation: This lesson is aimed at your readers who are not yet self-monitoring their reading. Hearing how silly it sounds when you read the wrong word is an important understanding. When you confer with a child, you can refer to this mini-lesson by saying something like, "Remember what you noticed when I was reading *George and Martha*? I notice that sometimes you are not listening to yourself read. As you're reading today, I'm going to tap the table when something doesn't make sense. When you hear that, I want you to stop and try to figure out what went wrong. Let's see if that helps you keep a careful watch over your own reading."

Demonstration: To begin this demonstration, start reading the book aloud without giving any indication of what you are going to do. Miscue a word and continue reading to see if the children notice that what you read didn't make sense. See chart below for examples of miscues I make for *George and Martha*. It is interesting to notice which children pick up on the miscue first. Say, "Oh, you mean something didn't make sense? What should I do?" "You're right, I should stop and reread! We call that strategy Pause, Think, and Check for Understanding. It's right here on our decoding strategy wheel." "OK, let me see if I can figure out the word. I will use the picture clues and the context of the sentence to help me. That's what readers do when they notice something doesn't make sense."

p. 10	George carefully poured the rest of his soup into his lemons [loafers] under the table.
p. 12	"I didn't want to heart [hurt] your feelings," said George.
p. 16	"Maybe the banana [basket] is too heavy," said Martha.
p. 20	"Now what have I done? There goes my floating [flying] machine!"
p. 40	One day when George was skiing [skating] to Martha's house, he tripped and fell.
p. 44	The dentist replaced George's missing tooth with a lovely green [gold] one.

Invitation: "Readers who pause, think, and check for understanding are keeping a careful watch over their reading. Pay attention to make sure what you are reading makes sense."

MINI-LESSON: Integrating the Decoding Strategies—Foundation Lesson

Preparation: Select a few sentences from a book you will be reading to the class. Choose sentences with challenging words. Write sentences on sentence strips or an interactive whiteboard document.

Explanation: We've observed that one of the greatest challenges is to teach children how to integrate the decoding strategies in order to be able to use them flexibly and efficiently. Students tend to rely on one strategy and use it over and over, instead of using several strategies to figure out the word.

Demonstration: "Readers, when you come to a word you don't know, what do you do?" Listen and discuss responses. "If the first strategy doesn't work, what do you do next? After that?" Introduce and demonstrate the sequence of strategies found in the sidebar as you try to figure out the challenging word in each sentence. Release the responsibility by inviting a student or two to help you model the process. Once you've tackled the unknown words, read the book.

> **REREADING STRATEGIES**
>
> First, skip the word and read through the sentence
>
> Then, reread the sentence and get my mouth ready to say the tricky word
>
> Next, reread again checking for clues—picture clues, context clues, letter/word clues
>
> Finally, reread one last time.

CD Resource 4.2

Invitation: "Readers, when you come to a word you don't know, think about what to do. First, skip and read through. Then, reread and get your mouth ready. Next, reread and check for clues. Finally, reread to check the meaning. Notice if that helps you to figure out the word."

MINI-LESSON: Integrating the Decoding Strategies—Follow-Up Lesson

Preparation: Select a picture book or Big Book that offers opportunities to demonstrate the use of multiple decoding strategies. For this demonstration we use *To Market, To Market* (Miranda, 1997).

Explanation: In *Growing Readers* (2004), Kathy Collins suggests the following mini-lesson to show readers how to be more flexible when using decoding strategies, instead of relying on one or two or giving up too quickly.

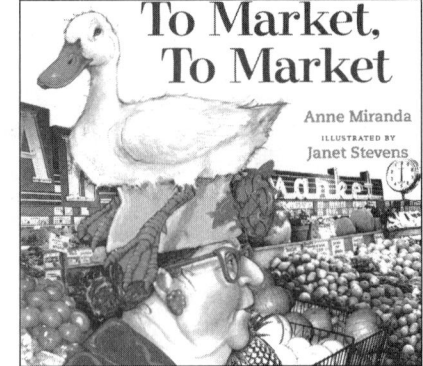

Demonstration: Begin your demonstration by using the toolbox analogy. Say, "When Mr. Zavala has to fix something at school, he brings a toolbox. He has to try different tools to find the right one to do the job. If he only had one tool in his box, and it didn't work, he couldn't fix the problem. The reading strategies we've learned are like the tools in Mr. Zavala's toolbox; we have to decide which tool makes sense and use that one. I'm going to read aloud and think aloud as I read so that you can see what readers do when they come to a word they don't know. Pay attention, because when I'm finished we're going to talk about what you noticed." Following are some ways you can model strategy use with the text.

p. 4. Cover the word *pig*	First, I'm going to **get my mouth ready** to figure out the word. Hmmm! Let me try to use the **picture clues**. I know it now! The word is *pig*! I'm going to quickly **reread** to be sure it makes sense and matches the sounds.
p. 8. Cover the letters *lump* in the word *plump*	Let me **get my mouth ready** to try to figure out this word. Well, I still can't figure it out, so I'll **look through the word for sounds I know.** I've got it now, the word is *plump,* but I'm not sure what that means. Let me **reread** to figure out the meaning of the word.
p. 10. Stop at the word *live*	[Misread *live* (long i) as *live* (short i).] Wait, I used the sounds, but that is not making sense! Let me **reread** to try to correct my miscue.
p. 17. Stop at the word *disappear*	[**Look for chunks** to figure out the word, but misread it by pronouncing the *pear* in *disappear* so it rhymes with *air*.] I used the chunks, but that doesn't make sense. Let me **reread** to try to correct my miscue.
p. 18. Pause at the word *stubborn* to ponder its meaning	**Reread** the words around *stubborn* and use the **picture clues** to try to figure out the meaning of the word. I notice that the lady is struggling to pull the goat into the market, so *stubborn* must mean that you want to keep doing something even if it's hard, and you don't want anyone to help you.
p. 25. Skip the word *chewing* because you can't figure it out.	**Skip and reread** *chewing* and use the picture clue and beginning sound to figure out the word.

Invitation: "Readers, did you notice that when I used one strategy that didn't help me, I tried another and another? Did you see how I didn't give up? That's what readers do. Try that today as you are reading and notice what happens."

MINI-LESSONS FOR COMPREHENSION STRATEGY INSTRUCTION

The focus for this month is to guide students to activate their schema and search for clues in the text and illustrations to predict or think ahead as they read. Predicting increases a reader's engagement. Often, when reading a picture book aloud, we will stop reading in the middle of the book, leaving our listeners "in suspense." Doing this not only gives children more time to ponder, but it also helps readers when they have to stop reading a book and pick it up again later that day or the next. It is interesting to hear how they respond if you simply ask, "So, did anyone do any thinking about the story we started earlier/yesterday?" "What do you think might happen next?" Finding natural ways to weave predicting into your day helps to make the concept part of children's thinking. A few examples might include the following:

- If it is pouring rain outside, ask, "Can anyone predict whether we will be going outside for recess today? Why or why not?"
- If a child has a wiggly tooth on Friday, say, "I'm predicting that Lauren will come back to school on Monday without her tooth. What do you think?"
- When sharing the lunch choices, say, "I notice that pizza has been the hot lunch for the past several Fridays. I'm predicting that you'll have pizza again this Friday. What do you think?"

MINI-LESSON: Predicting—Peek and Predict

Preparation: Select a book for an upcoming lesson or unit of study that has a detailed illustration on the cover. Wrap the book in a piece of bulletin board paper.

Explanation: We learned about this idea in the book *99 Ideas and Activities for Teaching English Learners With the SIOP® Model* (Vogt & Echevarria, 2008). Similar to the morning message idea Predict the Title found on page 109, the aim of this lesson is to show children how we predict as we read, and that the more we read, the easier it is to predict because we have more information.

Demonstration: Begin the demonstration with, "Readers, you will never guess what I have here." Take out the wrapped book. "This is the book we are going to read for our reading workshop lesson today, but first we are going to peek and predict." Tear off a little bit of the paper to reveal part of the cover illustration and invite students to share what they see and what they are thinking. As you continue to unwrap the cover, invite students to make predictions and revise their predictions, based on the new bits of illustration that appear.

Invitation: "Today we took a peek at the cover a little at a time. The same thing happens as you read a story a little at a time. You make predictions based on what you've already read, and the more you read and learn about the characters and the action in the story, the easier it is to predict what will happen in that story. When you reach the end, you finally see the whole picture and can think about the big idea or the author's message."

MINI-LESSON: Preview and Predict Read-Aloud/Think-Aloud—Foundation Lesson

Preparation: Copy and display the strategy song "Making Predictions" (CD Resource 4.3) and the Comprehension Strategy Wheel (CD Resource 3.5). The challenge of creating lessons for predicting is finding picture books that a majority of your students haven't already read or heard. We've suggested books that lend themselves to predicting; the books listed on page 117 work well for modeling prediction, while we recommend the books on page 118 for thinking about prediction with your students in a follow-up lesson. But you will have to determine whether your learners are familiar with them.

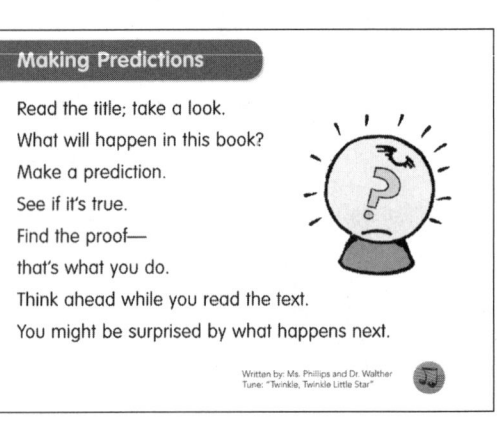

CD Resource 4.3 and IWB_Song_4.3

Explanation: Previewing the book sets the stage for reading by giving students a framework for what the text contains. Then, as you read aloud and think aloud, students will see how you make predictions about a story based on your prior knowledge and experiences.

Demonstration: Introduce the strategy by locating it on the Comprehension Strategy Wheel and singing the strategy song "Making Predictions." If you have an interactive whiteboard, display IWB_Song_4.3 and press the musical note to play the tune. Read aloud the title of the book, look carefully at the cover illustration, and read the back cover blurb if there is one. Predict what the book might be about based on your preview. Then continue reading and predicting aloud as you go. Use the following phrases as you think aloud:

- I predict . . .
- I think this will happen because . . .
- The clues I can use to prove this are . . .
- I'm thinking _____ might happen because . . .
- Wow! My prediction matched the author's thinking.
- My prediction was different from the author's idea.

Invitation: "Readers, when you read a book, remember to preview it just like I did today, by reading the title, looking carefully at the illustrations, and reading the blurb. Then, ponder what the book might be about. As you read, revise your predictions based on your new learning. Remember, it is OK if your predictions don't match the author's ideas, as long as they make sense."

Title and Author	Brief Summary
Badger's Fancy Meal (Kazsa, 2007)	Badger is tired of the "same old, same old"—apples, worms, and roots. So he leaves his den in search of a "fancy meal." First, he tries to make a mole taco but the mole slips away. Then, he tries to make a rat burger but the rat wiggles away. Next, he tries to make a rabbit-banana split but the rabbit jumps away. Finally, when he yells, "I'm so hungry that I could eat a horse!" he gets kicked back to his den, only to find his food is missing. The text and illustrations offer abundant opportunities to ponder and predict.
The Great Fuzz Frenzy (Stevens & Stevens Crummel, 2005)	When an unsuspecting dog drops a fuzzy tennis ball down a prairie dog hole, the creatures engage in some "fuzzy foolishness." Pause and predict when Pip Squeak cries, "SOMEONE HAS STOLEN OUR FUZZ!" and on the page that reads "SWOOP! The sky went black." Of course, the page that shows Violet the dog as she's about to drop another ball in the hole sparks a lot of predictions!
The Wolf's Chicken Stew (Kasza, 1987)	A hungry wolf is craving chicken stew and "was about to grab his prey . . ." when he changes his mind. Instead, he decides to fatten up the chicken. "So . . ." he bakes goodies for her. "But as he peeked into the chicken's house . . ." the wolf finds a surprise!

MINI-LESSON: Preview and Predict Read-Aloud/ Think-Together Follow-Up Lesson

Preparation: Select a book that lends itself to predicting. We've included a few suggestions on page 118.

Explanation: Release the responsibility to your listeners by inviting them to share their ideas. As you read aloud and think together, students will join you in making predictions about a story based on their prior knowledge and experiences.

Title and Author	Brief Summary
Agatha's Feather Bed: Not Just Another Wild Goose Story (Deedy, 1991)	We've introduced this story to many teachers and they either like it or they think it is a little odd. Either way, it is ideal for predicting. Agatha is an old woman who believes "everything comes from something." When a gaggle of naked geese appear on her windowsill, she makes them warm cloaks to replace their feathers, which make up her bed. In a surprise ending, we find out that the cloaks were made from her long white hair.
Dark Night (de Monfreid, 2009)	Felix heads to the forest on a dark night and is frightened by a wolf, a tiger, and a crocodile. Fortunately, he meets a clever rabbit who helps to him scare the ferocious beasts away.
The Incredible Painting of Felix Clousseau (Agee, 1988)	Felix Clousseau is an unknown painter who gains fame when his paintings come to life. But chaos erupts, and he is sent to prison. Fortunately, one of his paintings saves the king's crown. Felix is freed and "returns to his painting."

Demonstration: Review the strategy by locating it on the Comprehension Strategy Wheel and singing the strategy song "Making Predictions." Use *The Inside Tree* (Smith, 2010) for this read-aloud/think-together lesson, which offers ideal places to pause and predict, and then return to it to highlight three read-aloud words. See chart on page 123. Here are some suggestions to get you started.

Text on Book Page	A Few Questions to Spark Your Conversation
Cover	This book is called *The Inside Tree*. It's written by Linda Smith and illustrated by David Parkins. Let's take a look at the cover illustration. What do you notice? When you think about the title and look at the illustrations, what do you predict might happen in this story? Let's begin reading to see if your predictions match the author's ideas.
"It was a perfectly cozy arrangement until . . ."	Notice the three dots that the author chose to use here. What does that tell us as readers? What do you predict might happen to change Mr. Potter's cozy arrangement?
"Somehow, it didn't seem right that the tree was never invited in or allowed to sit by the fire . . ."	I'm wondering, is it easier to make a prediction now that we've read a bit of the story? Do you notice a pattern here? What do you think Mr. Potter is going to do now? What makes you think that?
"Everything was perfect until . . ."	Oh my goodness! What is going to happen now? Think and share with your partner.
"There he saw one of the loneliest cows he had ever seen."	Yikes! What will Mr. Potter do next? Why do you think that? I can't wait to read to find out. Let's read the big ending.

When responding to students' predictions, try to make nonjudgmental comments such as,

"That's an interesting idea. What made you think that?"

"Does anyone have a different idea?"

"Does anyone have the same thinking?"

"Wow! I never noticed that before. That's why we reread!"

"I never would have thought of that."

"What is your thinking behind that prediction?"

Invitation: "Readers, when you read a book, remember to preview it just like we did today, by reading the title, looking carefully at the illustrations, and reading the blurb. Then, think about what you predict the book might be about. As you read, revise your predictions based on your new learning. Remember, it is okay if your predictions don't match the author's ideas as long as they make sense."

MINI-LESSON: Using Visual Information to Set a Purpose for Reading and Predicting

Preparation: Gather a few of Steven Kellogg's books or other picture books like the ones listed here, in which key illustrations appear before the title page.

Title and Author	Brief Summary
Yes Day! (Rosenthal, 2009)	A boy wakes up to find that today is his favorite day of the year, a day when his parents grant his every request—Yes Day! Discuss the clues in the illustrations that help readers infer whether each of the boy's requests was granted. Invite students to write their own Yes Day! book for their families.
Shark vs. Train (Barton, 2010)	Two boys reach into a toy box. One pulls out a toy shark, one pulls out a train toy. Then the debate begins about who will win. Readers discover that it all depends on the kind of activity! An engaging, boy-appealing read-aloud.

Explanation: We've noticed that many authors and illustrators are choosing to begin the book before the title page. Steven Kellogg has been doing this for years. Readers have to preview the illustrations on the pages leading up to the first page of the story or they will miss key information. Once you make a habit of looking at all the front matter carefully, you will discover many hidden treasures on the endpapers, copyright page, and title page. These discoveries will help your young writers as well.

Demonstration: "Readers, today we are going to notice how this author and illustrator help us as readers by showing us some important information in the illustrations before the book even begins." Preview and discuss the pages leading up to the title page. Then, enjoy the book. Pause to notice how the pictures at the beginning lead to a better understanding of the story.

Invitation: "As you are reading today, notice if any of the authors and illustrators of your books chose to give you a visual preview before the title page. If so, bring that book with you to sharing today so we can see what you've found."

MINI-LESSON: Using Schema and Connections to Predict

Preparation: We usually use a series book (see page 105 for suggestions) for this lesson. You can either read a few books in the series prior to this lesson, to familiarize students with the characters, plot structure, and so on, or you can find a new book in a familiar series that your students haven't already read or heard.

Explanation: From the beginning, we want readers to truly understand that self-monitoring readers integrate decoding strategies to figure out unfamiliar words while at the same time using comprehension strategies to understand the author's meaning. This mini-lesson emphasizes how readers use their schema and make connections in order to make sensible predictions.

Demonstration: Open your demonstration with, "Let's think a little bit more about how we make predictions. As I'm reading this new book in the series, I want you to think about what you already know about the series and how that helps you predict what might happen next." After reading, discuss what students noticed. Ask, "What do you use to help you predict?" Create a chart of ideas similar to the one found in the sidebar.

Invitation: "Readers pay attention to what they are reading. They use their schema and make connections to help them better understand the author's message. As you are reading today, notice if those strategies help you as a reader."

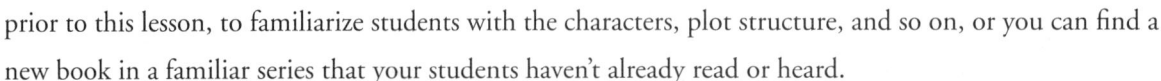

PREDICTING STRATEGIES

When I predict I use . . .

Clues in the illustrations

Clues in the text

My schema

    Experiences—I've had a similar experience so I think about what I might have done in that situation.

    Series Books—If it is a series book, I think about what I already know about how the character acts.

Connections

    Books—I remember that something like that happened in another book I've read or heard.

    Series Books—If it is a series book, I think about the other book's pattern or structure and notice if this is the same.

CD Resource 4.4

READ-ALOUDS THAT SPARK COMPREHENSION CONVERSATIONS

Title, Author, Focus, and Brief Summary	A Few Questions to Spark Your Conversation
The Secret Message (Javaherbin, 2010) **Focus:** Predicting **Summary:** Based on an ancient Persian poem, "Parrot and the Merchant" by Rumi, this is a tale of a wealthy merchant who keeps a parrot in his shop to attract customers. When the merchant asks the parrot what he wants from India, the parrot requests that the merchant tell his wild bird friends about him. Their secret message leads to the parrot's escape to freedom.	Think about the title, *The Secret Message*. What do you think this story might be about? Explain the thinking behind your prediction. What does the author mean by "the bird sang of longing?" Let's see if we can infer the meaning of the word *longing* by rereading this section. Why do you think the parrot asked the merchant to tell the wild parrots about his cage? Wow! I didn't expect the birds to do that. What do you think is going on? Why do you think the author chose the title *The Secret Message*? What would you have called this book?
The Magic Fish (Littledale, 1966) **Focus:** Vocabulary **Summary:** The Magic Fish grants a greedy fisherman's wife every wish she desires, but she still isn't satisfied.	What words might you use to describe the wife? [*greedy, demanding, selfish, bossy, ungrateful, mean*] Did you notice any repeated parts in this book? Why do you think Freya Littledale chose to repeat those words/parts? How do you think the wife is feeling at the end of the book? Why do you think she is feeling that way? What would you have done if you were the fisherman? How would the story have changed if the fisherman had said no to his wife? What is the big idea of this book? What is the author trying to tell us? What might happen next?
Too Many Tamales (Soto, 1993) **Focus:** Predicting **Summary:** While helping to make tamales, Maria puts on her mother's wedding ring, then forgets about it. Later, when it is time to eat the tamales, she realizes the ring is lost. Will Maria find the ring?	How do you think Maria is feeling when she realizes the ring is lost? Why do you think she is feeling that way? What do you think will happen next? How do Maria's feelings change at the end of the story? What is the big idea of this book? Do you think the title *Too Many Tamales* fits the story? Why do you think Gary Soto chose this title? If you were to give this book a different title, what would it be? While reading, discuss the words *dusk, kneaded, chattered,* and *batch*. Use the context of the sentence and picture clues to figure out what each word means.

MINI-LESSONS FOR VOCABULARY DEVELOPMENT: STUDYING VERBS AND ADJECTIVES

In the October chapter, we introduced compound words to show children how breaking words apart and thinking about word parts is one strategy they can use to better understand the meaning of a word. In the vocabulary lessons that follow, we focus on verbs and adjectives. These mini-lessons will be most beneficial if students already have a basic understanding of nouns, verbs, and adjectives. Teach the lesson on verbs to demonstrate how authors choose specific verbs carefully to match their intended message. The adjective lesson will guide learners to understand the connection between adjectives and the nouns that they describe.

> ### FLUENCY FUN! POPCORN HOP!
>
> As the name indicates, in this activity one child at a time pops up to read a line in the poem. To prepare for this fluency-building activity, assign numbers to the lines in the poem and project them on an interactive whiteboard. We usually use Stephanie Calmenson's poem "Popcorn Hop," found in her book *Kindergarten Kids: Riddles, Rebuses, Wiggles, Giggles, and More!* (2005). Assign each child or group a number, and then read the poem, number by number, to avoid having several children pop up at the same time (Vardell, 2009).

MINI-LESSON: Verbs—Shades of Meaning

Preparation: Select a book in which the author uses different verbs to indicate how the characters are speaking. For example, in *Doodleday* by Ross Collins, the characters *shrieked, asked, said, gasped, cried, yelled,* and *bellowed.* Write each past-tense verb on a separate index card.

Explanation: It is important that readers notice the verbs the author uses to indicate how the character is speaking. This leads to reading with expression and also an understanding of how the character is feeling when he or she is speaking.

Demonstration: After reading *Doodleday* for pleasure, return to it and notice the different verbs. Show children the verb cards, and compare and contrast their meanings. Ask questions like, "What is the difference between *said* and *asked*? Do we read those sentences in different ways?" and "If you had to put the verbs in order from quietest to loudest, how would you arrange them?"

Invitation: "As you are reading today, notice the verbs the author chooses to use to describe how the character is talking. If you find new verbs that we haven't talked about, jot them on a sticky note and we'll share them later. Happy reading!"

MINI-LESSON: Adjectives—Making Connections
Interactive Whiteboard Lesson 4

Preparation: If you have an interactive whiteboard, then access lesson IWB_Lesson_4. If not, create a deck of adjective cards. To spark your thinking, see the adjective chart below.

Explanation: The purpose of this mini-lesson is to help readers make real-life connections between adjectives and the nouns that they might describe.

Demonstration: Flash an adjective card. Depending on your grade level, learners can write, draw, or shout out a noun that connects to that adjective. Challenge your students to think of as many as they can before you move on to the next adjective card.

Can you name something that is . . . ?					
SHAPE	**SIZE**	**COLOR**	**TEXTURE**	**WEIGHT**	**PERSONALITY**
square	enormous	golden	hairy	flimsy	terrifying
rounded	minuscule	fuchsia	furry	light	ferocious
long	gigantic	crimson	scaly	heavy	monstrous
thin	massive	carroty	spongy	wispy	friendly
triangular	teeny	violet	jagged	hefty	gloomy

Adapted from: *Month-by-Month Trait-Based Writing Instruction* (Walther & Phillips, 2009)

Invitation: "As you are reading today think about the adjectives an author uses to describe the characters or settings. When you read those adjectives, picture someone you know who looks or acts like that. Making this connection will help you to imagine what the character is like."

READ-ALOUDS WITH RICH VOCABULARY		
Title and Author	**Brief Summary**	**Words to Highlight and Kid-Friendly Definition**
The Inside Tree (Smith, 2010) (Make-believe)	Mr. Potter's house is warm and comfortable until he decides to invite a dog and a tree inside.	**eerie**: spooky or scary **fetched**: went somewhere, picked something up, and brought it back **parlor**: a room in a house that is used for having people over and talking
If I Built a Car (Van Dusen, 2005) (Make-believe)	Jack describes every detail of his spectacular fantasy car.	**contemplate**: to think about something very carefully **concoction**: something that is made by putting together lots of different parts or ingredients **capture**: to catch something or take control of something
The Wolf's Chicken Stew (Kasza, 1987) (Make-believe)	A hungry wolf is craving chicken stew and is about to grab his prey when he changes his mind. Instead, he decides to fatten up the chicken by baking for her.	**craving**: a really big desire for something **critters**: little animals or creatures **scrumptious**: delicious

MINI-LESSONS FOR READING RESPONSE

As we continue to add to your menu of response options, our purpose is to embed this type of thinking into students' schema. As you continue to model and practice different responses to reading, students can choose the type of response that makes sense to them. In this chapter, the mini-lessons focus on expanding readers' understanding of character by recording the character traits that are indicated in the text. Readers can record what they learn about a character from reading the character's words or their thinking, noticing how the character acts, and paying attention to the way the author describes the character. Next, there are two responses that will help readers summarize their understanding of a text by recording the beginning, middle, and end or writing a book blurb.

MINI-LESSON: Creating Character Webs

Preparation: Gather a collection of books that are peopled by characters with distinct, observable traits. Some books that work well for this lesson include *Amazing Grace* (Hoffman, 1991), *Bridget's Beret* (Lichtenheld, 2010), *No, David!* (Shannon, 1998), and *Thomas' Snowsuit* (Munsch, 1985). Children record their thinking on the web page in their Read, Think, and Respond Book (CD Resource 1.4). Enlarge a copy of the web page for your demonstration.

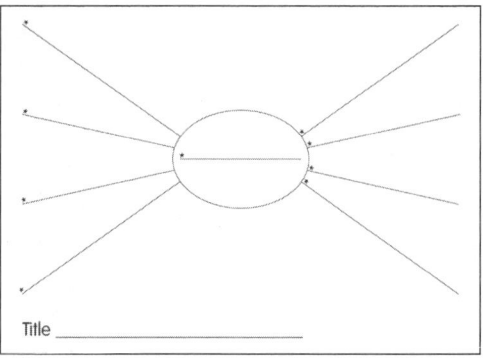

CD Resource 1.4

Explanation: As readers, we learn about characters from what they say, do, and think, and the way the author describes them or the illustrator portrays them. The aim of this response-to-reading lesson is to guide students to identify a character's traits by gathering information from the text and illustrations.

Demonstration:
- Read a portion of the text to or with your students.
- Invite them to tell you things they have learned about the main character. You'll notice that students often begin by telling you about things the character "does." To focus the conversation, point out specific clues in the text and use the following prompts:
  - Listen to what the character says right here. What does that tell you about him or her?
  - Notice what the character is doing here. What does that tell you about him or her?
  - Listen to the words the author uses to describe the character. Could we use some of the same words?
- Add their thoughts to the enlarged character web page.
- Continue reading and adding ideas to the web.
- Discuss how they can use what they know about that character to help when reading other books with the same character, or connect that character to a different character in another book. (Adapted from *Literature Is Back!*, Fuhler & Walther, 2007)

Invitation: "Why is it important to think carefully about the characters? Ponder that as you read today and we'll talk more about that when we share."

MINI-LESSON: Noticing the Beginning, Middle, and End

Preparation: Select a book with a clear beginning, middle, and end. This seems like an easy task, but over the years we've had little luck in finding simple books to introduce this retelling activity to our youngest readers. We've had better luck using nursery rhymes because they are simple. Just in case you have these books in your guided reading collection, we've found *Frog's Lunch* by Dee Lillegard and *Mr. McCready's Cleaning Day* by Tracey Shilling to work well. Another title to consider is *Duck on a Bike* (Shannon, 2002). Children record their thinking on the three-column notes page in their Read, Think, and Respond Book (CD Resource 1.7). Enlarge of copy of the three-column notes page for your demonstration.

CD Resource 1.7

Explanation: This idea comes from Linda Hoyt's book *Revisit, Reflect, and Retell* (1999). The goal here is to guide students as they identify the three main parts of a story, and then use these parts to help them retell the story to others.

Demonstration:

- Show students how to label the three columns on their response sheet with beginning, middle, and end by labeling the parts on your enlarged copy of the page.
- Begin reading the text to your students.
- After reading the beginning of the story, pause and demonstrate how to draw a quick sketch to show what happened at the beginning of the book. Invite listeners to draw on their three-column notes sheet a pencil sketch of what happened at the beginning.
- At this point, you can determine, based on the needs of your students, whether you want to continue to model sketching both the middle and the end of the story or if you can simply read the middle and end and invite listeners to draw the other two pictures on their own. Once students are back in the seats, they can add color and detail to their illustrations. You can challenge your early finishers to add a quick caption or written description to their illustration.
- After the students have finished their drawings, they think and share with partners or meet with a small group to show and discuss their pictures. Invite them to tell why they drew each illustration, and explain how the drawings relate to the story.

Invitation: "As you read today, make a picture in your mind of the beginning, middle, and end of the story. This will help you better remember the story so that you can tell someone else about it."

MINI-LESSON: Writing a Book Blurb

Preparation: Gather a stack of books with engaging back cover blurbs. Read and discuss the common characteristics of a book blurb, creating an anchor chart like the one shown below.

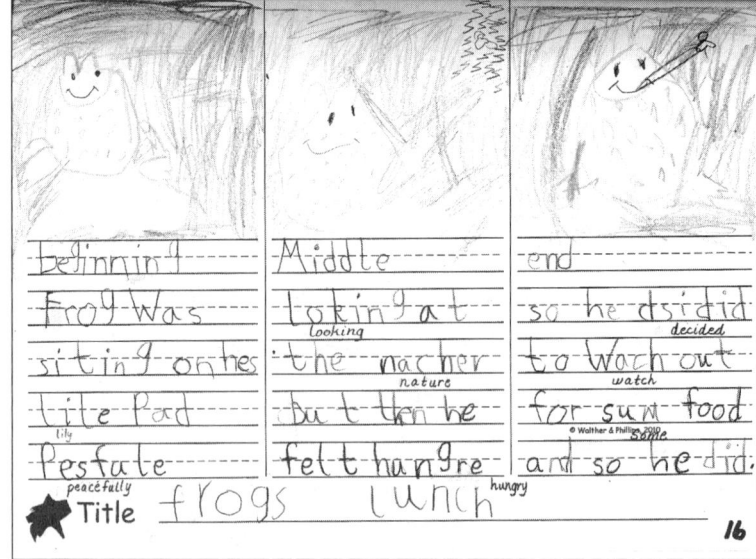

Sama responds by retelling the book *Frog's Lunch.* Beginning: Frog was sitting on his lily pad peacefully looking at nature. Middle: But then he felt hungry. End: So he decided to watch out for some food and so he did.

Explanation: Teaching children how to write a back cover blurb not only helps them capture the essence of the story, but it also introduces them to a helpful prereading strategy.

Demonstration: For your demonstration, choose a familiar picture book that does not have a back cover blurb. Model writing a blurb for that book. If you choose, you can rewrite the blurb on a sticky note and affix it to the book. After students have had time to practice, ask them to choose their best blurb and revise, edit, and display it with the book.

Invitation: "Readers, now is your chance to write a blurb for one of your favorite books. Pick a familiar book from your book box or the shelf that doesn't have a blurb and craft an inviting blurb to entice others to read it." (Adapted from *Month-by-Month Trait-Based Writing Instruction*, Walther & Phillips, 2009)

Helpful Hints for Writing Blurbs

Keep it short.

Tell readers enough to make them want to read the book, but not too much.

Don't give away the ending.

Book Blurb Anchor Chart

A first grader's back cover blurb

Part 3: Genre Study—Real and Make-Believe Stories

During this genre study, post a chart near your meeting area to collect your students' thinking. Begin by asking readers to share their prior knowledge about the differences between real and make-believe stories. Read aloud and discuss a real story, focusing on the real elements. Invite listeners to share the real elements that you and your students noticed in the book and record their thinking. The next day, read aloud and discuss a make-believe story, focusing on the make-believe elements. List the make-believe elements that you and your students discovered in the book. After you have shared a number of titles and are confident your students have a firm understanding of the two kinds of texts, it is time to release the responsibility to students. Before independent reading time, give each student a sticky note. Ask them to label the book they are reading as either real or make-believe. During sharing time, invite students to share their books, the label, and the characteristics they used to identify the type of book. Continue this conversation throughout the year to keep this learning fresh in students' minds (adapted from *Literature Is Back!*, Fuhler & Walther, 2007).

Real stories have . . .	Make-believe stories have . . .
• people acting like people • animals acting like animals • places that are real • events that can happen in real life	• animals or objects acting like people talking • wearing clothes • doing people things • places that are imaginary • events that are magical

GENRE STUDY: REAL AND MAKE-BELIEVE PAIRINGS	
Title and Author	**Brief Summary**
Big Red Barn (Brown, 1956/1989) (Real)	A book written by Margaret Wise Brown, author of the classic *Goodnight Moon*, that depicts the animals' day on a farm.
Moo Who? (Palatini, 2004) (Make-believe)	When Hilda Mae Heifer gets hit with a cow pie and loses her "mi-mi-moo," she tries out other animals' sounds until she gets her moo back.
Chicken Soup by Heart (Hershenhorn, 2002) (Real)	Rudie cooks a batch of chicken soup using Mrs. Gittel's secret ingredient—stories!
Chicken Soup (Van Leeuwen, 2009) (Make Believe)	All the farm animals "skedaddled" when Mrs. Farmer took out the big pot to make chicken soup—except little chickie, who is suffering from a cold and having a hard time hiding because she keeps sneezing. Enjoy the surprise ending!
The Missing Mitten Mystery (Kellogg, 2000) (Real)	As Annie and her dog Oscar search for her missing mitten, she imagines all of the things that could have happened to it. The story is real, but some of Annie's imaginative ideas are make-believe, so it often leads to an interesting discussion.
The Mitten (Brett, 1989) (Make-believe)	There is so much to look at and talk about in this classic retelling of a Ukrainian folktale about a boy named Nicki who loses the mitten that was lovingly knitted by his Baba.
Perfect Snow (Reid, 2009) (Real)	Scott and Jim are excited about the snow. At recess, Scott wants to make snowmen and Jim starts a snow fort. In the end, they work together to make a massive snowman fort.
Snowmen All Year (Buehner, 2010) (Make-believe)	In the third book of the Snowman series, the boy imagines all the things he would do with his non-melting snowman throughout the year.
Skunkdog (Jenkins, 2008) (Real)	Dumpling is an obedient dog whose owners love her, but because she has no sense of smell, she has no dog friends. When the family moves to the country, Dumpling finds a loyal, but smelly, new friend—a skunk!
Superdog: The Heart of a Hero (Buehner, 2004) (Make-believe)	Dexter the dachshund is determined to be a hero and he works very hard to achieve this goal.

Meeting the Needs of ALL Learners

As we look for ways to differentiate our reading instruction to meet the needs of the diverse learners in our classrooms, we always come back to the same question: "How can we possibly fit one more thing into our busy teaching day?" With this question firmly planted in our minds, we've tried to keep the ideas in this section manageable, yet powerful, knowing that, especially for striving and reluctant readers, we may have to try multiple ideas before we find the one that works. If you chose to use the Reading Boost Bag idea we shared in the September chapter, we're hopeful that your striving readers are making progress. We would expect that the series books you introduced in October have hooked other readers. We're sure that you, like us, still have a few students who haven't found their reading interests and are not reading enough. For them, we offer another suggestion—graphic novels. For advanced readers we will create an opportunity for them to engage in a debate.

SENSIBLE STRATEGIES FOR STRUGGLING READERS: THE APPEAL OF GRAPHIC NOVELS

If your students are like ours, we're sure you've seen an increase in the number of children, especially boys, who live in a video-game world. They talk about video games, write about video games, act out the games at recess, and sometimes their pencils and supplies transform into the characters, and then a battle scene erupts, complete with sound effects! Chances are, the stories that we love will not have the same appeal for readers with media-based interests. So, in addition to infusing a lot of nonfiction read-alouds into your repertoire (we'll talk more about that in the April/May chapter) we suggest introducing graphic novels. In the past few years, many publishers have picked up on this idea and have

Add graphic novels to your classroom library.

created graphic novels geared toward our youngest readers. We've highlighted a few of our favorite series below. Consider adding a "graphic novel basket" to your classroom library and see what happens!

Name of Series/ Publisher	Title, Author, and Brief Summary
Babymouse/ Random House	*Babymouse #13: Cupcake Tycoon* (Holm, 2010) Babymouse is determined to raise the most money and win the grand prize in the school library fundraiser.
Guinea Pig Pet Shop Private Eye/ Graphic Universe/ Lerner	*The Ferret's a Foot* (Venable, 2011) In the third book of this series, Sasspants and her sidekick Hamisher are trying to solve another pet shop mystery.
Phonics Comics/ Innovative Kids	*Teeny Genie* (Katschke, 2009) The Teeny Genie is helping kids who need him with one wacky wish after another.
Sticky Burr/ Candlewick	*Sticky Burr: Adventures in Burrwood Forest* (Lechner, 2007) Scurvy Burr and his pals do not accept Sticky Burr until he saves the village from a pack of wild dogs. A graphic novel interspersed with pages from Sticky Burr's journal.
Toon Books/ Candlewick	*Stinky* (Davis, 2008) Stinky and his pet Wartbelly enjoy their smelly days in the swamp until a kid comes along. Will Stinky and the kid become friends?

TARGETING TALENTED READERS: LET'S HAVE A DEBATE!

Bring your talented readers together for a debate. Debating promotes critical thinking and helps students organize information, ask questions to clarify differing points of view, and analyze alternative points of view. These are just a few of the essential 21st-century skills that students will be using as they prepare and debate (Partnership for 21st Century Skills, 2009). To begin this experience, introduce readers to the Mercy Watson series by Kate DiCamillo. Invite them to read and enjoy the books. Next, ask them to consider whether they think the Mercy Watson books are real or make-believe, based on the criteria you created in the genre study chart found on page 127. Divide the class into two small groups. Provide time for groups to formulate their arguments and locate the evidence in the text or illustrations to support their argument. Provide students with some helpful language for debating their point of view, including the following.

To give your reasons, say . . .	When you disagree, say . . .
I believe . . .	I disagree because . . .
The reasons why I think this are . . .	But what about . . .
To start with . . .	Shouldn't we consider . . .
So, I'm convinced that . . .	

Then, make time for each group of students to share their arguments in front of the class.

Final Thoughts

We predict that as you finish this chapter, you are looking forward to a much-needed winter break. Use the precious days ahead to read a few good books, enjoy time with your family, or spend an entire day in your pajamas! Then, as you prepare to begin school again, reflect upon all that your students have accomplished thus far. If your students had their school photos taken early in the year, it is fun to look at them now and see how much they've grown. We all know that the same growth is occurring on the inside; it is just so much harder to notice when you are with them day after day. Think back to those learners who came without any knowledge of letters or sounds—what do they know now? How about those children who were just learning English? As primary grade teachers, you do remarkable work—celebrate your successes! Give yourself a pat on the back! Then, set new goals, turn to the next chapter, and begin a new year!

CHAPTER 5: JANUARY

Retelling, Comparing, and Contrasting Stories

Not all of your readers make connections between stories. As you've probably noticed, many students are unfamiliar with traditional tales—including folktales, fairy tales, and nursery rhymes. Some children have seen the movie version but are surprised to find out that the same story originally appeared in a book. In this chapter, we've put together a menu of mini-lessons that will help you provide your students with essential story sense and guide learners as they make connections between texts to better understand the tales. Although you will find traditional tales sprinkled throughout the chapter, we conclude with a genre study highlighting these titles. Make it a New Year's resolution to give your students the gift of surrounding them with the tales that are an essential part of their reading history.

Part 1: Reading-Related Morning Message Ideas and Samples

As you read through the messages found in the upcoming pages, think about how you can select a message to launch the learning and begin a conversation that continues throughout your day or week. Can you use a decoding strategy message similar to the one described below to introduce a book you plan to read and discuss? Would a vocabulary-based message be helpful for highlighting words that will help your ELLs better understand an upcoming unit of study in science or social studies? We've found that January is a perfect time to review and reinforce some of the conversational rituals that we introduced in the September chapter. Our point is that, with limited time in the teaching day, the morning message provides a quick yet powerful teaching opportunity if we design each message to meet our students' short- or long-term learning goals.

MORNING MESSAGE IDEA: SELF-MONITORING/DECODING—GET YOUR MOUTH READY

Oftentimes, if readers simply verbalize the first sound of an unknown word, they have a better chance of figuring it out. We introduce this strategy in the mini-lesson on page 85. To save precious instructional minutes, choose sentences from a book you are planning to read. The sentences in the sample message on this page are found in the amusing book *Interrupting Chicken* (Stein, 2010).

MORNING MESSAGE IDEA: COMPREHENSION—STORY ELEMENTS

Try this message when you want to review story-related vocabulary such as character, setting, action, problem, and solution. If this story-related vocabulary is new to your students, you will want to begin using the terms when reading aloud and conversing about stories, as these terms are helpful when discussing stories and making connections between tales. Nursery rhymes lend themselves well to introducing these concepts to your learners. Interest-

> **MORNING MESSAGE SAMPLE**
>
> Get Your Mouth Ready
>
> Does the word pop into your head?
>
> Why don't you c____ inside? (come)
>
> Don't t____ to strangers! (talk)
>
> Now get b____ into bed. (back)
>
> I'll read one of y____ favorites. (your)

MORNING MESSAGE SAMPLE

Jack and Jill went up the hill
To fetch a pail of water
Jack fell down and broke his crown
And Jill came tumbling after

Characters: Jack and Jill
Location: the hill
Action: fetching water
Problem: they fell down
Solution: ?

Humpty Dumpty sat on a wall
Humpty Dumpty had a great fall
All the king's horses and all the king's men
Couldn't put Humpty together again

Character: Humpty Dumpty
Location: the wall
Action: sitting on wall
Problem: he had a great fall
Solution: ?

ingly, we've noticed that many nursery rhymes end without solving the problem. See if your students notice this, too! To add some higher-level thinking to this message, invite students to create their own ending for each nursery rhyme.

MORNING MESSAGE IDEA: VOCABULARY BUILDING—FAMILIAR WORDS WITH NEW MEANINGS

Interactive Whiteboard Morning Message 5

This message is targeted for our youngest learners and ELLs because it helps them discover and learn new meanings for familiar words. Prior to the message, write words with accompanying sentences on cards for the pocket chart; if you have an interactive whiteboard, display IWB_MM_5. You may also want to add clip art pictures to support students' understanding. Begin by displaying the first word in the pair along with the sentence and illustration. Then, discuss the alternate use of the word and, if applicable, invite students to act out the meaning of the word. We've provided a few words to get you started. We suggest discussing only two or three word pairs during one message time. Then, post and reinforce the words by using them throughout the week and inviting students to point them out when they read or hear them.

MORNING MESSAGE SAMPLE

duck	duck
The **duck** swam in the pond.	**Duck**! The ball is going to hit you!
fall	fall
Leaves change colors in the **fall**.	Humpty Dumpty had a great **fall**.
bug	bug
An ant is a **bug**.	Don't **bug** your sister.
pack	pack
There are 24 crayons in a **pack**.	It's time to **pack** your backpack.
school	school
We read and think in **school**.	A **school** of fish swims together.
bat	bat
A **bat** eats bugs.	Hit the baseball with the **bat**.
bark	bark
The tree has brown **bark**.	I heard the dog **bark**.
orange	orange
I will color the pumpkin **orange**.	I ate an **orange** for lunch today.
trunk	trunk
An elephant has a long **trunk**.	The **trunk** was filled with books.
ball	ball
The kids are playing with the red **ball**.	Cinderella went to the **ball**.

MORNING MESSAGE IDEA: READING RESPONSE—
USING KEY WORDS AND PHRASES TO RETELL

In order to successfully complete this message, learners will need to be familiar with the tale you would like them to retell. If your students lack this background knowledge, you will find lists of familiar tales on pages 142 and 150. To complete this message, display the first key word. Invite students to turn to their think-and-share partner and take turns retelling the beginning of the story. To continue, add words and provide time for students to retell the story bit by bit. For an added challenge, invite students to "tag team" retell—Partner 1 tells about the first word or phrase, Partner 2 tells about the second word or phrase, and so on.

MORNING MESSAGE SAMPLE

Can you use these key words and phrases to retell "Goldilocks and the Three Bears"?

Three Bears

cooling porridge

out for a walk

Goldilocks

porridge

chairs

beds

ran away

Can you use these key words and phrases to retell "Henny Penny"?

Henny Penny

acorn fell

the sky is falling

Cocky Locky

Ducky Lucky

Goosey Loosey

Foxy Loxy

cave

| POETRY POWER: POEMS FOR JANUARY ||
Title	Brief Summary
Polar Bear, Arctic Hare: Poems for the Frozen North (Spinelli, 2007)	As the cold wind blows (or cooler winds, if you live somewhere warm), read poems about the plants and animals of the Arctic, like lemmings, caribou, and the snow flea.
Sharing the Seasons: A Book of Poems (Hopkins, 2010)	This anthology contains 48 poems, 12 for each season. Enjoy the winter poems now, and save the spring and summer poetry for later in the year.

MORNING READ-ALOUDS: SPIN-OFFS OF TRADITIONAL TALES	
Title, Author, and Focus	**Brief Summary**
The Book That Zack Wrote (Long, 2011) **Focus**: Read Like a Writer	Zack creates an action-packed story in his composition notebook that follows the familiar pattern of "The House That Jack Built."
The Boy Who Cried Ninja (Latimer, 2011) **Focus**: Traditional Tale	In this spin-off of "The Boy Who Cried Wolf," Tim is actually telling the truth when he says a ninja ate the cake and a giant squid ate his backpack. To prove to his parents that he is telling the truth, he lures the creatures into the open where they can see them.
Chicken Big (Graves, 2010) **Focus**: Read Like a Writer	When Chicken Big is born, his coop-mates try to figure out what this humongous creature could be. You and your students are sure to laugh your way through this quirky, cartoonlike tale that has hints of the classic "Chicken Little" woven throughout. Notice that all of the transition words and phrases in this book are big and bold.
Clever Jack Takes the Cake (Fleming, 2010) **Focus**: See page 145	Jack bakes a special cake to bring to the princess. Along the way, his cake is eaten bit by bit by different characters. In the end, he tells the princess about his adventures, giving her the best gift of all—a story.
The End (LaRochelle, 2007) **Focus**: Fairy Tale	This backward fairy tale begins with the ending and continues in a cause-and-effect pattern to reveal the events leading up to "The End."
Interrupting Chicken (Stein, 2010) **Focus**: Reading and Writing	Little Red Chicken keeps interrupting her papa's bedtime reading of the classic folktales until they are out of stories. But she can't go to bed without a story, so she decides to write one of her own.
The Plot Chickens (Auch & Auch, 2009) **Focus**: Writing a Story	When Henrietta decides to write a book, she finds a helpful guide to composing a story that lists eight rules, including the following: 1. You need a main character. 2. You need to hatch a plot. 3. Give your main character a problem. 4. Develop your plot by asking, "What if?"
Tackylocks and the Three Bears (Lester, 2002) **Focus**: Series Book	Tacky and his companions are performing the Three Bears play for Mrs. Beakly's school, and Tacky gets the role of Goldilocks.
Thea's Tree (Jackson, 2008) **Focus**: Letter Writing	Thea plants a seed, and then writes letters to science experts in an attempt to discover the strange happenings surrounding her (Jack-and-the) beanstalk-like plant. Pair with *Jack and the Beanstalk* by Steven Kellogg (1991).
The Three Silly Billies (Palatini, 2005) **Focus**: Traditional Tale	The toll bridge troll stops the three silly billy goats, the Three Bears, Little Red Riding Hood, and Jack. Pair this with Paul Galdone's *The Three Billy Goats Gruff* (1973b).

Part 2: A Menu of Reading Workshop Mini-Lessons

As your bank of mini-lessons grows, keep in mind that you can choose to teach each lesson to the whole class or to a small group of learners. Also, you can teach the same type of lesson again and again by simply changing the text. We put the lessons in the book in a month-by-month format as an organizational structure to support you, but we want you to use your decision-making power to select the lessons that will take your learners to the next level. The focus of this chapter is on retelling stories, making connections between stories, and noticing similarities and differences between books and also words.

MINI-LESSONS FOR SELF-MONITORING/DECODING STRATEGY INSTRUCTION

> **WHERE ARE THE BOOKS ABOUT DR. MARTIN LUTHER KING, JR.?**
>
> You may have noticed that this book list does not contain any books about Dr. Martin Luther King, Jr., even though we celebrate the national holiday honoring him in January. We do teach a little bit about Dr. King prior to the holiday, but we recommend that you hold off on reading all the books about him until later in February. For more details on the rationale behind this decision, see page 153.

It's important that we not lose sight of the meaning of individual words. As Linda Hoyt says, "When teachers remind readers to think about meaning, especially after sounding out a word, they are coaching the reader to self-monitor understanding and empowering the child as a comprehender" (Hoyt, 2005, p. 151).

MINI-LESSON: Self-Monitoring at the Word Level

Preparation: Prepare a chart or interactive whiteboard document similar to the one pictured below. The sentences in this sample appear in the book *Tackylocks and the Three Bears* (Lester, 2000).

Readers Self-Monitor! Remember to Keep Watch Over Your Reading

We're going to _____ a play...

Right on time the _____ arrived...

Onto the stage _____ the three penguin bears...

Just then Mrs. Beakly _____ to pick up her class.

Tackylocks... by Helen Lester

- We're going to _____ a play. [perform]
- Right on time the _____ arrived... [audience]
- Onto the stage _____ the three penguin bears... [waddled]
- Just then Mrs. Beakly _____ to pick up her class. [arrived]

Explanation: The aim of this mini-lesson is to remind readers how important it is to monitor their comprehension at the word level.

Demonstration: To begin, invite students to read a sentence aloud, inserting a sound effect like "Hmmm" in the blank space. Reread the sentence and ask listeners to suggest words that would make sense in the blank. Record a few of their responses. Then, insert the beginning sound in the blank and ask them to revise their thinking based on the new information. Discuss how using the context of the sentence along with sound clues helps readers figure out unknown words.

Invitation: "Reading is challenging because not only do we focus on reading the words, but we also have to think about the meaning of those words. I know you're up for the challenge today, so let's read!"

MINI-LESSON: Self-Monitoring—Present and Past-Tense Verbs

Preparation: Make a list of the present- and past-tense forms of familiar words, such as *want/wanted, paint/painted, count/counted, rest/rested, yell/yelled*.

Explanation: As you have probably noticed, past-tense verbs are challenging for beginning readers. When young readers see an *-ed* ending, they tend to pronounce it with the /ed/ sound like this, "I walk-ed to school" instead of the /t/ sound that it makes in that particular word. Introducing the different sounds of the *-ed* ending including /t/, /d/, and /ed/ is helpful for young readers. Use this lesson to discuss past-tense verbs and the different sounds the *-ed* ending represents.

Demonstration: To familiarize students with past-tense verbs and *-ed* endings, play the following game.

Today I help, yesterday I _____ [helped].
Today I talk, yesterday I _____ [talked].
Today I play, yesterday I _____ [played].
Today I jump, yesterday I _____ [jumped].

Once students get the hang of this orally, ask them to get out a small dry-erase board and marker to play again. This time listeners will write the past-tense word on their board.

Invitation: "Word detectives, I'm going to read these past-tense verbs. Listen to the *-ed* endings. Do you notice anything about the sounds you hear? Let's sort the words according to the sounds you hear."

MINI-LESSONS FOR COMPREHENSION STRATEGY INSTRUCTION

Life revolves around making connections. We connect with people who have similar interests. We select books and make other entertainment choices based on whether we can connect with the content. When we read a book that echoes another, we naturally think to ourselves, "That reminds me of that other book I read." Structuring conversations that lead children to compare and contrast texts builds students' ability to make meaningful connections among texts. In addition, these conversations give children the necessary background knowledge needed to compare and contrast texts in writing. Above all, helping children make meaningful, lasting connections to literature will propel them to read, and read even more.

MINI-LESSON: Let's Retell a Story Read-Aloud/Think-Aloud—Foundation Lesson

> **Retelling**
>
> When readers share their retelling,
> they tell us about the book.
> First, they remember important parts,
> the characters, setting…
> yes, that's how it starts.
> Add the problem and the solution.
> Then tell how the story ends.
> Readers R – E – T – E – L – L
> to help comprehend!
>
> Written by: Dr. Walther
> Tune: "Take Me Out to the Ballgame"

CD Resource 5.1 and IWB_Song_5.1

Preparation: Copy and display the "Retelling Song" (CD Resource 5.1). Gather a collection of stories that lend themselves to retelling.

Title and Author	Brief Summary
Grandpa's Teeth (Clement, 1997)	**Somebody** Grandpa **wanted** his teeth back **but** he couldn't find them anywhere **So,** he called the police **Then,** he appeared on the television show *Unsolved Crimes* **After that,** everyone in town began smiling **Finally,** the town gave him new teeth **In the end,** his old dog Gump had his teeth.
Andrew's Loose Tooth (Munsch, 1998)	**Somebody** Andrew **wanted** his tooth to come out **but** it was stuck! **So,** Mom and Dad tried to pull it with their hands and pliers **Then,** the dentist used a rope and car **After that,** the tooth fairy used her hands and a hammer **Finally,** Louis used pepper **In the end,** Andrew sneezed his tooth out.

Explanation: The aim of this mini-lesson is to provide learners with a framework and language to guide their retelling. You've probably seen this helpful retelling framework: Somebody, Wanted, But, So, Finally, In the End. We've adapted the language a bit to reflect the multiple events that occur in many stories. This lesson introduces students to the language they can use to move their retelling along.

Demonstration: Introduce the Retelling Song, and invite children to sing along. If you have an interactive whiteboard, display IWB_Song_5.1 and press the musical note to play the tune. Then read aloud a favorite tale and demonstrate for students how you would retell the story. After the retelling, ask students what they noticed about your retelling and jot their answers in your notebook or on a chart similar to the one above. You may have to retell the story a few times before listeners can identify the different parts of your retelling.

Invitation: "If you finish a book today, take a few minutes to think about how you would retell the story. We'll share a few retellings during sharing time."

MINI-LESSON: Let's Retell a Story Read-Aloud/Think-Together—Follow-Up Lesson

Preparation: Copy and display the "Retelling Song (CD Resource 5.1). Gather a collection of stories that lend themselves to retelling.

Explanation: When you've read a good story, what do you want to do? You want to tell others about it. When a child can retell a story, we know that he or she has truly understood the key ideas and details of the text, and is able to recall them. In this lesson, we release the responsibility by inviting listeners to join us in retelling a story that we read aloud.

> **RETELLING TIPS**
>
> **When readers share their retelling, they . . .**
>
> name the main characters (The main character . . .)
>
> tell about the main character's goal (wanted . . .)
>
> tell about the problem (but . . .)
>
> tell about the main events in order (So, Next, Later, After that . . .)
>
> tell how the problem was solved (Finally . . .)
>
> tell how the story ended (In the end . . .)
>
> share their thinking about the story.
>
>   I noticed . . .
>
>   I think . . .
>
>   The big idea was . . .
>
>   This story reminded me of . . .

CD Resource 5.2

Demonstration: Review and discuss the retelling guidelines that you developed in the foundation lesson; you may want to sing the Retelling Song again. Read aloud a favorite picture book or a book with short chapters like *Poppleton in Winter* (Rylant, 2001). The chapters that work well for this lesson are "Icicles" and "The Sleigh Ride." After reading, students retell the story to a partner following the guidelines.

Invitation: "It's your turn to retell a story today. Take turns telling your think-and-share partner about the story you just heard. Listen carefully, and help your partner out if he or she asks for help."

MINI-LESSON: Using Key Vocabulary to Sequence, Predict, and Retell

Preparation: Select six to nine key words and/or phrases from the story. Write them on large index cards and copy Key Vocabulary Sheets for students (CD Resource 5.3).

Key Vocabulary Cards for *Muncha! Muncha! Muncha!* by Candace Fleming			
Mr. McGreely	tall wooden wall	he was angry
he was FURIOUS!	three hungry bunnies	the sun went down
small wire fence	Muncha! Muncha! Muncha!	watched his garden grow

Key Vocabulary Cards for *Tops and Bottoms* by Janet Stevens			
crops grew	went to work	an idea
lived happily	lazy bear	bear slept
clever hare	planted, watered, and weeded	vegetable stand

Sample Key Vocabulary Sheet; CD Resource 5.3 is a blank template you can use to create your own sheets.

Group students into pairs or triads.

Title and Author	Brief Summary
Muncha! Muncha! Muncha! (Fleming, 2002)	Mr. McGreely just wants to grow vegetables, but three hungry bunnies kept eating them. No matter what Mr. McGreely builds to keep them out, the clever bunnies keep outsmarting him. Enjoy the sequel to this story, *Tippy-Tippy-Tippy, Hide!* (Fleming, 2007)
Tops & Bottoms (Stevens, 1995)	Clever Hare and his family tell Lazy Bear that they will split the crops in half, tops or bottoms. He chooses tops, and Hare outsmarts him by planting root crops.

Explanation: This lesson idea is adapted from Linda Hoyt's "Word Sorts for Literature" lesson found in *Revisit, Reflect, & Retell* (2000, p. 25). We recommend dividing the mini-lesson into two segments as indicated below.

Readers use key words or phrases to retell a story.

Demonstration:

Part 1

- Without showing students the title or cover of the book, give each group a copy of the Key Vocabulary Sheet and invite them to work together to cut apart the cards and arrange them in an order that makes sense. After the cards are in order, learners take turns telling their story to the group. At this point, you may have to model for students how to add their own words in between the words and phrases on the cards to make a story. Without this scaffolding, students tend to simply read the words on the cards in order, rather than using them to tell a complete story. Once they've completed one version of the story, challenge students to mix up the cards and create another version.
- Read the story aloud.
- During reading, pause and work together to put your large cards in the pocket chart in the correct sequence, retell the story up to that point, and query students about predictions. Demonstrate how you retell the story using key words and phrases from the story.

Part 2

- Reread the story, then invite students to work with their group to put the words in order to match the author's story and retell it once again.

Invitation: "Readers, did you notice how we used key words and phrases from the story to help us with our retelling?"

MINI-LESSON: Text-to-Text Connections Read-Aloud/Think-Aloud—Foundation Lesson

Preparation: Gather different versions of traditional tales from your classroom, school, or public library. For this study, you might consider setting aside a special shelf or basket so that the tales are easily accessible for interested students during independent reading. We've included an anchor text and a few different versions of three traditional tales below.

Goldilocks and the Three Bears **Anchor Text:** ***The Three Bears*** **(Galdone, 1972)**	
Goldie and the Three Hares (Palatini, 2011)	Loud, obnoxious, and demanding Goldilocks falls down the rabbit hole after being chased by the bears. She hurts her foot, so the Hare family has to take care of her until they can't stand it any longer and scare her away by threatening to call "Da Bears."
Me and You (Browne, 2009)	You will find a lot to talk about in this unique version of the Goldilocks tale told from two points of view: the narrator, Baby Bear, and the lost girl alone in the city. Notice and discuss Anthony Browne's use of color and the big ideas in this book.
Rubia and the Three Osos (Elya, 2010)	This retelling of the traditional Goldilocks tale offers readers a new twist by sprinkling Spanish words throughout the text (with a glossary for pronunciations) and a new surprise ending.
Henny Penny/Chicken Little **Anchor Text:** ***Henny Penny*** **(Galdone, 1968)**	
Chicken Little (Emberley, 2009)	"Bonk! Eep!" An acorn has fallen on Chicken Little's head. As he runs into his feathered friends, readers will join in on the "Bonk!"s and enjoy the unique ending to the tale.
Chicken Little (Kellogg, 1985)	Foxy Loxy lures Chicken Little and her friends into his "Poultry" truck by disguising himself as a "Poul-ice" officer willing to take them to headquarters. Readers will also enjoy *Earthquack!* (2002), Margie Palatini's twist on the story.
Foolish Rabbit's Big Mistake (Martin, 1985)	In the book's foreword, Rafe Martin shares the origin of "perhaps the oldest version of the familiar 'Henny Penny' story." In this version, a foolish little rabbit spreads a rumor that the earth is breaking up, until a lion shows him that it was only an apple falling from a tree.
The Little Red Hen **Anchor Text:** ***The Little Red Hen*** **(Galdone, 1973a)**	
Mañana, Iguana (Paul, 2004)	Iguana wants to throw a spring party, but since her friends Conejo (rabbit), Tortuga (turtle), and Culebra (snake) are unwilling to help, she doesn't invite them. Luckily, they renew their friendship by helping her clean up. Includes a glossary of Spanish words and pronunciations.
The Little Red Pen (Stevens & Stevens Crummel, 2011)	In this twist on the traditional tale, Little Red Pen tries to grade all the papers without the help of her fellow school supplies. Things heat up as the school supplies work together to save Little Red Pen from the dreaded trash can.
The Red Hen (Emberley, 2010)	In this bright and bold version, Red Hen discovers a recipe for a "simply splendid cake" but, naturally, she can't find anyone to help.

Explanation: This lesson underscores the importance of schema by demonstrating that knowledge of an anchor text helps readers understand different adaptations of the same tale.

Demonstration: Again, we suggest spending at least two days on this demonstration and then continuing with the follow-up lessons as you read another version of the same tale. On the first day, after reading the anchor text of the traditional tale, discuss and chart the elements. The following day,

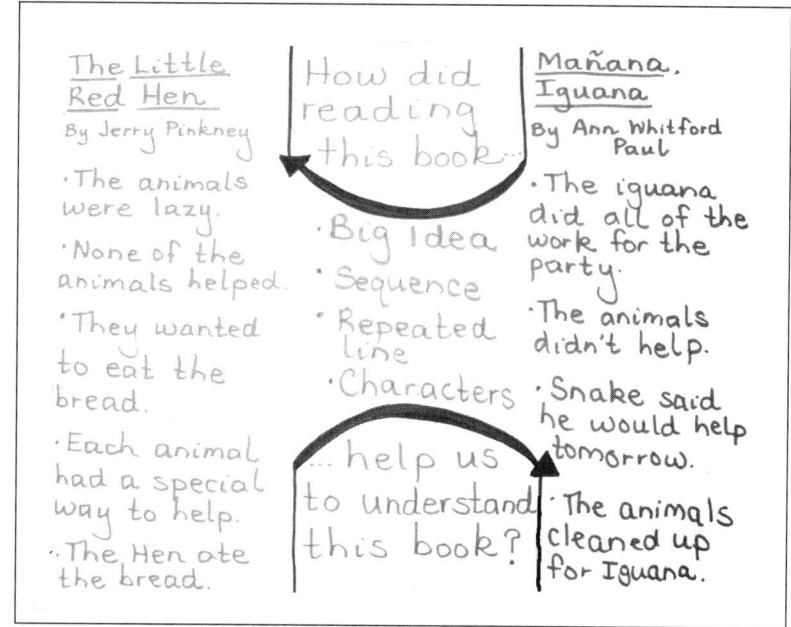

Create a chart like this to record text-to-text connections.

read a different version of the tale. Complete a chart like the one shown above to draw students' attention to how you are using your previous knowledge of the anchor text to make sense of an adaptation.

Invitation: "Girls and boys, story schema is so important to readers. Did you see how much that helped me today? That's why we read so many books together—so you will have a lot of stories to think about as you read new ones."

MINI-LESSON: Text-to-Text Connections Read-Aloud/Think-Together—Follow-Up Lesson

Preparation: Select a version of the traditional tale that differs from the one you read during the Foundation Lesson.

Explanation: The goal here is to expand on the thinking you began in the Foundation Lesson on page 142 and invite students to join in the discussion from both a reader's and a writer's perspective.

Demonstration: Review the previous days' goals by saying, "Readers, we've learned that knowing the anchor version helps us predict what the characters might do, how the story/plot may be organized, and what the big idea is. Let's notice how the author chose to make the tale his or her own." Some questions to extend students' thinking appear here:

- What changes did the author make?
- Why do you think he/she did this?
- How is the story the same?

- How is it different?
- Which version did you prefer? Why?
- What elements did the author change?
- Did he/she change the characters, setting, problem, solution, and/or villain?
- How would you go about writing your own version?
- What would you change or keep the same?

After this mini-lesson you can gradually release the responsibility to students by having them work with a partner or small group to compare and contrast two other tales. If you feel students need more scaffolding and support, guide them in small groups using other tales. You could also extend the learning to writing workshop and invite students to create their own version.

Invitation: "Did you know that you will find elements of the familiar tales in many of the books you read? You might find a villain like the Big Bad Wolf or Foxy Loxy, or you may notice that it is an "add-on" story like 'Henny Penny.' We'll continue to notice and share as we read more books."

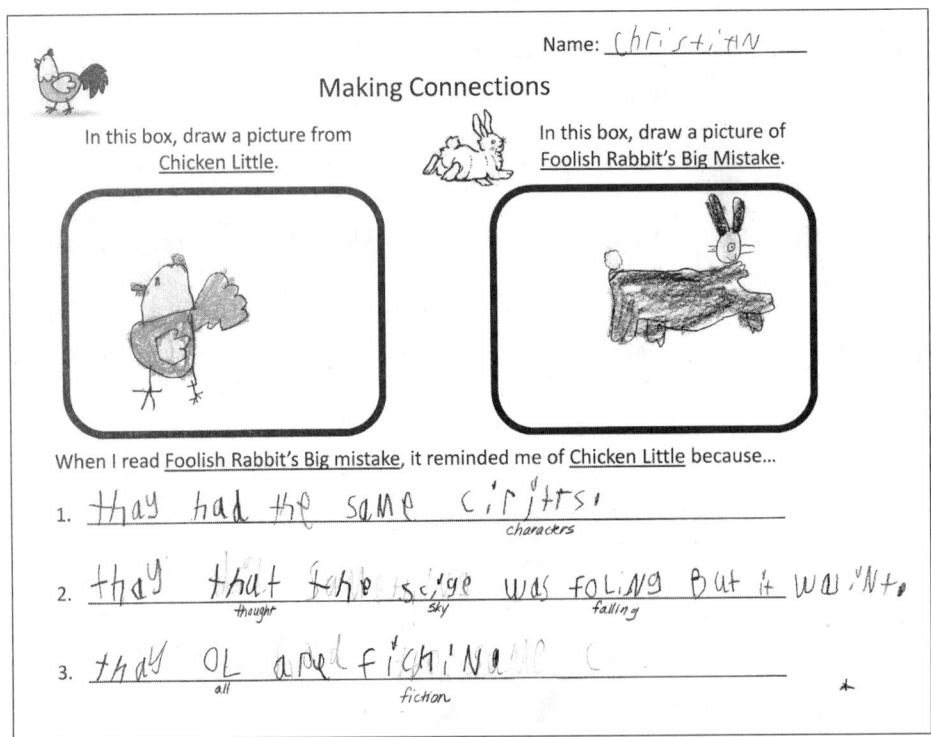

Christian connects *Chicken Little* and *Foolish Rabbit's Big Mistake* and writes:
1. They had the same characters
2. They thought the sky was falling, but it wasn't.
3. They all are fiction.

READ-ALOUDS THAT SPARK COMPREHENSION CONVERSATIONS	
Title, Author, Focus, and Brief Summary	**A Few Questions to Spark Your Conversation**
Clever Beatrice (Willey, 2001) **Focus:** Making Connections **Summary:** Beatrice outsmarts the massive and burly giant.	The blurb on this book reads, "What happens when a very little girl makes a bet with a very large giant?" Turn and talk about what you think will happen. What does it mean to be "sharp as a tack?" Is there another way you could say this? The rich giant likes to "gamble with his strength," which means he likes to play a game, have a race, or do another kind of challenge to win money. Would you gamble with the giant? What other words besides *clever* could you use to describe Beatrice? Does she remind you of any other characters? (the pig from *My Lucky Day*, page 148, or Jack from *Clever Jack Takes the Cake*).
Clever Jack Takes the Cake (Fleming, 2010) **Focus:** Making Connections **Summary:** Jake bakes a special cake to bring to the princess. Along the way, his cake is eaten bit by bit by different characters. In the end, he tells the princess about his adventures, giving her the best gift of all—a story.	Think about the title *Clever Jack Takes the Cake*. What do you think this story might be about? Why do you think that? Troll page: Oh, no! I see a troll! What story does this remind you of? Woods page: Jack just lit one of the candles. What do you predict is going to happen next? Now that the story is over, what are you thinking? Do you have any questions? Notice who is hiding in the woods on the endpapers!
Ten Birds (Young, 2011) **Focus:** Making Predictions **Summary:** Ten birds are trying to figure out how to reach the other side of the river. The first one, named "Brilliant," uses stilts. Bird No. 2, dubbed "Quite Advanced," bubbles underwater. Wait until you find out what the one they call "Needs Improvement" chooses to do.	Notice all the stuff on the riverbank. What is it? Why do you think it is there? Ten Birds Page: Do you have any predictions now that you know what the birds are trying to do? Did you notice how Cybèle Young uses the objects to form the numbers? Very clever! Let's talk about the big idea. What are you thinking? [Sometimes the best solution to a problem is the simplest one.]

FLUENCY FUN!
HOW DOES PUNCTUATION GUIDE THE READER?

To prepare for this activity, write a text similar to the one shown here. Invite students to read the chart, and then discuss how punctuation and other text conventions signal the reader to read in a certain way. Continue the conversation by reading *Punctuation Station* (Cleary, 2010) to review the punctuation marks and what they indicate. Using a Big Book or other enlarged piece of text (poems work well for this lesson), highlight the various punctuation marks, discuss their purpose, and read the text the way the author intended.

MINI-LESSONS FOR VOCABULARY DEVELOPMENT: STUDYING SYNONYMS AND ANTONYMS

To boost vocabulary development and make connections between background knowledge and newly learned vocabulary, learners need opportunities to use new words in multiple contexts. The two mini-lessons that follow are simply quick introductions to the concepts of synonyms and antonyms. To continue the learning, point out synonyms and antonyms when you notice them in books you read aloud and use transition times to sneak in a quick synonym or antonym challenge. For instance, say, "I'm going to say a word. If you can think of a synonym for that word, raise your hand. Let's see how many synonyms we can think of before it's time to leave for lunch."

MINI-LESSON: Learning About Synonyms
Interactive Whiteboard Lesson 5A

Preparation: Access IWB_Lesson_5A if you have an interactive whiteboard. If not, draw a quick picture of a snowman, a cup of hot chocolate, and a New Year's hat. Write the word *cold* on the snowman, *hot* on the mug of hot chocolate, and *happy* on the New Year's hat. Then write synonyms and non-synonyms on the chalkboard or index cards. If you are looking for a book to read about synonyms try, *Big, Bigger, Biggest* (Coffelt, 2009).

Explanation: The purpose of this lesson is to help learners understand that synonyms are words that have the same, or nearly the same, meaning as another word. Synonyms enable writers to select the right word for a specific situation. Children strengthen their knowledge of synonyms by identifying and discussing words that are not synonyms.

Demonstration: Invite the students to identify, discuss, and erase (or tear up, if written on index cards) the words that are not synonyms.

Which of these words are not synonyms?	
cold (snowman)	chilly, happy, freezing, frosty, round, icy, big
hot (chocolate)	steamy, sweet, burning, scorching, boiling, tasty
happy (New Year)	joyful, party, cheery, delighted, glad, celebrate

Invitation: "Today we learned about words that mean the same, or nearly the same, as another word. These words are called synonyms. Synonyms are helpful to you writers because they help you choose the right word to communicate your idea. As readers, synonyms are helpful because they can help you better understand the meaning of an unknown word."

MINI-LESSON: Learning About Antonyms—Antonym Memory Game
Interactive Whiteboard Lesson 5B

Preparation: If you have an interactive whiteboard, then access IWB_Lesson_5B. If not, print and copy the antonym memory game cards (CD Resource 5.4).

Explanation: To introduce the concept of antonyms, create an antonym memory game. Students can play this game as a whole class or with a partner during Explore the W.O.R.L.D. time.

Demonstration: Children work with a partner to play the Antonym Memory Game, or you can play as a class on the interactive whiteboard.

all/none	come/go	dirty/clean	dry/wet	empty/full
fancy/plain	front/back	go/stop	good/bad	little/big
above/below	beginning/end	bottom/top	cry/laugh	dull/bright
enemy/friend	enter/exit	friend/stranger	lead/follow	loose/tight

Invitation: "Today we learned about words that are opposite words. They are called antonyms. Thinking about the antonym can help us better understand the word."

READ-ALOUDS WITH RICH VOCABULARY		
Title and Author	**Brief Summary**	**Words to Highlight and Kid-Friendly Definition**
Once Upon a Time, The End (Asleep in 60 Seconds) (Kloske, 2005)	In an attempt to get his child to sleep, an exhausted dad shortens many traditional tales and adds his own funny endings.	**nimble**: able to move quickly **refreshed**: regaining energy; feeling better again **sensitive**: having strong feelings
My Lucky Day (Kasza, 2003)	When a pig knocks at the door, Mr. Fox begins to prepare for a feast, but the clever pig outwits him.	**filthy**: very dirty **exhausted**: tired or worn out **useless**: not able to make happen what you want to happen
Puss in Boots (Perrault, 1990)	Your students will enjoy listening as they marvel at Fred Marcellino's stunning illustrations of Charles Perrault's familiar tale, which won the Caldecott Honor.	**rascal**: a person who is dishonest or gets into mischief **sympathetic**: showing someone that you understand how they feel **unison**: saying or doing something at the same time

MINI-LESSONS FOR READING RESPONSE

After working together to compare and contrast stories during read-aloud and while guiding readers, it makes sense to teach children how to do this in writing. The thinking behind this response helps reinforce the importance of making connections from one text to another. Then, to guide students in writing an opinion piece, demonstrate, discuss, and practice how to write a book review. Remember to add these options to your growing menu of responses to reading.

MINI-LESSON: Comparing and Contrasting Texts

Preparation: Select two or more texts that have similar elements. There are many traditional tale titles in this chapter that work well for this type of response. It is helpful if you read one of the books earlier in the day so that you are ready to begin this lesson with the second book. Prepare Read, Think, and Respond Book H-Chart (CD Resource 1.3) and a large copy for your demonstration.

Explanation: In this response, students will demonstrate their ability to articulate the similarities and differences between two texts.

Demonstration: After completing both books, say, "Let's think about what these books have in common and what makes each book unique." To guide students' thinking, you might ask about the story elements with questions like, "Who were the characters? Were they the same or different? Where did the stories take place?" and so on. At this point, you will have to decide how much scaffolding your students need. You could begin the demonstration H-Chart, and then invite children to finish their own response sheet or work on it with a partner. On the other hand, if they need more experience with this type of response, you might complete a class H-Chart together and repeat the lesson with another set of books, then release the responsibility to the students.

Invitation: "Thinkers, when you ponder the ways that books are the same and different, you are building your schema for the next books you will read so you can make meaningful connections and make predictions based on that schema. Remember, the more you read, the better you get!"

MINI-LESSON: Write a Book Review

Preparation: For the whole-class demonstration, select a book your students have enjoyed. Decide where you want to write your rough draft—chart paper, overhead, or interactive whiteboard.

> **Let's Write a Book Review**
>
> Introduce the book to your readers—don't give away the ending!
>
> Talk about what you liked (or didn't like) about the book. Explain your reasons.
>
> Recommend this book (if you liked it) to your readers.
>
> Who else might like this book? Why would they like it?

Explanation: Book reviews are an authentic way to assess students' ability to summarize a story. Posting or sharing completed reviews helps to promote a book-loving community.

Demonstration: Begin by reading some children's book reviews to your students. Before you release to your students the responsibility of writing book reviews, write a few reviews together in a shared writing format following the guidelines below. Then, invite readers to write their own review and post them along with the books in your reading center.

Rough draft of book review

Invitation: "Readers, after I finish a good book I want to tell my friends about it. So I think about who might like it and I tell them enough about the book to see if they are interested in reading it. As you write your book reviews, think about the kids who will be reading your review and what you want them to know about the book."

Part 3: Genre Study— Traditional Tales

> I-W Reviews: Mercy Watson to the Rescue by: Kate DiCamillo
>
> This book is about a curious, crazy, trouble-making pig named Mercy. She loves buttered toast with a great deal of butter on it. She lives with the Watsons on Deckawoo Drive next to the Lincoln sisters. In this book, the Watsons need help and think Mercy will save them. Instead, Mercy goes to the Lincoln sisters' house and scares Baby Lincoln. Then, her sister Eugenia calls the fire department. We like when Mercy causes trouble with the Lincoln sisters. If you like hilarious books with a lot of action, you will love this book. This is the first book in the Mercy Watson series. So, go to the L.M.C. and check one out today!!

Final copy of book review

"Traditional tales become a part of a reader's personal literary history. As such, they serve as valuable links to other readers who can also relate to a familiar, shared literary heritage. In addition, tales from childhood become touchstones for different kinds of literature that will be read in the future" (Fuhler & Walther, 2007, p. 67). Therefore, a study of traditional tales is an essential part of core literacy instruction and will help you address specific standards set out in the Common Core State Standards. Whether you choose to weave traditional tales throughout the year or spend a month or so on an in-depth study, the benefits for your young readers are everlasting.

GENRE STUDY: TRADITIONAL TALES	
Title, Author, and Type of Tale	**Brief Summary**
The Boy From the Dragon Palace (MacDonald, 2011) Type of Tale: Folktale	In this retelling of a Japanese folktale, the Dragon King gives a poor flower seller a snot-nosed boy (yes, the boys will love this book!) who brings him luck and riches. But, when the ungrateful flower seller gets tired of making the boy shrimp every day, he sends him away and ends up with nothing.
Cinder Edna (Jackson, 1994) Type of Tale: Fairy Tale	Practical and down-to-earth, Cinder Edna lives next door to Cinderella. Compare how the two characters respond to the events and challenges they face. Then, compare this tale with versions from other cultures like *The Rough-Face Girl* (Martin, 1992) and *Mufaro's Beautiful Daughters: An African Folktale* (Steptoe, 1987).
Jack and the Beanstalk (Crews, 2011) Type of Tale: Folktale	In Nina Crews's modern, photo-illustrated version of this tale, the giant and the wife follow Jack down the beanstalk and return to normal size. It will be interesting to see what your students think of this ending.
Rapunzel (Gibb, 2010) Type of Tale: Fairy Tale	Based on the original story by the Brothers Grimm, this book will give your readers a schema for other adaptations such as the movie *Tangled* and the humorous book *Falling for Rapunzel* (Wilcox, 2003).

Pecos Bill (Kellogg, 1986) Type of Tale: Tall Tale	Kellogg's time-tested version of this Texas cowboy's tale.
Princess Zelda and the Frog (Gardner, 2011) Type of Tale: Fairy Tale	If you like photos of bulldogs dressed in clothes, you will like this silly version of *The Frog Prince*.
Seven Blind Mice (Young, 1992) Type of Tale: Fable	Young's version of the fable of the blind men trying to identify an elephant.
The Three Little Tamales (Kimmell, 2009) Type of Tale: Folktale	In this Southwest version of "The Three Little Pigs," Tía Lupe's famous tamales run for their lives and build different homes. Of course, Señor Lobo, the Big Bad Wolf, comes and threatens to blow their *casitas* from "here to Laredo." Share and compare other versions like Steven Kellogg's *Three Little Pigs* (1997), *The True Story of the Three Little Pigs* (Scieszka, 1989), or *The Three Little Wolves and the Big Bad Pig* (Trivizas, 1993).
Tortuga in Trouble (Paul, 2009) Type of Tale: Folktale	Join the characters from *Mañana Iguana* in a Spanish-laced retelling of "Little Red Riding Hood." Compare and share other versions like *Little Red Riding Hood* (Pinkney, 2007) and *Red Riding Hood* (Marshall, 1987).
Waking Beauty (Wilcox, 2008) Type of Tale: Fairy Tale	In this hilarious version of "Sleeping Beauty," the three fairies try to inform Prince Charming that he must wake the princess with a kiss, but he isn't listening.

Meeting the Needs of ALL Learners

If you've tried some of the ideas we've shared for boosting struggling readers, you've probably noticed that they all relate to helping kids connect with books. Surely, that is one of our top priorities. Again, the idea is simply to get more books into students' hands and also to send them into students' homes. We begin the Take-Home Book Club in January because it is much easier to model and manage at this time of the year. You'll find a sample letter to parents that introduces the Take-Home Book Club and provides suggestions for reading with children in CD Resource 5.5. As always, use your professional judgment to determine the best time to begin this program in your classroom. To challenge your talented readers, guide them as they produce a digital retelling of a traditional tale. You'll be amazed what the kids can create!

SENSIBLE STRATEGIES FOR STRUGGLING READERS: PROMOTING A LOVE OF BOOKS—THE TAKE-HOME BOOK CLUB

After a massive 20-year study, Mariah Evans and her colleagues (Evans, Kelley, Sikora, & Treiman, 2010) found that the number of books a child has at home increases the level of education he or she will attain. This is important information to share with parents, and it also gives us one more reason to send books home with students regularly. To this end, you have probably created your own plan for a take-home book program where students are consistently carrying books home to read with their family or to enjoy on their own. As you know, a well-stocked classroom library is essential to sustaining a take-home book program. If you are just beginning to build your library, you might consider other approaches to sending reading materials home.

First, as suggested in *Teaching Struggling Readers With Poetry* (Walther & Fuhler, 2010), create a three-ring "Poetry Binder" that contains reproducible songs, poems, and rhymes that you and your students have read together. Readers can take this binder home once a week to share the new poetry selections with their family. Next, enlist the help of your school librarian to assist students in locating just-right books to take home once a week. We like to send books home three times a week, on Monday, Wednesday, and Friday. Using the ideas we shared here, you could send a classroom library book home on Monday, a school library book home on Wednesday, and the students' own Poetry Binder home on Friday.

Students enjoy bringing their poetry binder home to share with their family.

TARGETING TALENTED READERS: DIGITAL RETELLING

Provide time for students to work on your classroom computer or in your school's computer lab to create a digital retelling of a familiar tale. Consider the following formats for this project.

- Record your students retelling a familiar nursery rhyme using a tape recorder, your computer, or by downloading Audacity, a free, open-source software program for recording and editing sounds. Place the recording along with a typed version of the rhyme in the Be a Listener center for others to enjoy.
- Teach students how to create a simple PowerPoint slide show or Photo Story to retell a traditional tale. To create a Photo Story, snap digital photos of children acting out key scenes of the tale. Then, add music from the library to fit the tone of the story.

Final Thoughts

Looking back, we began the year by acquainting children with the routines and procedures necessary to differentiate literacy instruction for all, while at the same time conversing about the different purposes for reading. We then zoomed in on real and make-believe stories along with those rooted in the oral tradition. Looking ahead to the second half of the year, we will shift our focus to other forms of literature including biography, poetry, and a focused study of informational text. Of course, wise teachers like you know that a balanced diet of different literary genres throughout the year gives students a well-rounded literary experience. If you don't already include a variety of different genres in your read-aloud fare, challenge yourself to do it, and then ask your students which kind of books they enjoyed most. You might be surprised by their answers!

CHAPTER 6: FEBRUARY

Questioning and Determining Importance to Understand Biographies

If you've taught the primary grades for many years, as we have, you may have noticed that studying famous Americans in the order of their holidays is like traveling backward in time. Typically, you begin with Martin Luther King, Jr., Day in January, move on to Lincoln's birthday on February 12th, and then end with George Washington. In addition, in the month of February, you are sharing books about famous African Americans from various time periods. This is confusing for young learners who already have a difficult time figuring out whether it is Tuesday or Wednesday! To address this issue, we've rearranged the order in which we teach about famous people and historical events, and now we introduce them in chronological order. We begin by reading aloud biographies about George Washington, and then

continue in chronological order by sharing picture books about the Underground Railroad. Next, we read biographies of Lincoln and stories that take place during the Jim Crow era. We then trek through historical-fiction titles that illuminate key events in the civil rights movement. Finally, we culminate our historical adventure by reading biographies of Dr. Martin Luther King, Jr. and other famous African Americans who followed his lead. We've spent many years collecting the books you'll find in this chapter (see timeline of picture books on pages 164–166) and have discovered that as we journey through time with our students, reading books like *Ruth and the Green Book* (Ramsey, 2010) and *Back of the Bus* (Reynolds, 2010), rich conversations occur. Invite your learners on a historical voyage as they build a deeper understanding of biographies!

Part 1: Reading-Related Morning Message Ideas and Samples

Morning messages serve different purposes depending on their content. The messages in this chapter provide students with the background knowledge for the mini-lessons and biographies that appear in this chapter. Building background is important for all young learners, but it is *essential* for ELLs and for students who may struggle with comprehension. Use the messages that follow to introduce the concept of prefixes and question words, and to build students' background knowledge about two elements found in biographies—chronological order and time lines.

MORNING MESSAGE IDEA: SELF MONITORING/DECODING—INTRODUCING PREFIXES

The morning message is ideal for a visual demonstration of how readers deconstruct words in order to discover their meanings. At the beginning of the year, you teach young learners to look for familiar letters or word chunks to help them decode. Then, you move on to compound words, made of two root words. As your readers become more proficient, they become ready to search unfamiliar words for familiar parts such as prefixes, suffixes, and root words. This message is helpful as you introduce affixes, specifically prefixes, and demonstrate how understanding these word parts helps readers make more precise predictions about the meanings of unknown words. To begin, explain that some words

> ## MORNING MESSAGE SAMPLE
>
> Circle the chunks/prefixes at the beginning of each word. Has the meaning of the words changed?
>
> | unfair | unhappy | disagree | discover |
> |---|---|---|---|
> | invisible | incorrect | unsafe | disobey |
> | increase | uncover | | |

change their meanings when letters are added to the original, or root word. Those letters, or the prefix, constitute a separate syllable that can change the meaning of the root word or make the original meaning more specific. Display the following words in your morning message and invite the students to underline the root words and circle the prefixes. Ask learners what they notice about the words listed in the message. Then, discuss how the prefixes changed the root words from their original meanings. Notice that the meaning of some words simply changes to the opposite, while other words have been changed entirely.

MORNING MESSAGE IDEA: COMPREHENSION—INTRODUCING QUESTION WORDS

From the first day of school, youngsters ask a multitude of questions, so we know they are familiar with question words. However, since one of the comprehension strategies found in this chapter is questioning, it is the ideal time to explicitly teach your students about question words. We use the morning message, in conjunction with higher-level picture books and biographies, to demonstrate how asking questions will help readers better comprehend what they are reading. For this message, simply display the /wh/ question words labeled with the question, "What do these words have in common?" Give the students an opportunity to share what they notice about these question words and jot down their observations.

MORNING MESSAGE SAMPLE

MORNING MESSAGE IDEA: VOCABULARY BUILDING—WHAT IS CHRONOLOGICAL ORDER?

Since you will be immersing your students in biographies, it is important to introduce key terms used in your discussions about biographical texts. Use the morning message as an opportunity to introduce one such term—chron-

MORNING MESSAGE SAMPLE

What does it mean to put things in order?
How many ways can you think of to put things in order?
How does an author organize a biography or put a biography in order?

ological order. Pose the questions found on page 155 to generate ideas and spark students' thinking about how writers organize a biography. Explain that chronological order is the order of events based on when they happened in time and that many biographies move through the subject's life in chronological order.

MORNING MESSAGE IDEA: READING RESPONSE—A TIME LINE OF OUR DAY

Interactive Whiteboard Morning Message 6

Now that your students understand a bit about chronological order, you can use that new learning as you work together to create a time line. Time lines are often found in biographies, serving to clarify the chronological order of events or to provide the reader with more detailed information of specific events. In this morning message, create a time line of your day at school. Brainstorm the main events of your school day. Then display IWB_MM_6 on the interactive whiteboard to create a time line of these events, or draw a line on the board or chart paper and fill in the events. The students should think about their day from a chronological perspective. You can also use this as an opportunity to discuss complete biographies, which tell about a person's life from birth to death. Partial biographies illuminate a specific event in a person's life, such as one school day, from beginning to end.

> **MORNING MESSAGE SAMPLE**
>
> What are the main events that happen within our school day? Let's create a timeline of our day in chronological order!
>
> Morning Message – Reading – Lunch – Writing – Math – Recess – Science/Social Studies – Dismissal

POETRY POWER: POEMS FOR FEBRUARY	
Title	**Brief Summary**
Another Jar of Tiny Stars: Children Select Their Favorite Poems (Cullinan & Wooten, 2009)	Introduce your students to different NCTE (National Council of Teachers of English) award-winning poets such as Nikki Grimes, Eloise Greenfield, and X. J. Kennedy by reading a few of their poems. This anthology is organized by poet and includes a biographical section called "About the Poets."
It's Valentine's Day (Prelutsky, 1983/1996)	Prelutsky's poetry collections are hard to beat when you are looking for engaging, kid-appealing seasonal poems.

MORNING READ-ALOUDS: FEBRUARY FAVORITES	
Title, Author, and Focus	**Brief Summary**
Abe Lincoln Crosses a Creek (Hopkinson, 2008) **Focus**: American History	In 1816, seven-year-old Abraham Lincoln and his friend Austin dare to cross a roaring creek on a fallen log. Austin rescues Abe from falling into the water and saves his life. Years later, when Abe becomes president of the United States, he still fondly remembers his old friend.
Fly Guy Meets Fly Girl (Arnold, 2010) **Focus**: Valentine's Day	Fly Guy and Buzz meet Liz and Fly Girl at the park. Fly Guy and Fly Girl imagine a life in which they fall in love, kiss, and get married.
The Moon Over Star (Aston, 2008) **Focus**: Read Like a Writer	Mae and her family live in the town of Star, where they await the news of the first lunar landing. Aston's expertly crafted text is filled with many techniques for writers to notice, such as first-person voice, time transitions, and rhythmic passages. Pair with *Mae Jemison* (Polette, 2003).
Of Thee I Sing: A Letter to My Daughters (Obama, 2010) **Focus**: American History/ Character Traits	Introduce your students to 13 of our country's icons and heroes, with a focus on their virtues, such as Georgia O'Keefe's creativity and Jackie Robinson's courage.
Our Children Can Soar (Cook, 2009) **Focus**: African-American History/Biographies	This moving book celebrates the achievements of ten African Americans, ending with President Obama. Illustrated by 13 artists, the book features a paragraph of additional information about each "pioneer of change" to spark students' interest, and further reading.
Patience Wright: American Sculptor and Revolutionary Spy (Shea, 2007) **Focus**: American History	Meet Patience Wright, a successful wax sculptor in America who moved to London to open a new studio. It was there that she learned secrets about the American Revolutionary War from her important British clients. Patience shared the information with military officers in America by sending secret messages hidden within the busts of her wax sculptures. Share this 40-page picture book over a period of two or three days. For a shorter book that also takes place during the American Revolution, consider *The 18 Penny Goose* (Walker, 1999).
Rosa's Bus: The Ride to Civil Rights (Kittinger, 2010) **Focus**: African-American History	In 1948, Bus #2857 rolled off the assembly line at the General Motors factory in Michigan. Travel along as you learn the story of Rosa Parks and the bus boycott from a unique point of view. The bus is now on permanent display at the Henry Ford Museum in Dearborn, MI.
Ruth and the Green Book (Ramsey, 2010) **Focus**: African-American History 	Ruth and her family are excited to be going on a road trip from Chicago to rural Alabama in their new 1952 Buick! They soon find out that, because of the Jim Crow laws, African-American travelers have limited choices for gas, food, and lodging along the way. Luckily, a friendly attendant at an Esso station gives them a copy of *The Negro Motorist Green Book* to help guide their way to friendlier places.

continued MORNING READ-ALOUDS: FEBRUARY FAVORITES	
Title, Author, and Focus	**Brief Summary**
Ruby Valentine Saves the Day (Friedman, 2010) **Focus**: Valentine's Day	After planning every detail of a Valentine's Day party, Ruby and her pet cockatoo, Lovebird, have to change their plans when snow prevents the guests from attending. This title is the sequel to *Love, Ruby Valentine* (Friedman, 2006).
These Hands (Mason, 2010) **Focus**: African-American History	Joseph's grandpa's hands can do many things, but back when he worked in the Wonder Bread factory, they were not allowed to touch the bread dough until workers united to change this practice. Floyd Cooper's distinctive illustrations add to this moving picture book about the Jim Crow era.

Part 2: A Menu of Reading Workshop Mini-Lessons

We are always looking for ways to integrate our reading, writing, and content-area instruction so that students can make connections among the difference processes and between new and known information. For us, the month of February seems to be one of those times when the integration is seamless. Through the chronological study of the social studies content, American history, you can introduce and practice the comprehension strategies of questioning and determining importance in biographies and other picture books. Then, after immersing students in the genre study of biographies in the reading workshop, consider guiding them to write biographies in writing workshop. See

During writing workshop, students interview each other and write a biography about their buddy.

Month-by-Month Trait-Based Writing Instruction (Walther & Phillips, 2009) for more information about this genre exploration. When our lessons flow into one another and overlap, it seems that we find more time for in-depth conversations with our students. We hope this helps you, too!

MINI-LESSONS FOR SELF-MONITORING/DECODING STRATEGY INSTRUCTION

Building on the background developed in the morning message on page 154, the mini-lessons that follow zoom in on prefixes. Patricia Cunningham reminds us that prefixes, suffixes, and roots are the "building blocks" of big words and that when children, especially ELLs, learn tools to decode, spell, and figure out the meanings of these words, they will not only be better spellers and decoders, but they will also increase their meaning vocabulary (Cunningham, 2009). Of course, you will need to determine if your learners are ready to develop this understanding. If you find that these lessons are not a good fit for your whole class, use them as you guide advanced readers in small groups.

MINI-LESSON: Look for Prefixes—Foundation Lesson

Preparation: Create a chart displaying the following prefixes: *dis-*, *un-*, and *re-*. Use these prefixes to engage your class in a discussion about their meanings, and then brainstorm a variety of words that begin with each prefix. This mini-lesson will take a few days to complete.

Explanation: Some words begin with the same chunk or set of letters, and these chunks can sometimes be referred to as a prefix. Prefixes are separate syllables that have predictable spellings and pronunciations and can change the meaning of the base word, or make the meaning of the base word more specific. Some prefixes change the meaning of the word to its opposite, such as *dis-* and *un-*, while other prefixes such as *re-* mean "back" or "again." With this understanding, your young readers will be able to decode and comprehend the meanings of an abundance of words. Note that the most common prefixes, *un-*, *re-*, *in-*, and *dis-*, will help learners figure out the meaning of more than 1,500 words (Cunningham, 2009b).

Demonstration:

- Present the prefix *dis-* and invite your students to brainstorm words that begin with these letters. Possible suggestions include: *disappear, discover, disorder, disobey, disagree,* and so on.
- Allow sufficient time for the students to ponder the words on the lists. Invite them to think and share with partners what they notice about these words. Ask, "Do you know any other words that look and sound like these words?"
- Record their thinking on the prefix chart.
- On subsequent days, repeat the brainstorming process for the prefixes *un-* (*uncover, unfair, unkind, unfriendly, unbelievable*) and *re-* (*replace, reopen, rewrite, replay, rewind*).
- Emphasize that the prefixes *dis-* and *un-* change the base word to its opposite and that the *re-* prefix changes the meaning of the base word to "back" or "again."

Invitation: "As you are reading, pay careful attention to any words you may come across that begin with one of the prefixes we discussed today. Jot them down on a sticky note so that we can add them to our chart."

MINI-LESSON: Look for Prefixes—Follow-Up Lesson

Preparation: This lesson targets the prefix *re-*. Write the following words on index cards, making sure you have one word card for each student. All of the words begin with the same prefix, but they can be divided into three categories: *re* (meaning "back"), *re* (meaning "again") and *re* (no meaning). To make it easier to sort the students by their category later in the lesson, color-code each word according to its category.

re ("back"): *refund, recline, rebound, recall, recede, replace, return, rewind*

re ("again"): *recount, recover, rebuild, recharge, refresh, refill, recreate, reopen, recycle, rewrite, replay, redo, redecorate, reusable*

re (no meaning): *receipt, recital, refrigerator, recess, refer, report, relax, result, resist*

Explanation: This lesson will emphasize the changes that occur to the base or root word when a prefix is added and how one prefix can change the word in different ways.

Demonstration:
- Pass one word card to each student.
- Allow sufficient time for students to read their word and discuss it with others. They can discuss their words in small groups, with partners, or they can mingle with all of their peers.
- Invite readers to look for similarities among their words. What do the words mean? How has the prefix changed the root word? Does the prefix have any impact on the word?
- Separate the children by their color-coded word cards. We typically direct them to different spots in the classroom. Once all of the students are sorted by color, give them an opportunity to share their word cards with one another, discuss what their words have in common, and try to determine and explain why they are grouped together. In other words, figure out what the prefix re- on their word card means.
- Invite each group to share their thinking about their words. Discuss the three different categories of words and how the prefix *re-* affected the meaning of each word.

Invitation: "When you come to a word you don't know, take a look at the beginning chunk. Is it a prefix you recognize? Ask yourself if you know any other words beginning with that prefix. Think about the meaning of the root word and how a prefix can change that meaning. Understanding how prefixes work will help you read and comprehend many challenging words."

MINI-LESSONS FOR COMPREHENSION STRATEGY INSTRUCTION

Part of what makes teaching the primary grades so delightful is young children's natural curiosity about the world around them. Kids have so many questions that they want answered. Inquiry-based learning begins with learners' questions and in that way increases engagement. It makes sense to draw on that sense of wonder when reading with students. Concluding a read-aloud by asking, "What are you still wondering?" provides a starting point for further reading, research, and discussions. In order to find the answers to their questions, students need to know how to determine the most important information in a text. We will explore how to do that in biographies in this chapter and also practice determining importance in informational texts in Chapter 8.

MINI-LESSON: Questioning Read-Aloud/Think-Aloud—Foundation Lesson

Preparation: Copy and display the strategy song "Questioning" (CD Resource 6.1) and the Comprehension Strategy Wheel (CD Resource 3.5). Select a book that will provide opportunities for you to ask questions before, during, and after reading. The following are some of our favorite books to use for reading aloud and thinking aloud:

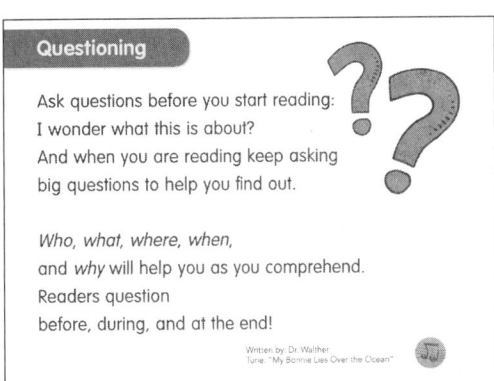

CD Resource 6.1 and IWB_Song_6.1

Title and Author	Brief Summary
A Bad Case of Stripes (Shannon, 1998)	Camilla Cream is worried about what everyone thinks of her, so she won't eat lima beans. That is, until a case of stripes and a clever old woman help her think for herself.
Barefoot: Escape on the Underground Railroad (Edwards, 1997)	In this dramatic picture book, the forest animals help Barefoot, an escaped slave, elude his pursuers.
The Island of the Skog (Kellogg, 1973)	Jenny and her mouse friends are tired of living in a hole, so they set off to find a peaceful island to call their own.

Explanation: As you prepare for this read-aloud/think-aloud demonstration, jot questions on sticky notes and place them in the book that you are going to read. Plan to model the types of questions you want your readers to ask, questions that delve into the text and push for deeper comprehension. In her book *Spotlight on Comprehension* (2005, pp. 112, 116), Linda Hoyt writes that the best questions do the following:

- demonstrate an understanding of events or facts
- reflect meaningful connections
- move the reader through the text
- question the author's meaning and purpose
- reveal application of schema or background knowledge
- examine the author's choice of craft techniques
- remain unanswered after reading, prompting further thought and investigation

Demonstration:
- Introduce the strategy and locate it on the Comprehension Strategy Wheel.
- Sing the strategy song "Questioning." If you have an interactive whiteboard, display IWB_Song_6.1 and press the musical note to play the tune.

- Review the question words—*who, what, where, when* and *why*.

For this read-aloud/think-aloud demonstration we use *A Bad Case of Stripes* (1998) by David Shannon. As you read the story, demonstrate how readers ask questions before, during, and after reading. We've provided a few questions here to get you started.

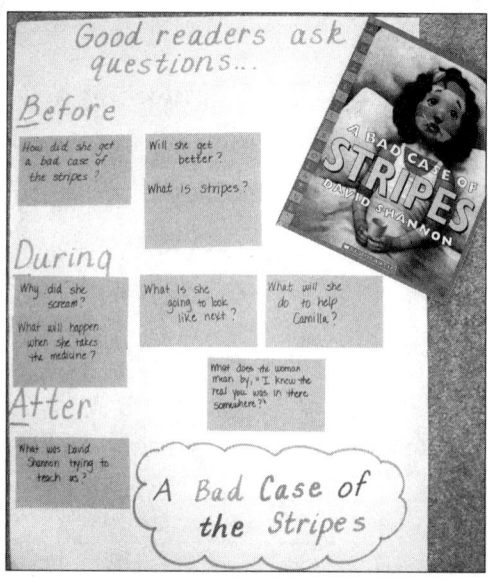

Record readers' questions before, during, and after reading.

Before
- How did she get a bad case of stripes?
- Will she get better?
- What are stripes? I've never heard of them before—this must be a make-believe book.

During
- Why did she scream? I'm going to keep reading to find out.
- What will happen when she takes the medicine?
- What is she going to look like next?
- What will she do to help Camilla?
- What does the woman mean by, "I knew the real you was in there somewhere"?

After
- What was David Shannon trying to tell us?

Invitation: "Readers, what did you notice today as I read? Did you notice that by asking questions, I couldn't wait to keep reading to discover the answers? Some of my questions were answered as I read, and other were not."

MINI-LESSON: Questioning Read-Aloud/Think-Together—Follow-Up Lesson

Preparation: Select a book that will provide opportunities for your students to ask questions before, during, and after reading. Some books that work well for reading aloud and thinking together include the following:

Title and Author	Brief Summary
Goin' Someplace Special (McKissack, 2001)	We view the segregation of 1950s Nashville through the eyes of 'Tricia Ann, who is going to her favorite spot: the integrated public library.
The Night I Followed the Dog (Laden, 1994)	A boy details his adventures following his dog to the exclusive "dog club."
A Sweet Smell of Roses (Johnson, 2005)	Minnie and her sister sneak out to join a civil rights march led by Dr. King.

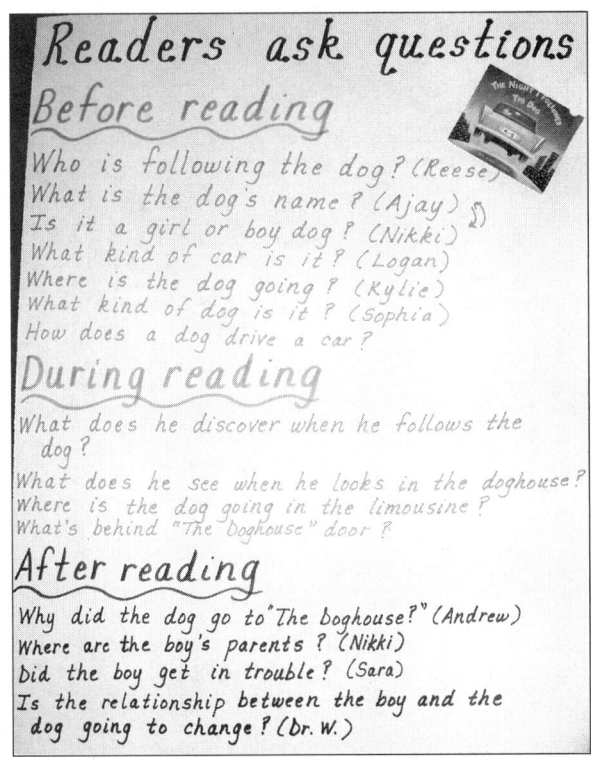

Readers' questions before, during, and after reading *The Night I Followed the Dog*.

Sara's thinking about the big idea of *A Sweet Smell of Roses*.

Explanation: In this lesson, we invite our listeners to ask questions before, during, and after reading while we give descriptive feedback as to how that question will help them as readers.

Demonstration: Read the title and back cover blurb, then look at the illustrations on the front and back cover. Ask, "What are you wondering before we begin reading?" Jot questions on sticky notes and post them on the chart. Continue this process as you read the book. Try not to interrupt the flow of the story by stopping too often. Conclude by asking, "What are you still wondering?" "What is the big idea in this story?"

Invitation: "How did asking questions help you as a reader? What did you notice about asking questions? Readers ask questions and continue reading to find out the answers. Readers are wonderers!"

MINI-LESSON: Questioning the Writer

Preparation: Prepare a chart similar to the one found on page 164. Select a piece of your writing to reread and revise.

Explanation: During reading workshop, we guide readers as they discover that asking questions not only helps them to activate and build their schema, but also strengthens their understanding of events or facts. Certainly, readers who question as they read are more motivated to move through the text by asking themselves, "What will happen next and why?" Ultimately, curious readers have a better understanding of the au-

QUESTIONING THE WRITER

BEGINNING

Does my title grab my readers?

Does my lead catch my readers' attention and tell them what I'm writing about?

MIDDLE

Is this part clear? Will my readers understand what I am trying to say?

Will my readers want to keep reading?

END

Will my ending make my readers laugh, cry, clap, or sigh?

CD Resource 6.2

Questioning the Writer — That's me!!

Beginning—
- *Does my title grab my readers?*
- *Will my lead make them want to read my piece?*

Middle— Is this clear? Will my readers understand what I'm trying to say?
- *Will my readers want to keep reading?*

End— Will my ending make my readers laugh, cry, clap or sigh?

Use these questions as young writers draft, reread, and revise their work; see CD Resource 6.2.

thor's meaning. So, why not apply the same strategy during the writing workshop? Use the questions on the chart to help young writers as they draft, reread, and revise their work.

Demonstration: Reread and revise a piece of writing in front of students, using the questions on the chart to guide your revisions.

Invitation: "Writers, as you reread your piece today, think about the questions you might ask yourself to make your writing even better. That's what writers do!"

A TIMELINE OF PICTURE BOOKS	
Time Period	**Title, Author, and Brief Summary**
George Washington 1732–1799 **Revolutionary War 1775–1783**	*George Washington and the General's Dog* (Murphy, 2002) Murphy highlights Washington's love of animals in this "easy reader" biography.
The Underground Railroad 1819– The first route of the Underground Railroad, a network of trails and hiding places that led fleeing slaves to the North, begins in a cave near a creek on what is now the Guilford College campus. **Harriet Tubman Escapes 1849**	*Barefoot: Escape on the Underground Railroad* (Edwards, 1997) See summary and mini-lesson for questioning on page 161. *Henry's Freedom Box: A True Story From the Underground Railroad* (Levine, 2007) After Henry's family is sold as slaves, he bravely escapes to freedom by shipping himself to the north in a wooden crate. *Underground: Finding the Light to Freedom* (Evans, 2011) A family heads for freedom by running barefoot through the dark woods and resting in a kind stranger's home.

Abraham Lincoln 1809–1865 Elected 1860 **Civil War 1861–1865** **Emancipation Proclamation** 1/1/1863 **Slavery Abolished** 13th Amendment outlaws slavery 1865	***A. Lincoln and Me*** (Borden, 2000) A young, awkward boy shares more in common than just a birthday with Abraham Lincoln. With the help of his teacher, the boy realizes that he has the potential for greatness, just like President Lincoln. ***Abe Lincoln: The Boy Who Loved Books*** (Winters, 2003) Winters's prose reads like poetry and spotlights Lincoln's love of learning. The biography ends, "He learned the power of words and used them well." ***Mr. Lincoln's Whiskers*** (Winnick, 1996) A true story of 11-year-old Grace, who wrote to Mr. Lincoln advising him to grow a beard.
Jim Crow Laws 1880s–1960s	***Freedom Summer*** (Wiles, 2001) Joe and Henry, who have been segregated because of the Jim Crow laws, are thrilled to find out that a new law will allow them to swim together in the public pool. Sadly, the boys realize that prejudice still exists when they discover that the water in the pool has been replaced with tar. ***Goin' Someplace Special*** (McKissack, 2001) See summary and mini-lesson for questioning on page 162. ***Finding Lincoln*** (Malaspina, 2009) Louis wanted to learn more about young Abraham Lincoln, and he knew the answers he needed would be found in a book at the library. But, because he is an African-American boy growing up in Alabama in 1951, the library is off-limits, until a brave librarian chooses to let him in after hours. ***Ruth and the Green Book*** (Ramsey, 2010) See summary on page 157.
Rosa Parks 1913–2005 Bus Ride: 12/1/1955 **Montgomery Bus Boycotts 1955–1956**	***Back of the Bus*** (Reynolds, 2010) See summary and Comprehension Conversation on page 169. ***Rosa's Bus: The Ride to Civil Rights*** (Kittinger, 2010) See summary on page 157.
Greensboro Sit-Ins 2/1/1960–6/25/1960 Ezell Blair Jr. (now Jibreel Khazan), David Richmond, Joseph McNeil, and Franklin McCain launch the Greensboro sit-ins. **www.sitins.com**	***Freedom on the Menu: The Greensboro Sit-Ins*** (Weatherford, 2005) See summary and Comprehension Conversation on page 169.
Ruby Bridges 1954– First Day at William Frantz Elementary in New Orleans: 11/14/1960 **www.rubybridges.com**	***The Story of Ruby Bridges*** (Coles, 1995) A few quotations from Ruby's mother and from her teacher help tell the story of the sole African-American girl to attend a court-ordered desegregated New Orleans school in 1960.
Dr. Martin Luther King, Jr. 1929–1968 "I Have a Dream" Speech 8/28/1963 **www.kingcenter.org**	***My Brother Martin*** (Farris, 2003) In this narrative, Christine King Farris recalls the early life of her younger brother, Dr. Martin Luther King, Jr., as they grew up in the segregated South. ***A Sweet Smell of Roses*** (Johnson, 2005) See summary and lesson on page 162.

	continued **A TIMELINE OF PICTURE BOOKS**
Review	***Climbing Lincoln's Steps: The African American Journey*** (Slade, 2010) See lesson and Comprehension Conversation on page 169. ***Let Freedom Sing*** (Newton, 2009) Based on the lyrics of the gospel song of the same name, this book is a celebration of the major events of the civil rights movement and leads the reader through time from Rosa Parks to Barack Obama. ***This Is the Dream*** (Shore & Alexander, 2006) The rhythmic text and powerful images show scenes of segregation in America. From bus boycotts and lunch counter sit-ins to marches and civil rights leaders, the author shows us how all of these events helped to change freedom and justice in America.

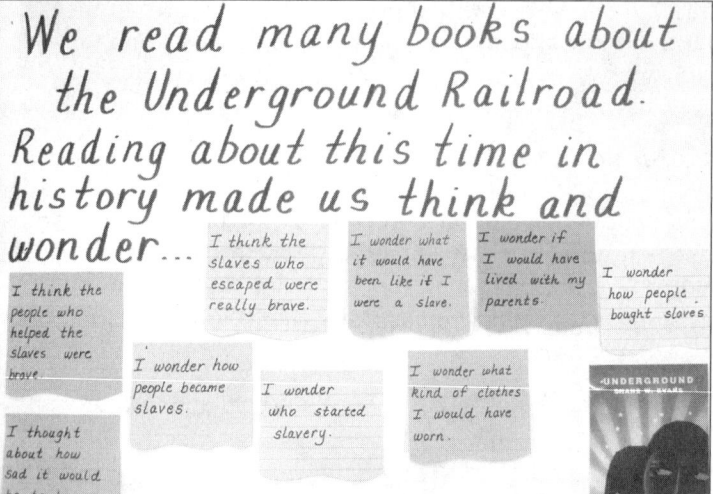

Learners' reflections about the Underground Railroad

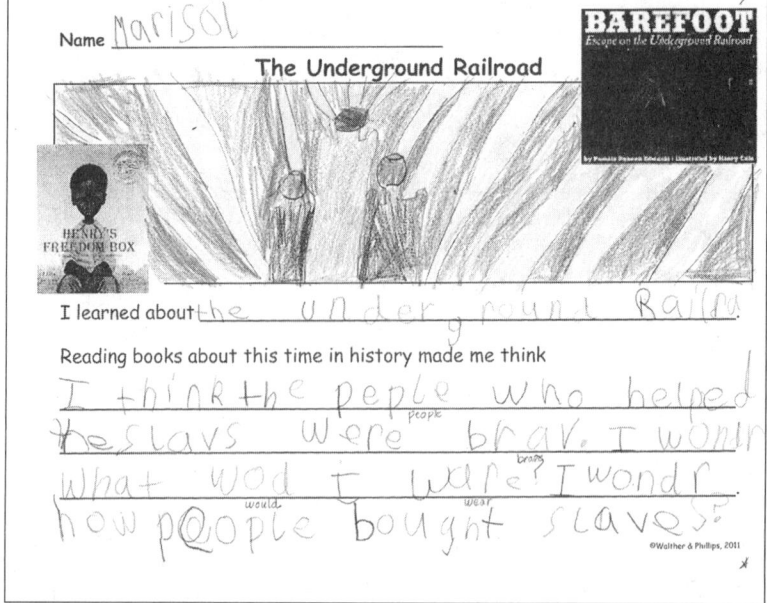

I think the people who helped the slaves were brave. I wonder what I would wear. I wonder how people bought slaves.

MINI-LESSON: Determining Importance in Biographies Read-Aloud/Think-Aloud—Foundation Lesson

Preparation:

- Copy and display the strategy song "Determining Importance" (CD Resource 6.3) and the Comprehension Strategy Wheel (CD Resource 3.5).
- Display and read aloud a biography of one page or less. The picture book *Our Children Can Soar* (Cook, 2009) includes one-paragraph biographies that are ideal for this lesson.

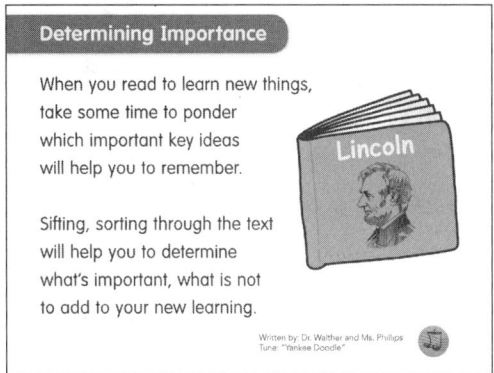

CD Resource 6.3 and IWB_Song_6.3

Explanation: The goal of this lesson is to help young learners observe your thinking as you model how to differentiate between fun facts and important ideas to help you understand and remember the text.

Demonstration: Introduce the strategy song "Determining Importance," and invite children to sing along. If you have an interactive whiteboard, display IWB_Song_6.3 and press the musical note to play the tune. Otherwise, sing the words to the tune of Yankee Doodle. Then read aloud the biography, thinking aloud as you differentiate "fun facts" and "important ideas." You might choose to mark them with two different colors or with the initials "FF" for fun facts and "II" for important ideas. Ask yourself questions like these:

- Is this information important?
- Why is it important?
- How will it help me understand this person?
- What makes this information more important than the fun fact?
- How will this help me remember what I learned about this person?

Invitation: "Readers, what did you notice today about my reading? What was I doing to determine the important information? How did the questions I asked help me to determine the key ideas? How can you use this strategy when you read?"

MINI-LESSON: Determining Importance in Biographies Read-Aloud/Think-Together—Follow-Up Lesson

Preparation:

- Display and read aloud a biography of one page or less. The picture book *Our Children Can Soar* (Cook, 2009) includes one-paragraph biographies that are ideal for this lesson.
- Make an enlarged copy of Determining Importance Response Sheet (CD Resource 6.4)

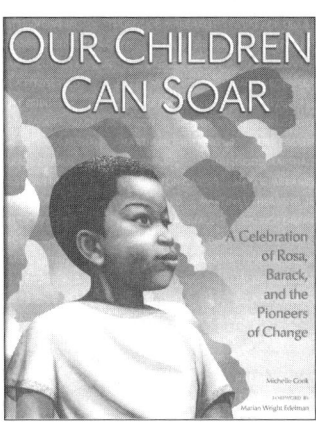

- Gather other biographies at various reading levels for children to read on their own.

Explanation: Certainly, guiding young learners to determine important information is going to take much more than one foundation lesson and this follow-up lesson. As always, let your learners guide you in deciding how much support they need in order to begin to independently apply this strategy. The aim of this lesson is to invite children into the decision-making process as you determine important information. As students identify the information that they deem important, remember to ask them to share the reasons behind their determination. Record their thinking on the Determining Importance Response Sheet.

Demonstration: While reading, ask students to join in and help you decide which "fun facts" and "important ideas" to highlight.

Invitation: "As you're reading and rereading today, sift and sort through the text to determine what information will help you understand and remember, and what is simply a fun fact. Write three important things you learned about the person on a sticky note and bring them with you when we share."

MINI-LESSON: Asking Questions to Determine Important Information

Preparation: Gather some sticky notes for jotting notes during the think-aloud and a selection of biographical texts such as books, passages, articles, Scholastic newspapers, and so on.

Explanation: During this think-aloud, you model the thought process behind asking questions to determine important information in the text. You will demonstrate that readers read nonfiction books to learn something new, and sometimes rereading is necessary to separate the important information from the fun facts.

Demonstration: "Today I am going to ask questions about specific parts of a biography to determine the important information about _____. As I am reading I'm going to think about the new information and decide if it is something that is important for me to remember about this person, or if it was just a fun fact."

Invitation: "Researchers, as you are reading biographies today and you come across some new information, reread it and think about how important it is to remember that new information. Is it something that will help you remember why that person is important, or is it just a fascinating fact that interests you? Jot down the important information from the text on a sticky note and we will share our new, and important, learning with each other."

READ-ALOUDS THAT SPARK COMPREHENSION CONVERSATIONS	
Title, Author, Focus, and Brief Summary	**A Few Questions to Spark Your Conversation**
Back of the Bus (Reynolds, 2010) **Focus:** Inferring **Summary:** It is December 5, 1955, as a young boy tells the readers about his bus ride with Mama on the day Rosa Parks was arrested.	What do you think the author means by, "She's got her strong chin on"? Why do you think the boy is "gettin' shaky legs"? Why does his mama have "Mrs. Parks' lightnin'-storm eyes now"? Let's talk about the ending. Why do you think he's "holding his marble out in the open"?
Climbing Lincoln's Steps: The African American Journey (Slade, 2010) **Focus:** Reading Like a Writer **Summary:** "Change. It happens slowly. One small step at a time." Slade repeats these powerful lines as she retells key moments in African-American history, including those that occurred on the marble steps of the Lincoln Memorial.	Did you notice the repeated lines in this book? Why do you think Suzanne Slade chose to repeat those particular words? Did you notice how throughout the book Suzanne Slade wove the idea of people taking small steps toward change? How could you do something like this in your own writing?
Freedom on the Menu (Weatherford, 2005) **Focus:** Inferring **Summary:** Set in 1960, this picture book tells the story of the civil rights sit-ins from the perspective of eight-year-old Connie, who is not allowed to sit at the lunch counter at Woolworth's for a banana split.	*Freedom on the Menu* is an interesting title. What are you thinking as you look at the cover? Do you have any prediction about what might happen? Let's take a minute to talk about a "lunch counter." Can you use the picture clues to try to figure out what that is? In the newspaper it says "Negro Students Stand Up By Sitting Down." What does that mean? Let's talk about the words *protests* and *picket*. It is important to understand those words to understand what is happening here. Why do you think it was the best banana split Connie ever had?

MINI-LESSONS FOR VOCABULARY DEVELOPMENT: STUDYING ROOT WORDS AND SUFFIXES

The two mini-lessons that appear here build on the lessons at the beginning of the chapter on prefixes. We begin by familiarizing students with common root words and then move on to focusing on suffixes.

MINI-LESSON: Studying Root Words

Interactive Whiteboard Lesson 6

Preparation: If you have an interactive whiteboard, access IWB_Lesson_6. If not, select a common root or base word that is the building block for many other words, like *play, work, light, form, time, fire,* or *ball.*

Explanation: The purpose of the lesson is to review the concept of base words that you introduced in the compound-word lessons and for children to discover all the different words they can make using a base word.

> ### FLUENCY FUN! TIME TRAVEL WITH TRANSITION PHRASES
>
> Write the following common transition phrases on large pieces of chart paper. Arrange the transition phrase charts in a "path" on the floor of your classroom and invite your students to line up with a partner. Have each pair read each phrase aloud as they follow the path of charts around the room. This is an engaging way for children to build reading fluency while familiarizing themselves with the common phrases that authors use to move their biographies through time.
>
> | In the beginning | and then | in the meantime | as soon as | at this point |
> |---|---|---|---|---|
> | as long as | after a while | at that time | in the past | at last |

Demonstration: To activate students' background knowledge, begin the demonstration by asking them what they already know about root words. Record their responses. Remind students that when they studied compound words they discovered that they were made up of two words. Display one of the words found in the chart on this page or display IWB_Lesson_6. Work with students to create as many words as you can that include the base word.

Invitation: "Word wizards, what did you learn today about root words? How will root words help you as a reader and a writer? See if you notice the root word that we worked with today in your reading."

work	time	fire	ball
fire/works	time/out	fire/place	eye/ball
home/work	over/time	camp/fire	meat/ball
work/sheet	any/time	fire/fly	ball/park
work/shop	day/time	fire/fighter	snow/ball
work/out	life/time	wild/fire	foot/ball
over/work	mean/time	fire/cracker	ball/game

MINI-LESSON: Studying Suffixes

Preparation: Prepare a piece of paper for each pair of students that is divided into three sections, and a large sheet or an interactive whiteboard document for your demonstration lesson. If available, read aloud *Big, Bigger, Biggest* (Sami, 2008).

Explanation: To determine whether your students are ready for a lesson on suffixes, informally assess if they are able to use the two words in a compound word and common prefixes to figure out the meaning of an unknown word. If so, then you want to begin by teaching the most common suffixes first. This lesson will focus on the common suffixes *-er* (more) and *-est* (most).

Demonstration: For your demonstration, select a base word from the chart below. Demonstrate how the meaning of the base word changes when you add the suffixes *-er* and *-est* by drawing three quick illustrations. For example, if you select the word *tall*, draw a short tree in the first section of your paper, a taller tree in the second section of your paper, and the tallest tree in the third section of your paper. Group students into pairs and provide each pair with a root word from the chart at right and a piece of paper divided into thirds. Invite students to illustrate the base word, and the base word with the suffixes *-er* and *-est*. Once students have finished, gather them together to share their drawings. Staple their pages together to make a resource for future discussions on suffixes.

tall	small	fast
long	slow	loud
quiet	short	cold
black	bold	calm
cheap	clean	cool
few	hard	light
mean	near	new

Invitation: "Today as you are reading, notice if any of the words have the *-er* or *-est* suffix. If you come across a word with one of those suffixes, write it on a sticky note and bring it over when it is time to share."

READ-ALOUDS WITH RICH VOCABULARY

Title and Author	Brief Summary	Words to Highlight and Kid-Friendly Definition
Abe Lincoln Remembers (Turner, 2001)	As the Author's Note points out, this is a fictionalized first-person account about "how Lincoln might have thought and felt" about the events of his time.	**debated:** talked about different sides of an subject or issue [in this case, slavery] **persuade:** to cause someone to believe something by giving them reasons or arguing **prevail:** to rise up as the winner or to control
The Librarian on the Roof! (King, 2010)	See page 174.	**essentials:** all the things you need to do something **resourceful:** able to use your imagination and think quickly to handle difficult situations **respectable:** showing good manners and making good choices
The Night I Followed the Dog (Laden, 1994)	A boy details his adventures following his dog to the "dog club."	**eventually:** at some time in the future, finally **fumbling:** searching for something in a nervous or clumsy way **glamorous:** fascinating or exciting

MINI-LESSONS FOR READING RESPONSE

The more that you know about your students as readers and thinkers, the better you will be able to help them improve both of those abilities. Reading or listening to students' questions before, during, and after reading opens a window into their thinking and gives you a way to determine whether they are truly understanding not only the literal meaning, but also the implied meaning of the text. Their after-reading questions often show you the depth of students' thinking and give you a direction to head in when selecting future books. To offer a different kind of response option for your mathematical learners, teach them how to make time lines of books. Keep in mind that this type of response is not limited to biographies. Readers could also make a time line of Rosie's day to summarize *Rosie's Walk* (Hutchins, 1968) or of the boy's day full of antics in *Yes Day!* (Rosenthal, 2009).

MINI-LESSON: Asking Questions Before, During, and After Reading

Preparation: Copy and display the Three-Column Notes page (CD Resource 1.7). Note that the samples of student work that appear on this page are based on the book *Fly Away Home* (Bunting, 1991).

Explanation: This response is the next step in releasing the responsibility to students after the foundation and follow-up lessons on pages 161 and 162.

Demonstration: For this demonstration, if you are doing it with the whole group, read the title and show the cover of the book. If you are working with students in a small group, invite them to do the same. Then, pause to record any "before reading" questions that they have in the first column on their page. Next, read and pause occasionally for students to record questions. After reading and discussion, ask students to write down

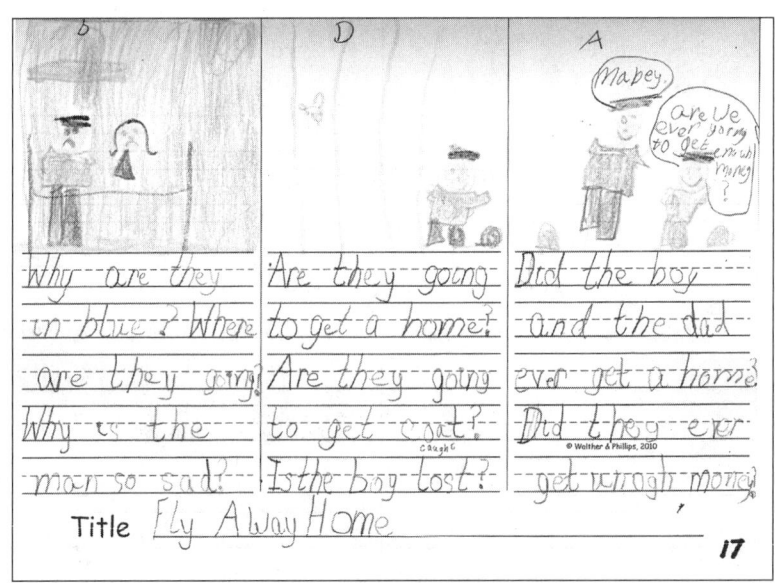

B—Why are they in blue? Where are they going? Why is the man so sad? D—Are they going to get a home? Are they going to get caught? Is the boy lost? A—Did the boy and the dad ever get a home? Did they ever get enough money?

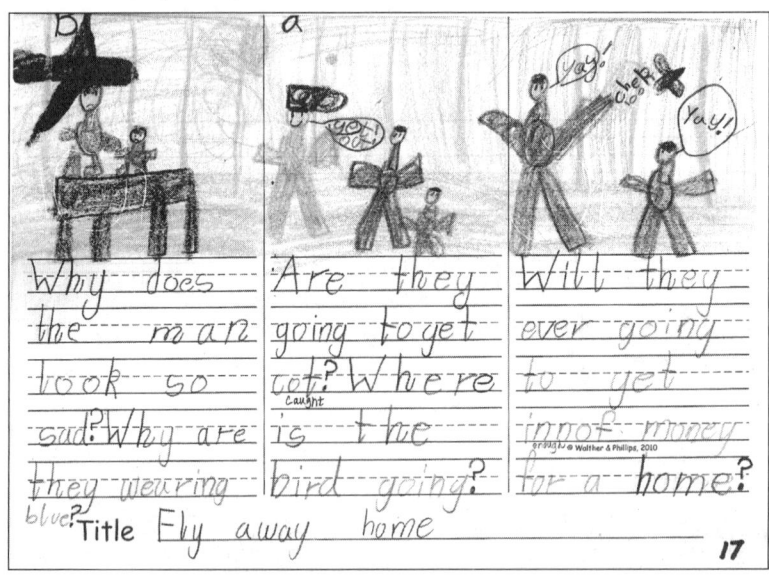

B—Why does the man look so sad? Why are they wearing blue? D—Are they going to get caught? Where is the bird going? A—Will they ever get enough money for a home?

any lingering questions.

Invitation: "Readers, today we are going to record our questions before, during, and after reading. It will be interesting to see how many of our questions are answered as we read along and how many remain after we are done."

MINI-LESSON: Creating a Time Line

Preparation: Gather some biographies or other books where the events occur over a period of time. Provide students with scratch paper for their rough draft of events and blank paper and a ruler for making a line.

Explanation: Time lines are a way for students to gather and visually present fast facts and information about people and events in history. Creating a visual time line helps children to better understand the time-order relationship between the events. Time lines are also helpful for young learners who are always wondering, "Is that person still alive?"

Demonstration: Demonstrate how to collect facts or events in chronological order on a piece of paper. Note that all of the "Picture Book" biographies by David Adler include a page at the end with "Important Dates" that you can use to model how to record dates in chronological order. Next, determine how many years, days, or hours you will need on your time line. Draw and label the time line accordingly. Finally, write or draw the events in the correct order. Release the responsibility to students by inviting them to create a large time line with a small group or with a partner. Once students are adept at creating time lines, add this option to your menu of reading responses.

Invitation: "Readers, time lines are one way to summarize historical events or important dates in a person's life. You can also use them to record what happens in a book. Time lines are a helpful visual tool when trying to picture the time order of events."

Part 3: Genre Study—Biographies

During this genre study, you and your students will read unique and interesting biographies about a diverse collection of people. Along with titles about famous men and women, numerous books have been penned about amazing human beings who were not as well known. We've selected titles that feature the hallmarks of well-written biographies for children because they include accurate information, boast a quick-paced narrative, are objectively written, and present various points of view (Fuhler & Walther, 2007). Biographies for children are written in different formats. We've defined each format so that you can share the following terms with your students.

- **Partial Biography**—Author takes an in-depth look at one part of a person's life.
- **Complete Biography**— recounts a person's life from birth to present or to the person's death if he or she is no longer living

- **Collective Biography**—describes the lives of several people with a common thread
- **Autobiography**—A person writes about his or her own life.

Enjoy learning alongside your students about people from various backgrounds as you read and reflect on the life stories illuminated in the pages of a book.

\multicolumn{2}{c}{**GENRE STUDY: BIOGRAPHY**}	
Title and Author	**Brief Summary**
Biblioburro: A True Story From Colombia (Winter, 2010)	Introduce your students to Luis and his trusty "biblioburros" Alfa and Beta, who carry books to young readers in the remote villages of rural Colombia.
Clemente! (Perdomo, 2010)	A young boy who is named after the heroic baseball player tells the story of Roberto Clemente, the first Latin-American baseball player inducted into the National Baseball Hall of Fame.
Jack's Path of Courage: The Life of John F. Kennedy (Rappaport, 2010)	This biographical sketch of the 35th president traces Kennedy's life from young adulthood through his presidency. As with Rappaport's other biographies, *Martin's Big Words* (2001) and *Abe's Honest Words* (2008), we recommend spending a few days reading this book aloud because there is so much to think and talk about.
Librarian on the Roof! (King, 2010)	This book is based on a true story about a Texas librarian who camped out on the roof of the oldest library in the state to raise money for the children's section. Notice how the illustrator chose to use vertical two-page spreads. Connect this title to other library-related biographies like *The Librarian From Basra* (Winter, 2005), *Biblioburro* (Winter, 2010), and *Miss Dorothy and Her Bookmobile* (Houston, 2011).
Mighty Jackie: The Strike-Out Queen (Moss, 2004)	On April 2, 1931, 17-year-old pitcher Jackie Mitchell made baseball history by striking out both Babe Ruth and Lou Gehrig.
Seeds of Change (Johnson, 2010)	A vibrantly illustrated picture book biography of Nobel Peace Prize winner and Kenyan environmentalist Wangari Maathai.
Sonia Sotomayor: A Judge Grows in the Bronx (Winter, 2009)	Written in both English and Spanish, this biography tells the story of young Sonia, who grew up in public housing in the South Bronx. Inspired by her hard-working mother, Sonia studied diligently, attended Princeton University, and after serving as both a lawyer and a judge, was appointed to the U.S. Supreme Court.
Testing the Ice: A True Story About Jackie Robinson (Robinson, 2009)	Sharon Robinson honors her father's memory not only as a competitive athlete but also as a loving family man.
A Weed Is a Flower: The Life of George Washington Carver (Aliki, 1965/1988)	A well-written biography about Carver, who was born into slavery but worked diligently to became a scientist devoted to helping southern farmers. Pair with *George Washington Carver* (Bowdish, 2004).
Wonder Horse: The True Story of the World's Smartest Horse (McCully, 2010)	Bill Key, also known as Doc Key, was born into slavery. He became a doctor who treated both humans and animals. He believed in treating animals with kindness, and with that mind-set he trained a horse he named Jim Key to do remarkable things.

Meeting the Needs of ALL Learners

At this point in the school year, your students have learned how to use many helpful strategies to decode unfamiliar words. However, we all know that there are still some words that just can't be decoded that easily. These are the high-frequency sight words that have appeared in poems, books, morning messages, word walls, and even flash cards throughout the school year. Many of your students have acquired most of these words, but there are some children who are still struggling. If you're like us, it is time to pull some tricks out of your teacher tote bag to help these struggling readers acquire those sticky sight words. For advanced readers, we challenge them to synthesize the knowledge they've learned from our trek through history by working collaboratively to create a visual time line.

SENSIBLE STRATEGIES FOR STRUGGLING READERS: POCKETS, PASSWORDS, AND STICKY NOTES

Begin by choosing a specific word that one of your students struggles to read. Write that word on a small card and have that child place the word in his or her pocket with the understanding that he or she will be asked to take out the word and read it to others throughout the day. Ask specific adults or peers who interact with your struggling student regularly to periodically ask what their "pocket word" is. He or she will then remove the pocket word and read it aloud. This oral practice can occur multiple times throughout the day or week until the student has memorized the word. However, keep in mind that in order to maintain the novelty of these practice opportunities, it is best not to overuse this strategy. You will also want to limit to a manageable number the pocket words and students using this strategy.

Another simple idea to help learners acquire those last few difficult sight words is to write a word on a large card and place the word card by your classroom door. This word becomes the classroom password! All of your students will enjoy tapping the card and reading the word aloud as they travel in and out of the classroom, but your striving readers will benefit from the additional reading practice. To avoid class disruptions, make sure your students whisper the word and tap gently as they pass in and out of the room. Think about how many times children leave the classroom to go to a special class, the library, lunch, recess, or even the bathroom! All of these opportunities to use the classroom password will provide additional reading practice for those students still learning their high-frequency sight words.

Finally, if all else fails, write the tricky sight word on a sticky note and place it in your struggling student's daily journal or book box. When you confer with that student about reading or writing, have the child read that difficult sight word to you. Chances are, you meet with that learner individually throughout the day for a variety of reasons. It only takes a second or two for him or her to read that sticky sight word aloud—and those practice opportunities really do add up!

Students work in small groups (above, left) to create a visual timeline (above, right).

TARGETING TALENTED READERS: CREATING A VISUAL TIME LINE

After completing your historical journey, ask students which person or historical era they found the most interesting. Then, divide talented readers into partners or small groups based on their interests. Provide each group with a large piece of bulletin board paper and gather the books you read about this person or time. To spark their thinking, brainstorm a list of words to describe that person or time, similar to the chart pictured here. Then, invite children to create a visual representation. Display the posters together in chronological order to create a visual timeline.

To help students with the timeline, brainstorm a list of words to describe the person or historical era.

Final Thoughts

As your historical voyage draws to a close, we're hopeful that the rich literary and historical experiences that you have shared with students through well-chosen books has given them a solid foundation on which to build future history lessons. If your learners are like ours, you probably have a few history buffs who will continue to read historical fiction and biographies for the rest of the school year and maybe for the rest of their lives. Just think, you might be the one to spark a lifelong interest!

CHAPTER 7: MARCH

Visualizing and Inferring to Peek Into Poetry

Poetry is all around us. It makes us think and feel—it brings music to our ears. When you weave poetry into your core literacy instruction by surrounding students with songs, poems, and rhymes, children develop an ear for language. Why do we spend so much time enjoying poems with our learners? Simply stated, because poets are masters at wordplay. What a wonderful message for young readers—let's play with words! We invite students to fiddle with words, to find pleasure in wordplay, and to ponder words and their meanings. Poems are also ideal texts for visualizing and inferring. During the year, we read a wide variety of poetry so that youngsters become familiar with different kinds of poems and specific poets. In this chapter, we further explore the genre of poetry. Join us in transforming your classroom into a playful poetry place!

Part 1: Reading-Related Morning Message Ideas and Samples

In keeping with the theme of playing with words, the message ideas presented here invite your students to play with, discuss, and wonder about words.

MORNING MESSAGE IDEA: SELF-MONITORING/ DECODING—DECODING TWO-SYLLABLE WORDS

> **MORNING MESSAGE SAMPLE**
>
> Let's decode these two-syllable words!
>
> | until | fastest | unlock | planet |
> |---|---|---|---|
> | pumpkin | insect | pocket | pretzel |
> | plastic | kicking | basket | insist |
> | cricket | monster | subtract | |

To begin this message, select four or five words from the list at right. Read the first word aloud and ask students to listen and clap once for each syllable. Next, display the word and cover the second syllable. Sound out and read the first syllable, the second syllable, and then blend them together. It will sound like this, /un/ - /til/ = *until*. Discuss the meaning of the word. Continue in the same fashion for the rest of the words you've chosen for that day. Save the remaining words for another morning message.

MORNING MESSAGE IDEA: COMPREHENSION— WORDS THAT EVOKE IMAGES

Use this message as a follow-up to the "Mental Images—Mind Music" mini-lesson on page 183. To prepare, choose words or phrases from poems or books that you plan to read to the class. For this message, we selected phrases from the poem " I Made Something Strange With My Chemistry Set" found on page 58 of *A Pizza the Size of the Sun* (Prelutsky, 1996). Read each phrase and discuss the image that particular phrase evokes. Ask questions like, "Do you know something else that looks/sounds/feels like that?" After discussing the image-evoking phrases, read and enjoy the poem!

> **MORNING MESSAGE SAMPLE**
>
> Use your senses! What do you visualize when you read these or phrases?
>
> gluey and blue
> half-scrambled eggs
> bubbled and slashed
> blubbery noise
> slobbery thing

MORNING MESSAGE IDEA: VOCABULARY BUILDING—QUIET WORDS AND NOISY WORDS

Interactive Whiteboard Morning Message 7

You might choose to set the stage for this morning message by reading an onomatopoeia-filled book like *Achoo! Bang! Crash! The Noisy Alphabet* (MacDonald, 2003) or a poem like "Clatter" by Joyce Armor (a reproducible copy appears in *Teaching Struggling Readers With Poetry*). If you have an interactive whiteboard, access IWB_MM_7 and invite students to categorize the words as "quiet" or "noisy" by dragging them to the appropriate column. If not, in your message space, draw a table with the headings Quiet Words and Noisy Words. Brainstorm words that are onomatopoeic and invite students to sort them according to whether each word is quiet or noisy.

MORNING MESSAGE IDEA: READING RESPONSE—CREATING LIST POEMS

Begin this message by thinking about a book you and your students just read or a topic of interest. Brainstorm words, feelings, and experiences pertaining to the topic. These become the building blocks of the poem. Orally play with the words, arranging and rearranging them in list format so that a natural rhythm emerges and then write it on the chalkboard. If you choose, you can also type the poem, reproduce it, and add it to students' Poetry Notebooks.

MORNING MESSAGE SAMPLE

Quiet Words	Noisy Words
hush	rumble
pitter-patter	thud
fizzle	bang
chirp	clang
hiss	smash
sputter	boom
rustle	crash

MORNING MESSAGE SAMPLE

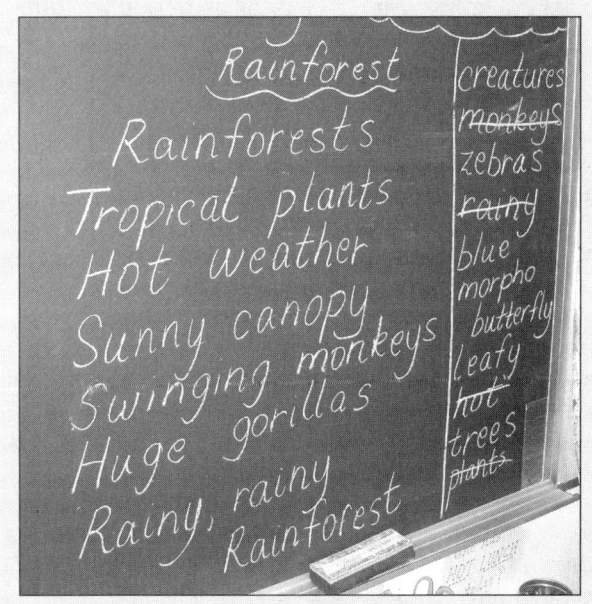

POETRY POWER: POEMS FOR MARCH	
Title	**Brief Summary**
Read a Rhyme, Write a Rhyme (Prelutsky, 2005)	A collection of poetry with "poemstarts" to get kids writing!
Shout! Little Poems That Roar (Bagert, 2007)	Your students will ask you to read the lively poems in this book over and over again.

MORNING READ-ALOUDS: INFERRING, IMAGINING, AND PLAYING WITH WORDS	
Title, Author, and Focus	**Brief Summary**
1+1=5 and Other Unlikely Additions (LaRochelle, 2010) **Focus**: Inferring	This book begins with the math equation 1+1=3. Upon turning the page, readers discover the answer is 1 unicorn + 1 goat = 3 horns. The book continues with more unique 1+1 equations. Clues in the illustrations will help careful readers infer the answers.
Billy & Milly: Short & Silly (Feldman, 2009) **Focus**: Wordplay	This ingenious picture book contains 13 short rhyming stories about Billy and Milly. Each story contains three or four rhyming words, which foster discussions about rhyme and how the images help to tell the story.
Birdsong (Sandall, 2010) **Focus**: Rhyming Text, Wordplay	"One small bird, in a tree. Kitcha kitcha Kee kee kee" begins this inviting book. Students will join in making the different bird sounds as the birds gather on the branch until a butterfly joins them and . . . "CRACK." Pair this with another noisy bird book, *Good-Night, Owl* (Hutchins, 1972).
Guess Again (Barnett, 2009) **Focus**: Rhyming Riddles	The endpapers in this book give readers a hint that they should expect the unexpected when trying to figure out the answers to these rhyming riddles.
The Imaginary Garden (Larsen, 2009) **Focus**: Imagination	Theo's grandpa moves to an apartment, but his balcony is too windy to plant a garden. So he and Theo work together to paint their own imaginary garden.
Mr. Putney's Quacking Dog (Agee, 2010) **Focus**: Wordplay	Meet Mr. Putney and his gang of unusual creatures as you enjoy a wordplay guessing game with your students. The book begins with the question, "Who wakes Mr. Putney up in the morning?" Followed by an armadillo saying, "Yo!" Of course, it is an Alarmadillo!
Rose's Garden (Reynolds, 2009) **Focus**: Inferring Big Ideas	Reynolds captures young Rose's adventurous spirit as she decides to plant a garden in a forgotten part of the city. When readers discover that Rose's faith, patience, and perseverance have paid off, they can infer the message of this fable: Anything is possible.
The Sea of Sleep (Hanson, 2010) **Focus**: Read Like a Writer	A baby otter and her mama float along on the sea of sleep enjoying the "peaceful beauty" that surrounds them. Notice the repeated stanza and beautiful language Hanson uses throughout the book.
Stanza (Esbaum, 2009) **Focus**: Writing Poetry	Stanza, the bully pooch, and his two nasty brothers torment the town, but Stanza has a secret—he spends every free moment writing poetry. Will his brothers find out?
Zoola Palooza (Barretta, 2011) **Focus**: Wordplay	Join the animal acts as Zoola Palooza rolls into town. This book is filled with homograph wordplay and humorous illustrations.

Part 2: A Menu of Reading Workshop Mini-Lessons

Poetry offers opportunities to create mental images and infer.

Since the focus of this chapter is on poetry, it makes sense that we would turn our attention to self-monitoring at the word level by focusing on multiple-meaning words. One of the reasons our language is challenging for ELLs is that many English words have more than one meaning. We'll explore multiple-meaning words in the mini-lessons for self-monitoring/decoding and again when we discuss homophones on page 188. The focus of the comprehension strategy instruction in this chapter will be on making mental images and inferring. We round out the chapter with a list of appealing poetry titles to add to your collection.

MINI-LESSONS FOR SELF-MONITORING/DECODING STRATEGY INSTRUCTION

Imagine the children in your classroom listening to you speak throughout the day. We don't think about how many times we say something like, "Wow! You are sharp thinkers," followed later by, "It's time to sharpen your pencils." Making a conscious effort to point out the differences in these word meanings is helpful for all learners but essential for ELLs.

MINI-LESSON: Understanding Multiple-Meaning Words—Foundation Lesson
Interactive Whiteboard Lesson 7

Preparation: Think about words you use every day that have multiple meanings. For this lesson focus on words in which the meaning changes depending on whether the word is used as a noun or a verb. Gather pictures or objects to represent the nouns below. If you have an interactive whiteboard, access IWB_Lesson_7.

Explanation: When discussing multiple-meaning words, a sensible place to begin is by distinguishing between nouns and verbs.

Demonstration: Show students the nouns on the whiteboard, on word cards, with pictures, or by using realia and invite a child or two to act out

> **NOUNS OR VERBS?**
>
> a pet/to pet
> a swing/to swing
> a tag/to tag
> a sled/to sled
> a skate/to skate
> a bat/to bat
> a list/to list
> a fan/to fan
> a roll/to roll
> a stamp/to stamp

CHAPTER 7: MARCH—VISUALIZING AND INFERRING TO PEEK INTO POETRY / 181

the related verb. Then, use each word in a sentence. Continue multiple-meaning word conversations during your read-alouds and in small groups as you guide readers.

Invitation: "Readers, notice how the meaning of a word changes depending on whether the writer or speaker uses it as a noun or a verb. That is something we will continue to ponder as we learn about words."

MINI-LESSON: Understanding Multiple-Meaning Words—Follow-Up Lesson

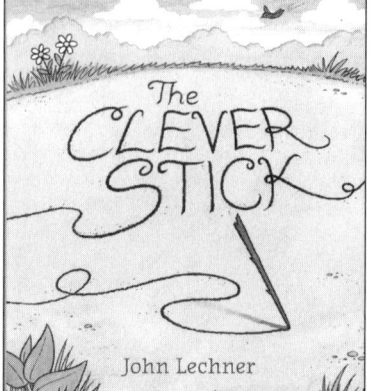

Preparation: Read aloud *The Clever Stick* (Lechner, 2009) or another book with multiple-meaning words. In *The Clever Stick* you will find the words *sharp* and *longed*. Create a list of school-related sentences that contain multiple-meaning words similar to the following:

> You are a *sharp* student. / It is time to *sharp*en your pencil.
>
> I hope we don't *run* out of paper. / Let's go outside and *run* around.

Write each pair of sentences on top of a piece of paper that is divided in half. Divide students into pairs.

Explanation: Multiple-meaning words are one of many aspects of the English language that make it difficult for young learners and also ELLs. This lesson provides students with hands-on practice reading and illustrating the meaning of words they hear every day in school. You can extend this learning by pausing during your read-alouds or while guiding readers in small groups to point out, quickly sketch, or act out words with multiple meanings.

Demonstration: After reading *The Clever Stick* or another book with multiple-meaning words, discuss those words and the various meanings of the same word. For example, in the book, the word *sharp* means to be smart, but it also means something pointy. Demonstrate illustrating two sentences with multiple-meaning words. Give each pair of students a paper with two sentences. Invite them to read the sentences, determine the meaning of the words, and then illustrate each sentence. Gather children together to share and discuss their sentences and illustrations.

Invitation: "As readers, you have to think about the way the author is using the word in a sentence to figure out the meaning. Remember to use the picture clues and word clues to help you to decide what the author means. Then, pause, think, and check for understanding!"

MINI-LESSONS FOR COMPREHENSION STRATEGY INSTRUCTION

In this chapter, we continue to encourage children to visualize, or make mental images, as we read books and poems aloud. Using these images helps readers draw conclusions, create unique interpretations of the text, and remember important details. In addition, incorporating images from reading enhances students' writing (Miller, 2002). Visualizing is critical for readers who are transitioning from picture books and transitional chapter books, like the Henry and Mudge series by Cynthia Rylant, to longer chapter books that have fewer illustrations. In addition, we will continue to add to students' knowledge of comprehension strategies by focusing on how readers use the information from the text along with their background knowledge to draw conclusions and formulate novel interpretations of the text. Inferring plays a critical role in reading in general, and specifically in reading poetry, because poets don't use as many words or write as literally as the authors of most books, so the reader has to "fill in the blanks" (Fuhler & Walther, 2007).

MINI-LESSON: Mental Images—Mind Music

Preparation: Record diverse sounds, different kinds of music such as parade music, holiday music, circus music, and/or songs that may evoke specific images, like "The Star Spangled Banner," "Take Me Out to the Ball Game," "Old MacDonald Had a Farm," and so on. Give each child a blank piece of paper divided into four sections.

Explanation: Are you a visual learner? Do you need to see something to clearly understand it? Readers who can visualize what is happening in a book comprehend the book better. The aim of this mini-lesson is to invite children to use their sense of hearing to create an image.

Demonstration: Explain the role the senses play in making mental images. "Readers, did you know that kids who remember stories are able to visualize or make a mental image of what is happening as they read? It is kind of like making a movie in your mind. Today we are going to use our sense of hearing to make images." Play a song clip and invite students to draw an image of what that particular song made them "see." Then, share and discuss images and how they felt when they heard the sound or music. Continue with other clips.

Invitation: "Think about what words an author might use to help you hear something that is happening in a book. He or she might use descriptive words, onomatopoeia, or words like *cried*, *screamed*, or *whispered* to tell you how a character is speaking. Can you hear the voices of the characters in your book? Pay attention to how they sound in your head."

MINI-LESSON: Mental Images—Using Senses to Describe

Preparation: Find a book where the author uses senses to paint a picture with words, such as these:

Title and Author	Brief Summary
The Black Book of Colors (Cottin, 2006/2008)	Imagine for a moment how you would describe the color red to a person who is blind. In this groundbreaking book, Thomas describes colors using his senses of touch, taste, smell, or hearing. The illustrations are raised black line drawings on black pages and the written text is also translated into Braille.
Hello Ocean (Ryan, 2001)	The author uses the five senses to vividly describe the ocean.

Explanation: Writers use sensory images to help readers visualize the story or poem. This lesson takes a look at that idea from a writer's perspective. When children spend a bit of time writing a piece with sensory language, the experience will make them more aware of that type of language in their reading.

Demonstration: After reading and discussing a sensory-rich book, poem, or excerpt from a book, work in a shared-writing format to create your own piece about a color or other object, such as the ocean, using sensory language. Once students are ready, invite them to try this on their own.

Invitation: "Writers, it is challenging to describe something using your senses. Now you know how much work authors do for you as a reader. As you are reading, notice the words and phrases that help you visualize the scene using your senses."

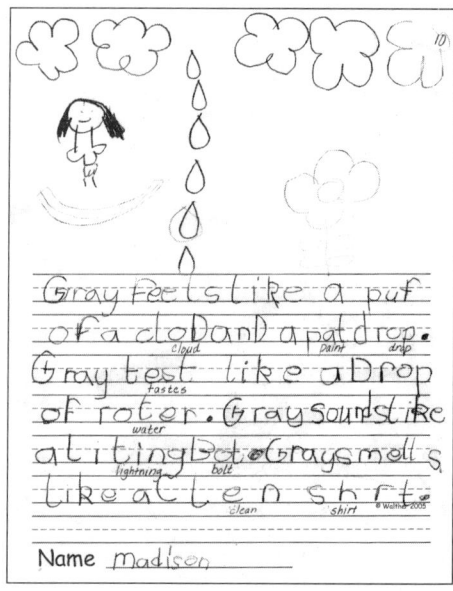

Madison uses sensory language to describe the color gray.

MINI-LESSON: Mental Images—Poetry

Preparation:

- Copy and display the strategy song "Mental Images" (CD Resource 7.1) and the Comprehension Strategy Wheel (CD Resource 3.5).
- Find a book told from two different points of view. Our favorite book for this lesson is *Duck! Rabbit!* (Rosenthal, 2009).

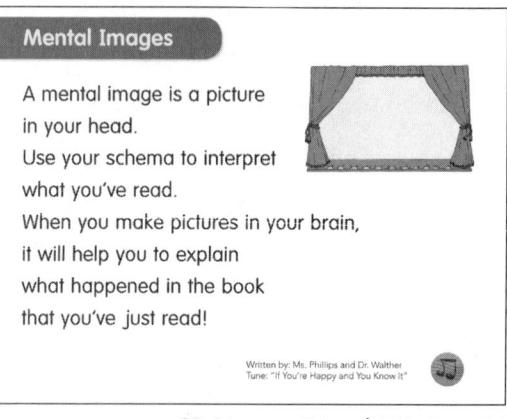

CD Resource 7.1 and IWB_Song_7.1

- Select a poem that will evoke a mental image. One of our favorites, "The Toaster" by William J. Smith, can be found in *Read-Aloud Rhymes for the Very Young* (Prelutsky, 1986).

Explanation: Our aim for this lesson is twofold. First, we want students to build on the knowledge from the previous lessons to listen carefully for sensory language that will help them visualize the content of the poem. Second, we want them to understand that every reader is going to have a different image because of his or her diverse schema and unique point of view.

Demonstration: To begin, read aloud *Duck! Rabbit!* Discuss why students think the two narrators "see" two different animals when they are looking at the same image. Connect their conversation with mental images by pointing out that all of their images will be different, just as they were when they listened to music or described a color. Next, read the poem to your students. Then, ask children to draw what they imagine or can infer from the clues in the poem. Share and discuss the images and the thinking behind them. Remind readers that using clues to create images or to infer helps them to better understand a poet or writer's ideas. Now, reread the poem, pinpointing the clues that children used. Wrap up the lesson by singing the strategy song "Mental Images." If you have an interactive whiteboard, display IWB_Song_7.1 and press the musical note to play the tune. Otherwise, sing the words to the tune of "If You're Happy and You Know It."

Invitation: "Making pictures in your mind is fun, isn't it? That's what makes reading so exciting—it's as if you have a movie right in your hands and you are the director!"

MINI-LESSON: Predicting vs. Inferring

Preparation: Select a picture book to read aloud. Almost any book will provide places for students to either predict or infer. A book that works well for this lesson is *What If?* by Laura Vaccaro Seeger (2010) because it uses only six words in varying combinations to tell a tale three different ways. This book will spark a conversation about friendship and considering the feelings of others. It is also ideal for pointing out the difference between predicting and inferring.

Explanation: When readers predict, they are thinking about what is going to happen next or in the future. On the other hand, when they infer, they are trying to read between the lines to figure out what is happening or why something is happening.

Demonstration: Read and have a comprehension conversation using the questions below to guide your discussions.

QUESTIONING PROMPTS	
Questions That Lead to Predicting	**Questions That Lead to Inferring**
What do you think might happen next? Why do you think that? Are there any clues in the text or illustrations that lead you to that prediction? Were you surprised by what happened? Did your prediction match the text or was it different from what the author wrote? Based on what we/you just read, do you want to revise your prediction?	Based on what we've read so far, what are you inferring here? What is the thinking behind your inference? Why do you think this is happening? What might have happened before this part/this story? What is the missing part? What has the author left out here? Why do you think the character said/did that? What did he/she mean by that? What is the big idea of this story? Why do you think the author is telling us this? How would the story have changed if ____ ?

CD Resource 7.2

Invitation: "Readers have a lot to think about as they read. They predict or think ahead of their reading and they infer or read between the lines. Doing this helps to keep your brain focused on what the author is trying to say. Happy reading!"

MINI-LESSON: Using Schema, Connections, and Mental Images to Infer Big Ideas

Preparation: Copy and display the strategy song "Inferring" (CD Resource 7.3) and the *Comprehension Strategy Wheel* (CD Resource 3.5). Select a book or poem that will offer readers opportunities to infer. We've included a few books that we found work well for inferring lessons here.

Resource 7.3 and IWB_Song_7.3

Title and Author	Brief Summary
Those Shoes (Boelts, 2007)	See Summary and Comprehension Conversation on page 187.
Zero (Otoshi, 2010)	In the sequel to *One* (2008), Otoshi explores the importance of numbers and the big idea of self-worth.

Explanation: "Visualizing and inferring don't occur in isolation. Strategies interweave. Inferring occurs at the intersection of questioning, connecting, and print" (Harvey & Goudvis, 2000, p. 96). When readers make inferences about what they read, it enhances their understanding of the text and increases their engagement with the written word. As they ask themselves, "What is really happening here?" and connect with a character or situation, the author's words begin to come alive in their mind. This is the goal of reading, isn't it?—the two-way communication between the author and the reader.

Demonstration: Introduce the strategy song "Inferring," and invite children to sing along. If you have an interactive whiteboard, display IWB_Song_7.3 and press the musical note to play the tune. Otherwise, sing the words to the tune of "Skip to My Lou." Then do your read-aloud. Using the questions found on page 185, lead a comprehension conversation that targets inferring.

Invitation: "Girls and boys, did you notice that as you read, you often have to infer, or read between the lines, to figure out what is happening in a text? Making mental images and connecting to your schema will help you to do this important kind of thinking."

READ-ALOUDS THAT SPARK COMPREHENSION CONVERSATIONS	
Title, Author, Focus, and Brief Summary	**A Few Questions to Spark Your Conversation**
Grandpa Green (Smith, 2011) **Focus:** Inferring **Summary:** Grandpa Green's great-grandson tells you about his great-grandfather's life as he follows his grandpa through the garden helping him with the little things he's forgotten to do or has left along the way.	Today we're going to read *Grandpa Green* by Lane Smith. What was Lane Smith's role in telling this story? [writer and illustrator] Do you know anyone who was born before computers or cell phones or television? Do you notice what the boy is doing? Who do you think the glove and shovel belong to? Can you infer what is happening here? Do you recognize any characters from the stories Grandpa read? Can you infer what Lane Smith means by, "At least to hear *him* tell it"? After reading: "What are you thinking? What did you notice? What are you wondering?"
Sparrow Girl (Pennypacker, 2009) **Focus:** Questioning **Summary:** In 1958, Chairman Mao declared war on the sparrow population in China, resulting in a plague of locusts and a three-year famine. This book is set during that time and tells the fictionalized story of Ming-Li, who defies the leader and rescues some sparrows.	*Sparrow Girl* is the name of the book we're going to read. What do you think it might be about? Before we start reading, do you have any questions? ". . . a tremendous din woke Ming-Li." I'm wondering what a *din* is. Let's keep reading to see if we can use the context clues to figure it out. When Older Brother finds out about Pigeon, his "face crumpled and his shoulders fell." Can you picture that? Can you infer how he is feeling here? Why do you think the farmers are having so much trouble with their crops? How do you think they will solve the problem? Does Ming-Li remind you of any other characters you know?
Those Shoes (Boelts, 2007) **Focus:** Inferring **Summary:** Jeremy really wants "those shoes"—the pair of high-tops that everyone else has—but Grandma can't afford them. Later, Jeremy finds a pair in a thrift store that are much too small, but gets them anyway. After much debate, Jeremy ends up giving his too-small shoes to another boy who is in need.	This book is called *Those Shoes*. What do you notice as you look at the cover? What are you thinking? What do you think Grandma means when she says, "There's no room for 'want' around here—just 'need'"? How do you think Jeremy is feeling when Mr. Alfrey gives him the hand-me-down shoes? Why do you think that? Let's reread this sentence: "The only kid not laughing is Antonio Parker." What does that tell you about Antonio? Why do you think Jeremy keeps saying, "I'm not going to do it!"? What are you inferring here? After reading: "What did you think of that story? What are you still wondering?"

FLUENCY FUN! POETRY PERFORMANCES

One obvious strategy for building fluency is repeated reading. To integrate this strategy into your classroom in a meaningful and joyful way, create opportunities for your students to practice and perform poetry for their classmates. To do this, gather a basket of poetry books, a plastic jar labeled "Poetry Performances," and some small slips of paper, and put them in or near your reading center or classroom library. During Explore the W.O.R.L.D. time or when they are done with their work, invite children to select a favorite poem to practice on their own or with a friend. Once they have practiced reading the poem enough that they can perform it fluently with expression, they write their name on a slip of paper and place it in the jar. To fill an extra minute here and there, draw a name from the jar and enjoy a poetry performance! Work with your students to develop criteria to determine if they are ready for a poetry performance. Here are the criteria we created with our students.

How to Prepare for a Poetry Performance
- Choose a poem that you, or you and your partner, enjoy
- Read the poem a few times. Notice the conventions the author uses as signals to the reader.
- Practice reading the poem aloud with style (read it smoothly with expression).
- Practice, practice, practice. If reading with a partner, practice reading it together (in unison) so it sounds like one voice.
- Write your name(s) on a poetry performance ticket and place the ticket in the jar.

When you have a few minutes, pull a ticket from the jar and enjoy a poetry performance!

MINI-LESSONS FOR VOCABULARY DEVELOPMENT: STUDYING HOMOPHONES

In this section, we continue our work on multiple-meaning words that we started at the beginning of the chapter. Homophones are the focus of the lessons that follow. As always, use what you know about your readers to determine the best teaching context for these lessons.

MINI-LESSON: Homophones—Foundation Lesson

Preparation: Read a book about homophones. For this lesson we read *Dear Deer: A Book of Homophones* (Barretta, 2007).

Explanation: Homophones are words that are pronounced the same but have different spellings and meaning. Words such as these pose a challenge for struggling readers and ELLs. Taking the time to introduce homophones and then pointing them out when you come across them in your read-alouds will help children become more familiar with this type of word.

Demonstration: After reading, go back and discuss some of the words in the book. Use visuals or invite students to act out the different meanings.

Invitation: "Word detectives, while reading, see if you notice any of the words we talked about today. Do you remember what they are called?"

MINI-LESSON: Homophones—Follow-Up Lesson

Preparation: Divide 15 pieces of paper in half and write a different set of homophones on each side of each page. Pair students with a word-study buddy.

hear/here	ate/eight	blue/blew	close/clothes	eye/I
hair/hare	knew/new	made/maid	one/won	red/read
sea/see	son/sun	tale/tail	mail/male	we/wee

Explanation: Certainly, two lessons on homophones will not be enough to cement this understanding for your young learners. After you've introduced homophones to your class and given them the opportunity to explore them with a partner, continue to highlight them when you read aloud and while guiding readers in small groups.

Demonstration: Use one of the homophone pairs to model how students will draw an illustration of the meaning of each homophone on their page.

Invitation: "Word detectives, you are going to work with your word-study buddy to create a poster that shows the meaning of each word on your paper. After you're finished, you'll share your work with the class."

READ-ALOUDS WITH RICH VOCABULARY		
Title and Author	**Brief Summary**	**Words to Highlight and Kid-Friendly Definition**
Birdsong (Sandall, 2010)	"One small bird, in a tree. Kitcha kitcha Kee kee kee" begins this inviting book. Students will join in making the different bird sounds as the birds gather on the branch until a butterfly joins them and… "CRACK."	**piercing**: when referring to a sound, extremely loud and high-pitched **splendid**: beautiful or grand **still**: not moving, calm

continued READ-ALOUDS WITH RICH VOCABULARY

Doodleday (Collins, 2011)	Harvey's mom warns him not to draw on "Doodleday" but he doesn't listen. When his drawings come to life and take over his house and neighborhood, his clever mom comes to the rescue.	**bellowed**: said something loudly and powerfully **furiously**: full of anger **nonsense**: rude or silly behavior
The Secret Shortcut (Teague, 1996)	At the beginning of the week, Wendell and Floyd are late for school because they've encountered space creatures, pirates, and a frog plague. To solve the problem, they decide to take a secret shortcut.	**clearing**: open land with no trees or bushes **dense**: thick and hard to see through **meandered**: walked back and forth

MINI-LESSONS FOR READING RESPONSE

By now your readers should be comfortable sharing their thinking in whole-group conversations, with partners, and in writing. To broaden their repertoire of responses to reading, we will share two poetry-related options. The first is simply writing poems about books. The second is a way for students to record their thought process as they read and think about a poem.

MINI-LESSON: Using Poetry as a Response to Reading

Preparation: Cut white drawing paper into about 50 3-by-8-inch strips for brainstorming words as a whole group and about 25 small strips per child for individual learners' words. Because our students bring index cards as a school supply, we use 3-by-5-inch cards cut in half so that they measure 1½ by 5 inches for students' paper strips/word cards. Keep a basket of extra word cards handy for students who need more than 25. If you have an interactive whiteboard, prepare an interactive whiteboard document to record students' words.

Explanation: Poetry is yet another way to teach students

A young writer plays with words to create a poem.

how to respond to their reading. In this mini-lesson, we'll share the process that we use to guide students in writing free-form poems.

Demonstration: Select a specific book or a topic that you and your students have read about. Invite students to share words or phrases about that topic, and record their responses on the 3-by-8-inch strips for use in the pocket chart or in your interactive whiteboard document. Then demonstrate how you can "play with the words," moving them around and adding other words, if needed, to create a poem. Once you've created one poem, mix up the words and try again. Continue with this demonstration until you feel that students are ready to try it on their own. At that time, give

Young poets play with words.

learners a bag of 25 small (1½-by-5-inch) paper strips. Invite them to record words about a book they've read, and then play with them until they've made a poem, adding words as needed.

Invitation: "Poets play with words to create a poem that tells about a specific topic or idea. Today you are going to create a poem about the book you've just read. If you need more paper strips, they are in this basket. Have fun playing with words!"

MINI-LESSON: Inferring With Poetry—Revising Our Thinking

Preparation: For this reading response mini-lesson, select a poem that offers opportunities to infer the meaning. We've found that many poems work well if you read them to students without reading the title. Two such poems are "Crayons: A Rainbow Poem" by Jane Yolen, found in *Poetry Speaks to Children* (Pashen, 2005), and "Cat Kisses" by Bobbi Katz, found in *Here's a Little Poem: A Very First Book of Poetry* (Yolen & Peters, 2007). Reproducible copies of these poems also appear in *Teaching Struggling Readers With Poetry* (Walther & Fuhler, 2010). Children record their thinking on the three-column notes page in their Read, Think, and Respond Book (CD Resource 1.7). Enlarge a copy of the three-column notes page for your demonstration.

Explanation: This lesson is designed to show learners how readers revise their thinking and understanding as they reread for meaning or have a conversation with a friend.

CD Resource 1.7

Demonstration: For this demonstration to be most effective, you will want to spend two days on it. This gives children time to really think about the poem. On the first day, read the poem aloud and invite students to write down their initial thoughts in first section of the three-column notes pages, labeled "I'm thinking . . ." Then, provide students with their own copies of the poem (with the title removed) to reread during the day. Encourage students to think about the poem when they have a few extra minutes. On the second day, reread the poem aloud and invite students to record their revised thinking (or same thinking) in the second box, labeled "After rereading, I'm thinking . . ." Next, provide time for students to read and discuss their thinking and responses with a peer. After their conversations, invite them to record their revised thinking in the third column, labeled "After talking, I'm thinking . . ." Finally, have a whole-class conversation about the poem and the process of reading, rereading, and talking, and how this process helped them to better understand or infer the meaning of the poem.

| I'm thinking . . . | After rereading, I'm thinking . . . | After talking, I'm thinking. . . |

Invitation: "What did you learn about yourself as a reader today? How did reading, rereading, and talking with a friend help you understand the poem? Remember what we did today when you are reading something that you find challenging. Rereading and talking about what you are reading will help you infer the author's meaning and better understand the text."

Part 3: Genre Study—Poetry

At the Illinois Reading Council Conference in March 2011, accomplished children's poet Jane Yolen spoke to teachers about sharing poetry with children. She stated emphatically that when children are learning a poem, first and foremost, let the children LOVE the poem. Read the poem once, and then read it again and again. Invite students who are interested to practice the poem and recite it from memory. When conversing about poetry, ask questions like, "How does the poem make you feel? What are the words that make you feel that way? What does the poem say to you?" Here you will find a small sampling of the wealth of fine poetry to read with your students.

GENRE STUDY: POETRY	
Title and Author	**Brief Summary**
Amazing Faces (Hopkins, 2010)	Chris Soenpiet's vibrant, realistic illustrations shine in this collection of 16 poems about people from diverse cultures. Two of our favorite poems are "Me x 2" by Jane Medina, about a child who speaks English and Spanish, and "I'm the One," Jude Mandell's poem about a boy who is excluded from the group. Some poems are more appropriate for intermediate-grade students.
Button Up! Wrinkled Rhymes (Schertle, 2009)	A collection of poems told from the point of view of different articles of clothing.

Falling Down the Page: A Book of List Poems (Heard, 2009)	This treasure trove of poems about life inside and outside school includes perfect poems for introducing various science topics, such as "Things to Do if You Are the Sun" by Bobbi Katz, or "Tree Song" by George Ella Lyon.
Guyku: A Year of Haiku for Boys (Raczka, 2010)	At the outset, Bob Raczka explains to readers that he wrote *Guyku* because these short but powerful poems are about nature, written in the present tense, and about stuff boys like to do!
Messing Around on the Monkey Bars and Other School Poems for Two Voices (Franco, 2009)	Build reading fluency with this assortment of poems about school, designed to be read aloud by two people. It includes a final section entitled "Adventurous Ways to Read the Poems."
My Dog May Be a Genius (Prelutsky, 2008)	Kids can't resist Prelutsky's humorous, kid-appealing anthologies illustrated by James Stevenson, which include *The New Kid on the Block* (1984), *Something Big Has Been Here* (1990), *A Pizza the Size of the Sun* (1996), and *It's Raining Pigs & Noodles* (2000).
Once I Ate a Pie (MacLachlan & Charest, 2006)	Poetic tales of 13 different dogs are written in free verse with a creative use of font size and word placement.
Orangutan Tongs: Poems to Tangle Your Tongue (Agee, 2009)	Your students will enjoy the challenge of repeating Agee's tongue-twisting rhymes like "Two Tree Toads" and "Purple Paper People."
Punctuation Celebration (Bruno, 2009)	Use this collection of 14 short, playful poems to introduce or review the various punctuation marks. Each poem is coupled with an example of a sentence, phrase, or paragraph using that particular mark.
Won Ton: A Cat Tale Told in Haiku (Wardlaw, 2011)	The story of a rescued shelter cat is told in a form of haiku called senryu, which is more concerned with human nature than nature itself. Pair this with *Oh, Theodore! Guinea Pig Poems* (Katz, 2007).

Meeting the Needs of ALL Learners

Poetry has endless possibilities for both striving and self-extending readers. Poems are ideal texts for guiding readers in small groups because they are short and easy to locate, yet rich in teaching opportunities. For example, select a poem filled with high-frequency sight words and, after chorally reading the poem a few times, invite learners to highlight the sight words, then reread the poem, clapping for each highlighted word. Obviously, poetry is helpful for fine-tuning fluency and much more enjoyable than other scripted methods. For advanced readers, choose poems with rich vocabulary. One of our students' favorite poems was Jack Prelutsky's "The Turkey Shot Out of the Oven," from *Something Big Has Been Here* (1990), which includes words such as *demolished, deafening, obscuring, displeasure,* and *chagrin*. We hope the two quick ideas found here help you begin "thinking poetry" for small-group instruction—you'll be happy you did!

SENSIBLE STRATEGIES FOR STRUGGLING READERS: HIGHLIGHTING WORD ENDINGS

Can You Dig It? and Other Poems (Weinstock, 2010) includes two poems that are ideal for focusing on word endings with either your struggling readers or ELLs. The title poem has many words with *-ed* endings, such as *cracked* and *aged*, so you can talk with your students about how the meaning of the word changes when the ending is added. For a poem that highlights *-ing* endings, choose "Diplodocus." For additional poetry-related lessons for struggling readers, see *Teaching Struggling Readers With Poetry* (Walther & Fuhler, 2010).

TARGETING TALENTED READERS: PUZZLING POETRY BOOKS

We recommend two poetry books that will tempt your talented readers to play with words in a unique way. In *Lemonade and Other Poems Squeezed From a Single Word* (2011), Bob Raczka writes each poem using different combinations of letters from just one word. After reading and thinking about this book with your students, challenge them to try their hand at their own single-word poems. In the amazing *Mirror Mirror: A Book of Reversible Verse* (Singer, 2010), Marilyn Singer introduces the concept of the "reverso." "When you read a reverso down," she writes, "it is one poem. When you read it up, with changes allowed only in punctuation and capitalization, it is a different poem." Invite your students to start with a simple three-line poem, then play with the words and punctuation to create their own reverso.

Final Thoughts

"Shout it! Shout it! POETRY! Fun for you and fun for me" wrote poet Brod Bagert in *Shout! Little Poems That Roar* (2007). Indeed, he says it well—poetry is fun. As teachers we need to take advantage of that. We can create joyful learning opportunities, celebrate language, and boost the reading skills of even the most reluctant reader by making poetry a part of our classroom routine every day. We encourage you to take the books and ideas your students enjoyed from this chapter and extend them across the school year to spread the joy of poetry.

CHAPTER 8: APRIL & MAY

Questioning and Determining Importance to Navigate Nonfiction

When we think about the skills that children are going to need as they continue through school and beyond, we recognize that one of our top priorities is helping them become wise consumers of information. Today's learners have instant access to facts at their fingertips. If they are looking for the answer to a question, they Google it and get hundreds of results. The next step is sifting through the results in order to identify reliable information. Understanding how to navigate nonfiction texts is a critical part of this process. Therefore, our students spend the last few months of school engaged in an in-depth study of how nonfiction texts work. To hone students' understanding of informational texts, we return to the comprehension strategies of questioning and determining importance. The chapter ends with a genre study that pairs fiction and nonfiction titles on the same topic to prompt discussions of the similarities and differences between the two types of texts. Prepare to embark on an exploration of the world of nonfiction with your learners!

Part 1: Reading-Related Morning Message Ideas and Samples

There is so much to explore in the genre of informational texts that the four messages here are just a starting point. You can reuse many of the messages found earlier in the book by giving them a nonfiction twist. For example, try the "Skip and Read Through Message" found on page 86 to introduce content-related vocabulary. On the other hand, instead of writing riddles about characters (page 112), write a riddle about a plant, a bug, or the sun. Think about shifting the responsibility of creating the message from yourself to your students. As described in our writing book, beginning in May we invite each student to be the "Writer of the Day" and take his or her turn creating, writing, and leading the class in the morning message. Often their ideas are much better than ours!

MORNING MESSAGE IDEA: SELF-MONITORING/DECODING— DECODING MULTISYLLABIC CONTENT-RELATED WORDS

Interactive Whiteboard Morning Message 8

For this message, display a collection of content-area words that vary in syllables; you may use IWB_MM_8 on the CD to get started. Invite students to sort the words by the number of syllables in each word. Once sorted, guide students to use letter and word chunks, prefixes, base words, and suffixes to decode each word. During your content-area instruction, provide experiences to help students gain an understanding of the meaning of each word.

MORNING MESSAGE SAMPLE

Let's Sort!

Can you read these words about Earth Day? How many syllables does each word have?

pollution   ecosystem
renewable   recycle
air   environment
endangered   natural
water   garbage

Topic	1 syllable	2 syllables	3 syllables	4 syllables	5 syllables
Weather	clouds, rain, fall, spring	lightning, thunder, winter, summer	hurricane, tornado	thermometer, humidity	precipitation, evaporation
Insects	egg, head	larva, pupa, adult, thorax	abdomen, predator, habitat	interaction	metamorphosis
Earth and Rocks	soil, rocks, crust, core	gravel, fossil, mantle, earthquake	minerals, igneous, volcano	metamorphic, geology	sedimentary

MORNING MESSAGE IDEA: COMPREHENSION—UNDERSTANDING TEXT FEATURES

In *Reality Checks* (2006), Tony Stead shares an idea for examining visual information in nonfiction texts by asking two related questions: "What can you see?" and "What can you prove?" This idea works well in the morning message. For this message, post or project a nonfiction text feature such as a map, labeled photograph, diagram, graph, and so on. Pose the two related questions and record students' responses. For example, when looking at a map of the United States, students may count 48 states, leaving out Alaska and Hawaii. So, on the "What Can You See?/What Can You Prove?" list they would say, "There are 48 states." The next day, analyze and revise the responses based on the visual information, providing an opportunity to teach children how to accurately read the visual information. In this case, point out the inset map of Alaska and Hawaii. Repeat this type of message with other nonfiction features.

MORNING MESSAGE SAMPLE

MORNING MESSAGE IDEA: VOCABULARY BUILDING—TEXT STRUCTURE SIGNAL WORDS

Informational texts are organized in various ways. The different nonfiction text structures include description, sequence, compare and contrast, cause and effect, question and answer, and problem and solution.

MORNING MESSAGE SAMPLE

Match the Signal Words and Phrases to the Informational Text Structures

Compare and Contrast Tell the similarities and differences between two or more facts, concepts, or ideas	Description Describe a topic by telling about the characteristics and giving examples	Sequence Organize facts in number or chronological order
alike	for example	first
unlike	resembles	after
compared to	the characteristics	next
on the other hand	such as	finally

CHAPTER 8: APRIL & MAY—QUESTIONING AND DETERMINING IMPORTANCE TO NAVIGATE NONFICTION / 197

To introduce various signal words that aid readers in identifying certain nonfiction text structures, invite learners to match the signal words to the corresponding text structure. This message would work well in the pocket chart or on an interactive whiteboard. In the sample, the signal words are correctly sorted. You will need to mix them up before beginning the message.

MORNING MESSAGE IDEA: READING RESPONSE—TRUE OR FALSE?

If you have not discovered Scholastic's True or False series, take a look! Each book has 22 content-related true-or-false questions. Each question is followed by a page turn with the answer found on the next page. The books are ideal for partner reading and are available on many topics in the primary-grade science curriculum, including storms, planets, rocks and minerals, and butterflies and caterpillars. The format of the books also sparks ideas for writing or for your morning message. To create interest in a topic or review content that you have already covered, write a few true-or-false statements. Read and discuss each statement to determine whether it is true or false. You may want to have a nonfiction book handy to read aloud to confirm the answers.

MORNING MESSAGE SAMPLE

True or False?

Insects have 6 legs. [True]

Spiders are insects. [False]

Insects have 2 body parts. [False]

The sun is a planet. [false]

Uranus is tilted on its side. [true]

Mars is a gas giant. [false]

POETRY POWER: POEMS FOR APRIL AND MAY	
Title	Brief Summary
Lemonade Sun and Other Summer Poems (Dotlich, 1998)	Save these poems for the end of the year, and then share the joys of summer as your read Dotlich's child-friendly poems.
Volcano Wakes Up! (Peters, 2010)	A day on an imaginary Hawaiian volcano is described from five different perspectives, including those of the fern, the lava flow cricket, the small black road, the sun and moon, and, of course, the volcano. The back matter tells a little about each perspective and may be helpful to read prior to reading the poems.

MORNING READ-ALOUDS: APRIL AND MAY—HOORAY!	
Title, Author, and Focus	**Brief Summary**
Arthur Turns Green (Brown, 2011) **Focus**: Earth Day	To celebrate Arthur's 35th anniversary, Marc Brown wrote this Arthur picture book, the first in almost ten years. In this adventure, Arthur and his classmates are working on a class project called "The Big Green Machine" to find ways to protect our planet.
Book Fiesta! Celebrate Children's Day/Book Day (Mora, 2009) **Focus**: Reading	In Mexico, April 30th is El Día del Niño, or the Day of the Child. This bilingual picture book celebrates both reading and children and would be a wonderful catalyst for a school-wide book fiesta.
The Boy Who Was Raised by Librarians (Morris, 2007) **Focus**: Nonfiction—Research	Melvin loves the public library and the reference-desk librarians. Whenever he's needed help with some research, they have been up for the challenge. Then he goes off to college, where he becomes a librarian himself, ready to help a young boy with his bug collection.
A Butterfly Is Patient (Aston, 2011) **Focus**: Read Like a Writer	The author-and-illustrator team behind *An Egg Is Quiet* (2006) and *A Seed Is Sleepy* (2007) join forces again in their distinctive style to inform readers about a variety of butterflies.
Christian the Lion (Bourke & Rendall, 2009) **Focus**: Nonfiction Features—Captions	This picture book is based on the true story of a young lion that was purchased from Harrod's department store in London by two men who cared for him and eventually set him free in Africa. The story is presented in a scrapbook style with captioned photos throughout, making it ideal for teaching students how to write captions!
Compost Stew: An A to Z Recipe for the Earth (Siddals, 2010) **Focus**: Earth Day	Read aloud this rhyming alphabet book to discover an A-to-Z recipe for making compost. Pair this with *Garbage Helps Our Garden Grow: A Compost Story* (Glaser, 2010).
Energy Island: How One Community Harnessed the Wind and Changed Their World (Drummond, 2011) **Focus**: Earth Day	The true story of how a teacher named Søren Hermansen led an energy independence project on Samsø Island in Denmark, and gradually convinced the community to join in. The island reduced its carbon emissions by 140 percent in just ten years.
Oh No! Or How My Science Project Destroyed the World (Barnett, 2010) **Focus**: Science	Part comic book and part 1950s monster movie, this nearly wordless picture book is a surefire hit for your graphic novel fans. What makes it even more delightful is that the main character is a pigtailed girl who is trying to control her prize-winning robot.
Our Tree Named Steve (Zweibel, 2005) **Focus**: Plants	In a letter to his children, a dad recounts all the family memories surrounding the tree that two-year-old Sari named "Steve." On the last page, readers have to infer what happened to the tree. Pair with Shel Silverstein's *The Giving Tree* (1964).
Tyrannosaurus Dad (Rosenberg, 2011) **Focus**: Father's Day	If you are looking for a comical Father's Day book to read at the end of the school year, try this one. Tobias's father is busy, hardworking, and a lot like other fathers, except he is a dinosaur. In the end, Dad joins Tobias and his friends for a fun field day baseball game.

Part 2: A Menu of Reading Workshop Mini-Lessons

As children make the transition from "learning to read" to "reading to learn," we support them by demonstrating that reading informational text is different from reading a fiction text. The mini-lessons that follow teach students how to use questions to determine the key ideas and details in a text in order to make connections between events, ideas, or information found in a nonfiction book. To be proficient readers of informational texts, readers have to understand how nonfiction texts are structured. To that end, we have included mini-lessons that highlight nonfiction text features and show how visual information helps readers understand the content.

Children need ample time to read informational texts.

MINI-LESSONS FOR SELF-MONITORING/DECODING STRATEGY INSTRUCTION

Proficient readers of nonfiction texts are adept at using the text features to locate key facts or additional information. We've designed the mini-lesson below to be repeated with different kinds of nonfiction features. The features you choose to focus on will vary, depending on the needs of your readers. This mini-lesson can be done with the whole class or while guiding readers in small groups.

MINI-LESSON: Using Visual Information to Pause, Think, and Check for Understanding

Preparation: Gather a few nonfiction texts or informational websites that contain text features such as headings, bold print, captions, maps, charts, graphs, and so on. Select a specific feature and display the page with that feature using a document camera or on an interactive whiteboard. A nonfiction Big Book also works well for this lesson.

Explanation: When children read nonfiction books they need to learn how to move back and forth between the text on the page and the visual supports the author has provided. The aim of this series of mini-lessons is to focus on one feature at a time and model how that particular feature will help readers access information.

Demonstration: Begin your demonstration by modeling how you access information from a visual feature in an informational text. Say, "Let's take a look at this [nonfiction text feature]. What can we learn from 'reading' this visual information?" Invite students to share their learning and record their responses. Point out how that feature relates to the rest of the text on the page. Continue with similar demonstrations throughout your study of nonfiction texts. Focus on the importance of taking time to pause, think, and check for understanding when viewing text features. Once students are familiar with different features, invite them to find features in the texts they are reading and share what they learn from that particular feature.

Students notice how the nonfiction features help them as readers.

Invitation: "Nonfiction experts, while you are reading today, notice how the features in the book help you as a reader. Remember to pause, think, and check for understanding as you read."

MINI-LESSONS FOR COMPREHENSION STRATEGY INSTRUCTION

Although readers use many of the same comprehension strategies to tackle informational text, they apply the strategy in a different way. For example, readers ask questions to determine the accuracy of the content, to clarify the visual information, and to check their understanding of the concepts presented in the text. Therefore, the types of questions a reader of nonfiction asks differ from those of someone reading a piece of fiction. Additionally, the purpose of visual information in a nonfiction text differs from that of illustrations found in a picture book. Because of this, readers need to know how to determine the importance of such features and use them to deepen their understanding.

MINI-LESSON: Questioning in Nonfiction Read-Aloud/Think-Aloud—Foundation Lesson

Preparation: Display the strategy song "Questioning" (CD Resource 6.1) and the Comprehension Strategy Wheel (CD Resource 3.5). Select a short, engaging nonfiction book or a chapter or section from a longer book.

Explanation: While reading nonfiction texts, the process of asking questions leads to deeper understanding and

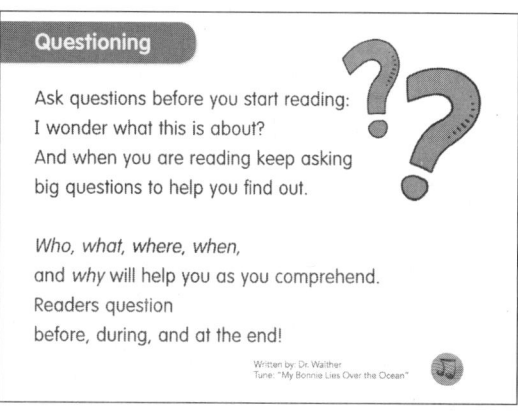

CD Resource 6.1 and IWB_Song_6.1

future discoveries. When we model how readers ask open-ended questions to further their learning, we show students how to pause, think, and check for understanding. While most questions target comprehension, other questions lead to critical thinking about the accuracy of the content and the author's bias. Still other queries spark further research to discover the answers to questions that remain after reading.

Demonstration: As you prepare for this read-aloud/think-aloud demonstration, jot questions on sticky notes and place them in the book you are going to read (so that you will have them ready for next year!). Plan to model the different types of ques-

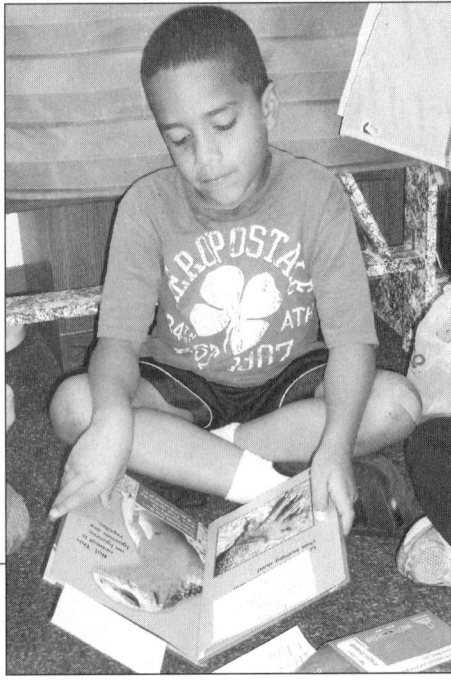
Readers jot questions on sticky notes.

READ-ALOUD/THINK-ALOUD QUESTIONS AND REFLECTIONS

Before Reading—What I'm thinking and wondering . . .
I wonder what I'll learn from reading this book.
I wonder when this book was published. Is the information current or out of date?
I wonder how the author has organized the information. Let me check to see if there's a table of contents or other clues.
I wonder what nonfiction features I will find in this book. I think I will take a quick picture walk to find out.

During Reading—What I'm thinking and wondering . . .
I'm not sure what this word means. I am going to finish the sentence and look at the text features to see if I can figure it out. Is there a glossary that can help me?
Wait! I don't understand this. I wonder what the author is trying to teach me here. Let me reread this part.
As I look at this photograph (graph, map, and so on), I'm wondering what I can learn about . . .
Why did the author choose this particular feature? What information can I learn from it?
Wow! This is really interesting! I wonder how the writer was able to make me feel so excited about this information.

After Reading—What I'm thinking and wondering . . .
The author didn't tell me anything about _____. I wonder where I could learn more about that.
Reading this book made me curious about . . .
If I were to pick three main ideas, they would be . . .
I wonder what the author wanted me to understand after reading this book.

(Adapted from Hoyt, 2002, pp. 119–120)

CD Resource 8.1

tions you want your readers to ask as they read informational texts. For different types of questions, see page 202. To begin this demonstration, review the questioning strategy by singing the strategy song "Questioning" and pointing it out on the Comprehension Strategy Wheel. If you have an interactive whiteboard, display IWB_Song_6.1 and press the musical note to play the tune. Then, continue by reading aloud and thinking aloud.

Invitation: "Readers, today I'd like you to choose a nonfiction book from your book box [or classroom library]. Think about the questions that pop up as you read. If it would help you to jot your questions down, take a sticky note and pencil with you. We'll share our questions at the end of reading workshop."

Encourage children to ask questions as they read nonfiction texts.

MINI-LESSON: Questioning in Nonfiction Read-Aloud/Think-Together Follow-Up Lesson

Preparation: Display the strategy song "Questioning" (CD Resource 6.1 and IWB_Song_6.1) and the Comprehension Strategy Wheel (CD Resource 3.5).

Explanation: In this lesson, we invite our listeners to ask questions before, during, and after reading while we give descriptive feedback as to how that question will help them as readers of informational text.

Demonstration: As you prepare for this read-aloud/think-together demonstration, read the title and back cover blurb, then look at the illustrations on the front and back cover. Ask, "What are you wondering before we begin reading?" Jot questions on sticky notes and post them on the chart. Quickly discuss how a particular question will help them as readers. Continue this process as you read the book. Try not to interrupt the flow by stopping too often. Conclude by asking, "What are you still wondering?" Close the lesson by singing the strategy song "Questioning."

Invitation: "Readers, today I'd like you to continue reading the nonfiction book you chose yesterday. Think about the questions that pop up as you read. If it would help you to jot your questions down, take a sticky note and pencil with you. Also, think about how asking questions helps you as a reader. We'll share our questions and our thinking at the end of reading workshop."

MINI-LESSON: Determining Importance Using Nonfiction Features— Foundation Lesson

Preparation: Gather informational texts that have clear and understandable features. It is helpful to keep your nonfiction titles separate from the fiction titles in your classroom library. Display the strategy song "Determining Importance" (CD Resource 8.2) and the Comprehension Strategy Wheel (CD Resource 3.5).

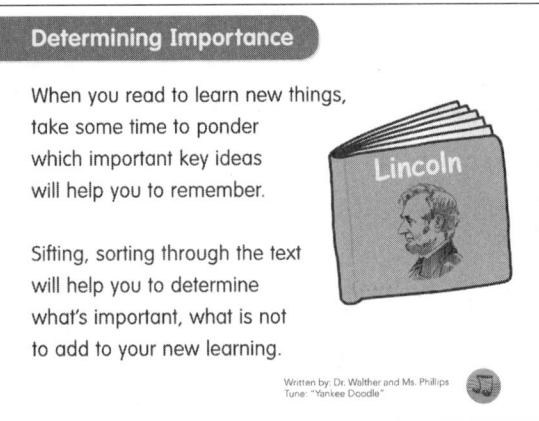

CD Resource 8.2 and IWB_Song_8.2

Explanation: The two Determining Importance Using Nonfiction Features lessons go hand-in-hand with the Pause, Think, and Check for Understanding lesson on page 112. The difference between the two is that in the lesson on page 202, you are guiding readers as they learn how to access information from various nonfiction features—in other words, teaching children how to read a map, understand a chart, or find a word in the glossary. In this lesson and the follow-up lesson, students are determining the purpose of the feature and figuring out how that particular feature helps them ascertain the most important information in the text. For example, features like the table of contents and chapter or section headings serve as advanced organizers for readers.

Demonstration: Introduce the strategy song "Determining Importance," and invite children to sing along. If you have an interactive whiteboard, display IWB_Song_8.2 and press the musical note to play the tune. Next, read aloud part of a nonfiction Big Book or other text that is brimming with nonfiction features. Pause to point out and discuss a feature, its purpose, and how it helps readers better understand the text and determine the most important information. Begin a chart to record your findings.

Invitation: "Readers, today as you are learning from a nonfiction book, notice any nonfiction features. Think about why the author chose to put it on that page and what you learn from studying the feature. How does that information add to what you've learned from the text?"

MINI-LESSON: Determining Importance Using Nonfiction Features—Follow-Up Lesson

Preparation: Gather informational texts that have clear and understandable features. It is helpful to keep your nonfiction titles separate from the fiction titles in your classroom library. For this mini-lesson, each child will need three or four nonfiction books.

Gather informational texts with clear and understandable text features.

Explanation: The goal of this mini-lesson is to release the responsibility to students as they determine the purpose of various nonfiction features.

Demonstration: Once students are familiar with nonfiction features, organize them into partners or small groups and give each pair or group three or four sticky notes. Send students on a scavenger hunt through a few nonfiction books to look for additional features and determine their purpose. Share and discuss the features and their purposes as you add to the chart.

Sara shares a nonfiction feature and its purpose.

Invitation: "Readers, today as you are learning from a nonfiction book, notice any nonfiction features and determine each feature's purpose. Think about why the author chose to put it on that page and what you learn from studying the feature. Record your thinking on a sticky note to bring with you when we share."

MINI-LESSON: Inferring Big Ideas with Earth Day Books

Preparation: Select a few books about Earth Day that offer opportunities to infer the big idea or central message of the texts. Below you will find a few of our favorites.

Title and Author	Brief Summary
The Great Kapok Tree: A Tale of the Amazon Rain Forest (Cherry, 1990)	A man enters the rain forest to chop down the Kapok tree and falls asleep. As he is sleeping, the animals tell him all the reasons to leave the tree standing.
Just a Dream (Van Allsburg, 1990)	Walter wants to live in the future but doesn't care about taking care of the Earth today. When he wakes up from a dream that takes him to a polluted future, his behavior changes.
Rain Forest (Cowcher, 1988)	Something is stirring in the rain forest and the animals are terrified. Readers have to infer what is happening until the danger is revealed near the end of the book.
The Wump World (Peet, 1970)	The Wumps are living happily in their world until the Pollutians invade and destroy their planet.

Explanation: To build on the inferring mini-lesson found on page 186, we've used the four Earth Day books listed here for inferring big ideas.

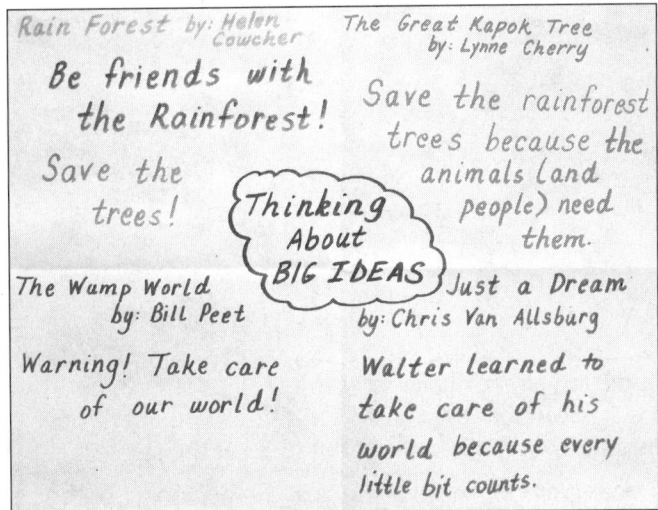

Record children's thinking about the big idea in these books about Earth Day.

An Earth Day morning message

Demonstration: As part of your regular read-aloud routine, read and discuss one book each day. After reading aloud, converse about the big idea or author's message. As a culminating activity, collect Earth-saving tips in the morning message. (See photo.)

Invitation: "Think about the big idea in the book we read today. What little things can you do to help our world?"

READ-ALOUDS THAT SPARK COMPREHENSION CONVERSATIONS	
Title, Author, Focus, and Brief Summary	**A Few Questions to Spark Your Conversation**
Cloudette (Lichtenheld, 2011) **Focus:** Inferring **Summary:** Little Cloudette wants to do big and important things like her fellow clouds. When a storm blows her to a new neighborhood, she discovers that even a little cloud can make a big difference.	"Usually Cloudette didn't mind being smaller than the average cloud." What are you inferring here? What does Tom mean by "Being small had lots of advantages"? How do you think Cloudette feels when the other clouds go off to do something important? "This gave Cloudette an idea . . ." What are you predicting? What makes you think that? What do you think Tom Lichtenheld is trying to tell us in this book? What is the big idea?

Redwoods (Chin, 2009) **Focus**: Fiction or Nonfiction? **Summary**: Readers must begin this book before the title page to see the boy picking up the book *Redwoods* while waiting for the subway. What follows is a clever blend of fantasy illustrations, and factual text about the giant trees.	Let's look at the title and wraparound cover. Do you think this is a fiction or nonfiction book? Notice the illustration before the title page—what is the boy doing? Wait! There are dinosaurs outside the subway window. What is going on here? Listen to the text. What are you thinking now, fiction or nonfiction? Wow, Jason Chin did something unique as an author and illustrator. Let's talk about it!
Stable (Lewin, 2010) **Focus**: Read Like a Writer **Summary**: Learn about the history of Kensington Stables in Brooklyn, New York, and the horses that still live and work there.	What schema do you already have for stables? Have any of you ever been to a stable? What did you do there? Can you infer from the cover illustration what this girl is going to do at the stable? What do you notice about the illustrations at the beginning of the book? How do they change as the book continues? What does Lewin mean when he says that the stable is a "relic of a bygone era"? How did the ending make you feel? What are thinking? What are you wondering?

MINI-LESSONS FOR VOCABULARY DEVELOPMENT: THE LANGUAGE OF NONFICTION

It is especially important for ELLs that we provide multiple ways for students to build background in order to understand content-related vocabulary. The two mini-lessons in this section are helpful because you can use either lesson to introduce words prior to any science or social studies unit.

MINI-LESSON: Preview-Predict-Confirm

Preparation: Choose a text rich with pictures and other visuals. For this lesson we used the book *Our Earth* (Rockwell, 1998). Divide the class into four or five small groups. Assign one child in each group to be the recorder. Have a set of

FLUENCY FUN! NONFICTION POETRY

Using poetry to introduce a nonfiction topic is an ideal way to weave fluency instruction into content-area teaching. There are many informational poetry collections to share with your students. Here are just a few titles to add fluency fun to your content-area instruction:

Days to Celebrate: A Full Year of Poetry, People, Holidays, History, Fascinating Facts, and More (Hopkins, 2005)

Scien-trickery: Riddles in Science (Lewis, 2004)

Spectacular Science: A Book of Poems (Hopkins, 1999)

Toad by the Road: A Year in the Life of These Amazing Amphibians (Ryder, 2007)

A World of Wonders: Geographic Travels in Verse and Rhyme (Lewis, 2002)

index cards and a marker ready for each group.

Explanation: Use this vocabulary-building activity developed by Hallie and Ruth Yopp (2006) to launch any content-area study. We suggest planning two days to complete the experience.

Demonstration: Show the students all the pictures and visuals in the book without reading any of the words. If you have a document camera or interactive whiteboard, you can display enlarged illustrations. Close the book and demonstrate making a prediction about the words you think the author might use in the book. Say something like, "I predict the author used the word *earth* in this book, because I saw many illustrations of the earth. I'll write that word on this index card." Invite learners to share another word or two and record them on index cards.

After previewing the book, a child predicts the words she might find in a book about the earth.

Invitation:

Day 1: "Today you are going to work with your group to predict what words you think the author used in this text. The recorder will write down the words as you take turns sharing your ideas. Happy predicting!"

Day 2: "Today I will show you the illustrations again, and then you can add a few more words to your collection. After writing the words, sort your words into meaning-based categories and label each group of words." When it is time to share, ask students to agree on one word that they think all the other groups *will* have and one word they think is unique and the other groups *won't* have. Share and discuss the words with the class. After the discussion, read the book to compare students' vocabulary with the vocabulary in the text.

MINI-LESSON: Categorizing Content-Area Words
Interactive Whiteboard Lesson 8

Preparation: Write down all the content-related vocabulary words that you will be using during an upcoming unit of study. We've included a few sample sorting activities in IWB_Lesson_8. To do on open-ended sorting activity in pairs or small groups, make a grid on a piece of paper and write one word in each section of the grid. Then, copy the paper and distribute to students. Invite learners to cut apart and sort the words into different categories, and then label each category. To do a teacher-directed sort, determine the categories prior to the sorting activity and work with students to sort the words into the predetermined categories.

Explanation: It goes without saying that the best way to develop a child's vocabulary in math, science, or social studies is through hands-on, interactive experiences. To that end, any lesson on content-area vocabulary should be coupled with real, concrete experience to provide a background for the word knowledge. There are many other resources that can help you develop these experiences. Our focus here is on guiding children as they learn the words and think about them in different contexts.

Demonstration: For your demonstration, select categories that make sense with the content-area words, and then invite students to sort the words into those specific categories. You can follow this teacher-directed sort with additional opened-ended sorting activities.

PLANTS		
Types of Plants	**Plant Parts**	**Plant Needs**
grass	roots	water
bushes	leaves	light
trees	stem	air
flowers	flower	soil

BODY UNIT			
Brain	**Heart**	**Lungs**	**Stomach**
computer	blood	expand	digest
think	pump	oxygen	swallow

ANIMAL UNIT			
Mammals	**Amphibians**	**Reptiles**	**Insects**
rabbit	frog	snake	ant
elephant	salamander	alligator	bee
wolf	newt	crocodile	ladybug
tiger	toad	chameleon	butterfly

Invitation: "When readers come across a new word, they think about what other words they already know that they can connect to the new word to help them understand its meaning. I just love learning new words, don't you?"

READ-ALOUDS WITH RICH VOCABULARY

Title and Author	Brief Summary	Words to Highlight and Kid-Friendly Definition
Gumption! (Broach, 2010)	Uncle Nigel and Peter go on an African expedition and encounter many challenges. With gumption, and the help of the animals, Peter manages to keep up with his uncle. Readers will enjoy the humorous pictures showing that Uncle Nigel has no idea that Peter's adventures are occurring. Pair this with *Officer Buckle and Gloria* (Rathmann, 1995) to discuss how both books' illustrations add to the humor of the story.	**expedition**: a trip that is taken for a certain reason **gumption**: bravery **peered**: looked hard or closely at something to see it better
Strange Creatures: The Story of Walter Rothschild and His Museum (Judge, 2011)	The story of a painfully shy boy who followed his dream and his love of animals to create a museum of natural history.	**overheard**: heard what someone was saying without his or her knowing **reluctantly**: unwillingly **revolutionize**: to completely change or transform something
Velma Gratch & the Way Cool Butterfly (Madison, 2007)	In trying to find a personal interest that will get her noticed, Velma discovers butterflies. This book includes interesting content-related vocabulary, such as *metamorphosis* and *migration*, for you to introduce to your students.	**lamented**: expressed sorrow (sadness) or complained **perched**: rested or sat on a branch or bar **precisely**: clearly and with attention to details

MINI-LESSONS FOR READING RESPONSE

To round out the menu of response options, we've chosen two quick ways that readers can demonstrate their understanding of a topic.

MINI-LESSON: Compile a Fact Web

Preparation: Copy and display a web graphic organizer (CD Resource 1.4). Select a short, engaging nonfiction book or a chapter or section from a longer book.

Explanation: In order to complete a fact web, students have to be able to determine the most important information that they have learned from reading the text.

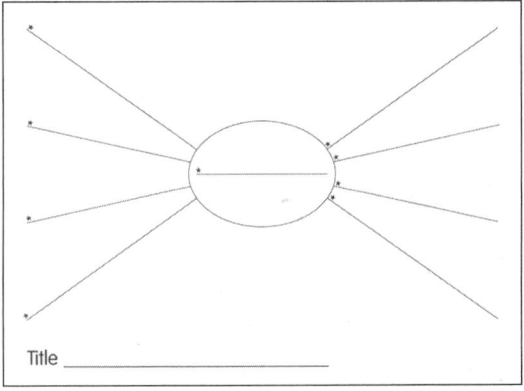

CD Resource 1.4

210 / MONTH-BY-MONTH READING INSTRUCTION FOR THE DIFFERENTIATED CLASSROOM

Demonstration: As you read aloud a nonfiction book, demonstrate how you determine the most important information using the nonfiction text features. Jot each fact on a sticky note. After reading the text, sort your sticky notes to determine the most crucial information. Record each important fact on the web.

Invitation: "Researchers, while you are reading today, jot on a sticky note the most important facts you've learned. Then, determine which of these fact you think should go on your fact web."

MINI-LESSON: List the Top Ten Facts You Learned

Preparation: Copy and display Top Ten Facts page (CD Resource 8.3). Select a short, engaging nonfiction book or a chapter or section from a longer book.

Explanation: In order to complete a Top Ten Facts page, students have to be able to determine the most important information that they have learned from reading the text. Then, to further their understanding, they will arrange the facts in number order from 1 (most important) to 10 (least important).

Demonstration: As you read aloud a nonfiction book, demonstrate how you determine the most important information, using the nonfiction text features. Jot each fact on a sticky note. After reading, arrange your sticky notes according to level of importance, from the most important fact to the least important. Record each important fact on the Top Ten Facts page.

Invitation: "Researchers, while you are reading today, jot on a sticky note the most important facts that you've learned. Then, determine which of these facts you think should go on your fact web and their order of importance. Fact number 1 should be the most important fact and fact number 10 will be the least important fact."

Part 3: Genre Study—Pairing Fiction and Nonfiction

When we look for ways to incorporate nonfiction into our busy day, pairing fiction with nonfiction titles simply makes sense. Reading a pair of books on the same topic provides opportunities to compare and contrast the texts from both a reader's and a writer's point of view. Fiction titles often lead students to ask questions that are quickly answered by doing a little research in a paired nonfiction book. Having paired sets at your fingertips makes this a bit easier. By reading aloud nonfiction books, we are balancing the types of books we read to children. Consider how this works in the science curriculum by sampling a few of the paired titles found in this genre study. To introduce this genre study, display and sing the "Nonfiction" song (CD Resource 8.4). If you have an interactive whiteboard, access IWB_Song_8.4 and press the musical note to play the tune.

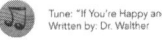

Books that tell stories are called fiction.
Books that help you learn facts are nonfiction.
Nonfiction books help you study.
You can read them with a buddy!
Learn about any topic with nonfiction.

Tune: "If You're Happy and You Know It"
Written by: Dr. Walther

CD Resource 8.4 and IWB_Song_8.4

GENRE STUDY: PAIRED FICTION AND NONFICTION	
Fiction Titles	**Nonfiction Titles**
Animals	
Barry B. Wary (Muir, 2011) *Scaredy Squirrel* (Watt, 2006) *Don't Eat the Teacher* (Ward, 1998) *Horton Hears a Who!* (Seuss, 1954/1982) *Sneaky Sheep* (Monroe, 2010)	*Spiders* (Bishop, 2007) *Flying Squirrels* (Jango-Cohen, 2004) *Surprising Sharks* (Davies, 2003) *Desert Elephants* (Cowcher, 2011) *Brave Dogs, Gentle Dogs: How They Guard Sheep* (Urbigkit, 2005)
Earth Day/Nature	
Ants in Your Pants, Worms in Your Plants! (*Gilbert Goes Green*) (deGroat, 2011) *Cloudette* (Lichtenheld, 2011) *I Stink* (McMullan, 2002) *The Rain Came Down* (Shannon, 2000) *The Rattlebang Picnic* (Mahy, 1994)	*Earth Day* (Trueit, 2007) *Clouds* (Rockwell, 2008) *Where Does the Garbage Go?* (Showers, 1974/1994) *Volcanoes* (Walker, 2008)

Meeting the Needs of ALL Learners

Dick Allington reminds us that children who do not read during the summer months experience a "summer reading loss." The two groups of learners most affected are struggling readers and children from economically disadvantaged backgrounds. To learn more about summer reading loss, go to Dr. Allington's Web site, teachersread.net. Although you may be reading this chapter in April, it is not too early to think about ways you can support your readers and their families during the summer months. In addition to sending a list of summer reading suggestions, you could e-mail your students' families a periodic "book blast" alerting them to new books or other reading-related events that they might want to check out at the local library. Also, a periodic message simply reminding parents how important it is to encourage summer reading could be a gentle nudge that makes a difference. For those readers who do not come from book-rich homes, consider collecting books from your classroom library and from other teachers who are cleaning and sorting their materials at the end of the year, to make a summer reading bag. For your advanced learners, summer reading is usually not a problem, so we've focused the Targeting Talented Readers section on extending the learning they've done about nonfiction to an independent study project to ask and answer questions as they learn more about a favorite animal.

SENSIBLE STRATEGIES FOR STRUGGLING READERS: SUMMER READING LIST

To combat summer reading loss, many of us compile or collect lists of suggested summer reading titles to share with children. While these are certainly a helpful resource, a personalized list may be more inviting to reluctant readers. In *The Reading Zone* (2007), Nancie Atwell suggests having students create their own Kids Recommend Pages and post them on the school or library Web site. You can view her Kids Recommend pages at www.c-t-l.org. To create the list, ask your students to suggest 10–12 beloved books that they believe will spark a reluctant reader's interest in reading. We have done this with our first graders for the past few years. In our classrooms, we ask each student to choose the one book or chapter that he or she wants to hear us read aloud again. To refresh their memories during the week that they are choosing their favorites, we place "old favorite" books all over the classroom. This helps learners select some of the books that you read early in the year, rather than the titles you most recently completed. Repeatedly these recommendations include titles that are part of a series. This makes sense for beginning readers, because when children become familiar with an author's writing style and characters, they gain the background knowledge and vocabulary needed to support them as they continue to read (Walther & Fuhler, 2009). During the last weeks of school, we post the titles on a chart, read them all aloud, and then send the list home to spark summer reading.

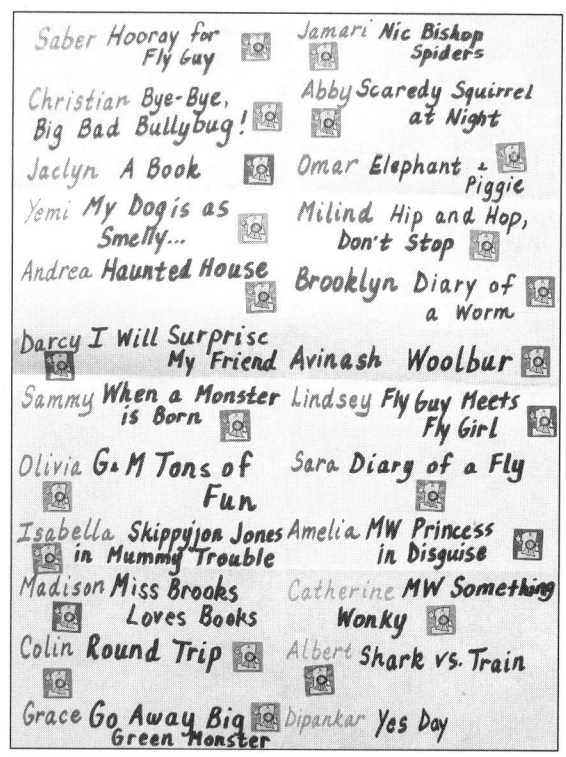

First graders' favorite read-aloud books make an ideal summer reading list.

TARGETING TALENTED READERS: ANIMAL RESEARCH

Invite students to select an animal that they are interested in learning more about. Then, to guide learners' research, ask them to write down the specific questions they have about that particular animal. Based on those questions, students collect nonfiction books, magazines, or digital information sources. We've found *Zoobooks* magazines to be a helpful resource for this project. Once children gather their research, provide different ways for them to present the information to the class. Encourage students to use text features to share this information with their readers.

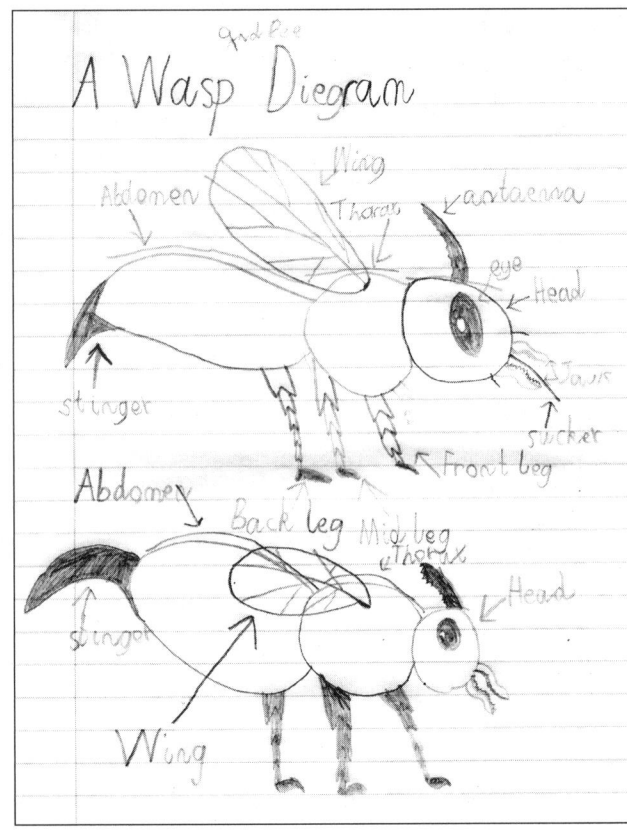

A child uses text features to share his learning with the class.

Final Thoughts

As always, the end of the school year is a time of both joy and sadness. When you look around your classroom during the last months of school, you observe children applying all that they have learned during the year. You marvel at their insightful observations about the books they read, and how they think, converse, and write about them. It is always sad to say good-bye to a class of students. The joy comes in looking ahead to next year, a fresh start. With renewed enthusiasm, we purchase professional books, attend conferences, and think about how we can refine our instruction. That is what dedicated, reflective professionals like you do. We'll be joining you in that reflection, and we will be thinking about you when you're at the beach, near the pool, digging in your garden, biking, running, or relaxing. Take time to rejuvenate—a new school year will be here before we know it!

PROFESSIONAL RESOURCES CITED

Allington, R. L. (2006). *What really matters for struggling readers: Designing research-based programs* (2nd ed.). New York: Allyn & Bacon.

Atwell, N. (2007). *The reading zone: How to help kids become skilled, passionate, habitual, critical readers.* New York: Scholastic.

Boushey, G., & Moser, J. (2006). *The daily five: Fostering literacy independence in the elementary grades.* Portland, ME: Stenhouse.

Calmenson, S. (2005). *Kindergarten kids: Riddles, rebuses, wiggles, giggles, and more!* New York: HarperCollins.

Celic, C. M. (2009). *English language learners day by day, K–6: A complete guide to literacy, content-area, and language instruction.* Portsmouth, NH: Heinemann.

Collins, K. (2004). *Growing readers: Units of study in the primary classroom.* Portland, ME: Stenhouse.

Cunningham, P. (2009a). *Phonics they use: Words for reading and writing* (5th ed.). New York: Pearson.

Cunningham, P. M. (2009b). *What really matters in vocabulary: Research-based practices across the curriculum.* New York: Allyn & Bacon.

Evans, M. D. R., Kelley, J., Sikora, J., & Treiman, D. J. (2010). Family scholarly culture and educational success: Books and schooling in 27 nations. *Research in Social Stratification and Mobility, 28*(2), 171–197.

Fountas, I. C., & Pinnell, G. S. (1996). *Guided reading: Good first teaching for all children.* Portsmouth, NH: Heinemann.

Fountas, I. C., & Pinnell, G. S. (1999). *Matching books to readers: Using leveled books in guided reading K-5.* Portsmouth, NH: Heinemann.

Fountas, I. C., & Pinnell, G. S. (2009). *The Fountas & Pinnell leveled book list, K–8+: 2010–2012 edition.* Portsmouth, NH: Heinemann.

Fuhler, C. J., & Walther, M. P. (2007). *Literature is back! Using the best books for teaching readers and writers across genres.* New York: Scholastic.

Graham, S., & Hebert, M. A. (2010). Writing to read: Evidence for how writing can improve reading. *A Carnegie Corporation Time to Act Report.* Washington, D.C.,: Alliance for Excellent Education.

Harvey, S. (2002). Nonfiction inquiry: Using real reading and writing to explore the world. *Language Arts, 80*(1), 12–22.

Harvey, S., & Goudvis, A. (2000). *Strategies that work: Teaching comprehension to enhance understanding.* York, ME: Stenhouse.

Hoyt, L. (2002). *Make it real: Strategies for success with informational texts.* Portsmouth, NH: Heinemann.

Hoyt, L. (1999). *Revisit, reflect, retell.* Portsmouth, NH: Heinemann.

Hoyt, L. (2000). *Snapshots: Literacy mini-lessons up close.* Portsmouth, NH: Heinemann.

Hoyt, L. (2005). *Spotlight on comprehension: Building a literacy of thoughtfulness.* Portsmouth, NH: Heinemann.

Johnston, P. H. (2004). *Choice words.* Portland, ME: Stenhouse.

Knipper, K. J., & Duggan, T. J. (2006). Writing to learn across the curriculum: Tools for comprehension in content area classes. *The Reading Teacher, 59*(5), 462–470.

Layne, S. L. (2009). *Igniting a passion for reading: Successful strategies for building lifetime readers.* Portland, ME: Stenhouse.

Miller, D. (2002). *Reading with meaning.* Portland, ME: Stenhouse.

Miller, D. (2008). *Teaching with intention: Defining beliefs, aligning practice, taking action.* Portland: ME: Stenhouse.

National Board for Professional Teaching Standards (2001). *Early childhood generalist standards* (2nd ed.).

National Governors Association Center for Best Practices (NGA Center) and Council of Chief State School Officers (CCSSO) (2010). *Common core state standards initiative.* Washington, DC (www.corestandards.org)

Nations, S., & Alonso, M. (2001). *Primary literacy centers: Making reading and writing STICK!* Gainesville, FL: Maupin House.

Partnership for 21st Century Skills. (2009). *A framework for 21st century learning.* Tucson, AZ: Author.

Richard-Amato, P. A. (2003). *Making it happen: From interactive to participatory language teaching* (3rd ed.). New York: Pearson.

Routman, R. (2003). *Reading essentials: The specifics you need to teach reading well.* Portsmouth, NH: Heinemann.

Routman, R. (2008). *Teaching essentials: Expecting the most and getting the best from every learner, K–8.* Portsmouth, NH: Heinemann.

Stead, T. (2006). *Reality checks: Teaching reading comprehension with nonfiction K–5.* Portland, ME: Stenhouse.

Vardell, S. M. (2009). Everyday poetry. *Book Links,18*(3), 44–47.

Vardell, S. M. (2011). Everyday poetry: Poetry tag. *Book Links,* ___.

Vogt, M., & Echevarria, J. (2008). *99 ideas and activities for teaching English learners with the SIOP® model.* New York: Pearson.

Walther, M. P., & Fuhler, C. J. (2009). Making every book count: Supporting summer readers. *Book Links, 18* (5), 45–46.

Walther, M. P., & Fuhler, C. J. (2010). *Teaching struggling readers with poetry: Engaging poems with mini-lessons that target & teach phonics, sight words, fluency & more—Laying the foundation for reading success.* New York: Scholastic.

Walther, M. P., & Phillips, K. P. (2009). *Month-by-month trait-based writing instruction: Ready-to-use lessons and strategies for weaving morning messages, read-alouds, mentor texts, and more into your daily writing program.* New York: Scholastic.

Yopp, H. K., & Yopp, R. H. (2006). Primary students and informational text. *Science and Children* 44(3), 22–25.

CHILDREN'S LITERATURE CITED

Chapter 2: September: Setting the Stage

Al Abdullah, R., & DiPucchio, K. (2010). *The sandwich swap.* New York: Hyperion.

Allard, H. (1977). *Miss Nelson is missing.* Boston: Houghton Mifflin.

Allen, S., & Lindaman, J. (2003). *Read anything good lately?* Millbrook.

Amado, E. (2011). *What are you doing?* Toronto: Groundwood.

Baker, J. (2010). *Mirror.* Somerville, MA: Candlewick.

Bloom, B. (1999). *Wolf!* New York: Orchard.

Bottner, B. (2010). *Miss Brooks loves books! (and I don't).* New York: Knopf.

Bruss, D. (2001). *Book! Book! Book!* New York: Scholastic.

Bush, L., & Bush, J. (2008). *Read all about it!* New York: HarperCollins.

Calmenson, S. (2005). *Kindergarten kids.* New York: HarperCollins.

Casanova, M. (2011). *The day Dirk Yeller came to town.* New York: Farrar, Straus and Giroux.

Cox, J. (2010). *Carmen learns English.* New York: Holiday House.

Czekaj, J. (2010). *Hip and Hop don't stop.* New York: Hyperion.

DiCamillo, K., & McGhee, A. (2010). *Bink and Gollie.* Somerville, MA: Candlewick.

Donaldson, J. (1999). *The gruffalo.* New York: Penguin.

Finchler, J., & O'Malley, K. (2006). *Miss Malarkey leaves no reader behind.* New York: Walker.

Fucile, T. (2009). *Let's do nothing!* Somerville, MA: Candlewick.

Gall, C. (2011). *Substitute creacher.* New York: Little, Brown.

Garland, M. (2003). *Miss Smith's incredible storybook.* New York: Dutton.

Gerstein, M. (2009). *A book.* New York: Roaring Brook.

Gore, L. (2010). *The wonderful book.* New York: Scholastic.

Haseley, D. (2002). *A story for bear.* Orlando, FL: Harcourt.

Hills, T. (2000). *Knock, knock! Who's there? My first book of knock-knock jokes.* New York: Little Simon.

Hills, T. (2010). *How Rocket learned to read.* New York: Schwartz & Wade.

Himmelman, J. (2010). *Pigs to the rescue.* New York: Holt.

Hopkins, L. B. (Ed.). (1990). *Good books, good times.* New York: HarperCollins.

Hopkins, L. B. (Ed.). (2011). *I am the book.* New York: Holiday House.

Husband, A. (2010). *Dear teacher.* Naperville, IL: Sourcebooks.

Hutchins, P. (1983). *You'll soon grow into them, Titch.* New York: Greenwillow.

Jeffers, O. (2007). *The incredible book-eating boy.* New York: Philomel.

Kalan, R. (1981). *Jump, frog, jump!* New York: Greenwillow.

Kirk, D. (2007). *Library mouse.* New York: Scholastic.

Lee, S. (2010). *Shadow.* San Francisco, CA: Chronicle.

Lester, H. (1995). *Listen Buddy.* New York: Houghton Mifflin.

Litwin, E. (2011). *Pete the cat: Rocking in my school shoes.* New York: HarperCollins.

Marshall, J. (1973). *George and Martha encore.* Boston: Houghton Mifflin.

Munson, D. (2000). *Enemy pie.* San Francisco, CA: Chronicle.

Murray, L. (2011). *The gingerbread man loose in the school.* New York: Putnam.

Nelson, K. L. (2011). *Let's look at sharks.* Minneapolis, MN: Lerner.

Newman, M. (2011). *Polar bears.* New York: Holt.

Nikola-Lisa, W. (1994). *Bein' with you this way.* New York: Lee & Low.

Numeroff, L. (2002). *If you take a mouse to school.* New York: HarperCollins.

Otoshi, K. (2008). *One.* San Rafael, CA: KO Kids Books.

Palatini, M. (2000). *Bedhead.* New York: Simon & Schuster.

Parr, T. (2005). *Reading makes you feel good.* New York: Little, Brown.

Pearson, S. (2011). *How to teach a slug to read.* Tarrytown, NY: Marshall Cavendish.

Phillips, B. (2007). *Super incredible! Knock-knock jokes for kids.* Eugene, OR: Harvest House.

Piehl, J. (2011). *Let's look at sloths.* Minneapolis, MN: Lerner.

Pinkney, J. (2009). *The lion and the mouse.* New York: Little, Brown.

Portis, A. (2006). *Not a box.* New York: HarperCollins.

Prelutsky, J. (1990). *Something big has been here.* New York: Greenwillow.

Recorvits, H. (2003). *My name is Yoon.* New York: Frances Foster.

Robbins, J. (2009). *Two of a kind.* New York: Atheneum.

Rosenthal, A. K. (2010). *One smart cookie: Bite-size lessons for the school years and beyond.* New York: HarperCollins.

Seeger, L. V. (2010). *What if?* New York: Roaring Brook.

Sierra, J. (2004). *Wild about books.* New York: Knopf.

Sierra, J. (2008). *Born to read.* New York: Knopf.

Spinelli, E. (2011). *Miss Fox's class shapes up.* Chicago, IL: Albert Whitman.

Steig, W. (1971). *Amos & Boris.* New York: Farrar, Straus and Giroux.

Taylor, S. (2006). *When a monster was born.* New York: Roaring Brook.

Thomson, B. (2010). *Chalk.* Tarrytown, NY: Marshall Cavendish.

Uegaki, C. (2003). *Suki's kimono.* Towanda, NY: Kids Can.

Watt, M. (2011). *You're finally here!* New York: Hyperion.

Whitcomb, M. E. (1998). *Odd Velvet.* San Francisco, CA: Chronicle.

Willems, M. (2010a). *City dog, country frog.* New York: Hyperion.

Willems, M. (2010b). *We are in a book!* New York: Hyperion.

Williams, S. (1989). *I went walking.* Orlando, FL: Harcourt.

Wilson, K. (2002). *Bear snores on.* New York: Margaret K. McElderry Books.

Wood, A. (1984). *The napping house.* Orlando, FL: Harcourt.

Wood, A. (1992). *Silly Sally.* Orlando, FL: Harcourt.

Chapter 3: October—Making Meaningful Connections

Adler, D. A. (1980). *Cam Jansen and the mystery of the stolen diamonds.* New York: Penguin.

Adler, D. A. (2004). *Bones and the big yellow mystery.* New York: Viking.

Aillaud, C. L. (2005). *Recess at 20 below.* Portland, OR: Alaska Northwest.

Allard, H. G. (1977). *Miss Nelson is missing.* New York: Houghton Mifflin.

Arnold, T. (2005). *Hi! Fly Guy.* New York: Scholastic.

Bang, M. (1999). *When Sophie gets angry—really, really angry . . .* New York: Scholastic.

Barrows, A. (2006). *Ivy and Bean.* San Francisco, CA: Chronicle.

Bunting, E. (1991). *Fly away home.* New York: Clarion.

Charlip, R. (1964). *Fortunately.* New York: Aladdin/Simon & Schuster.

Choi, Y. (2001). *The name jar.* New York: Knopf.

Coffelt, N. (2007). *Fred stays with me!* New York: Little, Brown.

Crimi, C. (2008). *Where's my mummy?* Somerville, MA: Candlewick.

Danneberg, J. (2000). *First day jitters.* Watertown, MA: Charlesbridge.

dePaola, T. (1975). *Strega Nona.* New York: Simon & Schuster.

dePaola, T. (1989). *The art lesson.* New York: Puffin.

DiCamillo, K. (2005). *Mercy Watson to the rescue.* Somerville, MA: Candlewick.

DiCamillo, K., & McGhee, A. (2010). *Bink and Gollie.* Somerville, MA: Candlewick.

Finchler, J. (1998). *Miss Malarkey won't be in today.* New York: Walker.

Fox, M. (1994). *Tough Boris.* Orlando, FL: Harcourt.

Frazee, M. (2008). *A couple of boys have the best week ever.* Orlando, FL: Harcourt.

French, J. (2010). *Diary of a baby wombat.* New York: Clarion.

Gomi, T. (1995). *My friends.* San Francisco, CA: Chronicle.

Grogan, J. (2007). *Bad dog, Marley!* New York: HarperCollins.

Hest, A. (1996). *Jamaica Louise James.* Somerville, MA: Candlewick.

Hobbie, H. (2010). *Everything but the horse.* New York: Little, Brown.

Judge, L. (2009). *Pennies for elephants.* New York: Hyperion.

Keane, D. (2009). *Sloppy Joe.* New York: HarperCollins.

Kellogg, S. (1979). *Pinkerton, behave!* New York: Dial.

Kellogg, S. (1986). *Best friends.* New York: Dial.

Laminack, L. (2004). *Saturdays and teacakes.* Atlanta, GA: Peachtree.

Lichtenheld, T. (2010). *Bridget's beret.* New York: Holt.

Lies, B. (2010). *Bats at the ballgame.* Boston: Houghton Mifflin.

Lester, H. (1988). *Tacky the penguin.* Boston: Houghton Mifflin.

Look, L. (2004). *Ruby Lu, brave and true.* New York: Atheneum.

Look, L. (2008). *Alvin Ho: Allergic to girls, school, and other scary things.* New York: Random House.

Lowry, L. (2002). *Gooney Bird Greene.* Boston: Houghton Mifflin.

Malaspina, A. (2010). *Yasmin's hammer.* New York: Lee & Low.

Marshall, J. (1972). *George and Martha.* Boston: Houghton Mifflin.

Mayer, M. (1968). *There's a nightmare in my closet.* New York: Dial.

McDonald, M. (2000). *Judy Moody.* Somerville, MA: Candlewick.

McDonald, M. (2005). *Stink: The incredible shrinking kid.* Cambridge, MA: Candlewick.

McElligott, M. (2010). *Even monsters need haircuts.* New York: Walker.

Monks, L. (2004). *Aaaarrgghh! Spider!* Boston: Houghton Mifflin.

Monks, L. (2009). *Eeeek, Mouse!* New York: Egmont.

Moore, J. (2007). *Freckleface strawberry.* New York: Bloomsbury.

Moulton, M. K. (2010). *The very best pumpkin.* New York: Simon & Schuster.

Munson, D. (2000). *Enemy pie.* San Francisco, CA: Chronicle.

O'Connor, J. (2006). *Fancy Nancy.* New York: HarperCollins.

O'Connor, J. (2008). *Fancy Nancy: Bonjour, butterfly.* New York: HarperCollins.

Osborne, M. P. (1992). *Dinosaurs before dark.* New York: Random House.

Parish, P. (1960). *Key to the treasure.* New York: Random House.

Park, B. (1992). *Junie B. Jones and the stupid smelly bus.* New York: Random House.

Pattou, E. (2001). *Mrs. Spitzer's garden.* Orlando, FL: Harcourt.

Pennypacker, S. (2006). *Clementine.* New York: Hyperion.

Preller, J. (1998) *Jigsaw Jones: The case of Hermie the missing hamster.* New York: Scholastic.

Recorvits, H. (2003). *My name is Yoon.* New York: Farrar, Straus and Giroux.

Rocco, J. (2011). *Blackout.* New York: Hyperion.

Roemer, H. B. (2004). *Come to my party and other shape poems.* New York: Holt.

Rumford, J. (2010). *Tiger and turtle.* New York: Roaring Brook.

Rylant, C. (1987). *Henry and Mudge: The first book of their adventures.* New York: Simon & Schuster.

Rylant, C. (1994). *Mr. Putter and Tabby bake the cake.* Orlando, FL: Harcourt.

Rylant, C. (1997). *Poppleton.* New York: Scholastic.

Schachner, J. (2003). *Skippyjon Jones.* New York: Dutton.

Schmid, P. (2011). *A pet for Petunia.* New York: HarperCollins.

Scillian, D. (2010). *Memoirs of a goldfish.* Ann Arbor, MI: Sleeping Bear.

Seeger, L. V. (2007). *First the egg.* New Milford, CT: Roaring Brook.

Sharmat, M. W. (1972). *Nate the great.* New York: Random House.

Siegel, R. (2010). *Grandma's smile.* New York: Roaring Brook.

Spinelli, E. (2008). *The best story.* New York: Dial.

Sullivan, S. (2010). *Once upon a baby brother.* New York: Farrar, Straus and Giroux.

Urbanovic, J. (2007). *Duck at the door.* New York: HarperCollins.

Viorst, J. (1972). *Alexander and the terrible, horrible, no good, very bad day.* New York: Atheneum.

Waber, B. (1972/2000). *Ira sleeps over.* New York: Houghton Mifflin.

Willems, M. (2007). *Today I will fly.* New York: Hyperion.

Williams, L. E. (2010). *The can man.* New York: Lee and Low.

Winters, K. (2010). *This school year will be the best.* New York: Dutton.

Yolen, J., & Peters, A. F. (2007). *Here's a little poem: A very first book of poetry.* Cambridge, MA: Candlewick.

Zemach, K. (2008). *Ms. McCaw learns to draw.* New York: Arthur A. Levine.

Chapter 4: November & December—Predicting in Real and Make-Believe Stories

Agee, J. (1988). *The incredible painting of Felix Clousseau.* New York: Farrar, Straus and Giroux.

Barton, C. (2010). *Shark vs. train.* New York: Little, Brown.

Brett, J. (1989). *The mitten.* New York: Putnam.

Brown, M. W. (1956/1989). *Big red barn.* New York: HarperCollins.

Buehner, C. (2004). *Superdog: The heart of a hero.* New York: HarperCollins.

Buehner, C. (2010). *Snowmen all year.* New York: Dial.

Collins, R. (2011). *Doodleday.* Chicago, IL: Albert Whitman.

Davis, E. (2008). *Stinky.* New York: Toon.

Deedy, C. A. (1991). *Agatha's feather bed: Not just another wild goose story.* Atlanta, GA: Peachtree.

de Monfried, D. (2009). *Dark night.* New York: Random House.

Ernst, L. C. (2006). *The gingerbread girl.* New York: Dutton.

Gerber, C. (2008). *Winter trees.* Watertown, MA: Charlesbridge.

Hershenhorn, E. (2002). *Chicken soup by heart.* Simon & Schuster.

Hoffman, M. (1991). *Amazing Grace.* New York: Dial.

Holm, J. L. (2010). *Babymouse #13: Cupcake tycoon.* New York: Random House.

Jarka, J. (2010). *Love that kitty!: The story of a boy who wanted to be a cat.* New York: Holt.

Javaherbin, M. (2010). *The secret message.* New York: Hyperion.

Jenkins, E. (2008). *Skunkdog.* New York: Frances Foster.

Kasza, K. (1987). *The wolf's chicken stew.* New York: Putnam.

Kasza, K. (2007). *Badger's fancy meal.* New York: Putnam.

Katschke, J. (2009). *Teeny genie.* Norwalk, CT: Innovative Kids.

Kellogg, S. (2000). *The missing mitten mystery.* New York: Dial.

Kimmell, E. (1989). *Hershel and the Hanukkah goblins.* New York: Holiday House.

Laminack, L. (2011). *Three hens and a peacock.* Atlanta, GA: Peachtree.

Lechner, J. (2007). *Sticky Burr: Adventures in Burrwood Forest.* Somerville, MA: Candlewick.

Lester, H. (2010). *Tacky's Christmas.* Boston: Houghton Mifflin.

Lewis, J. P. (2009). *Spot the plot: A riddle book of book riddles.* San Francisco, CA: Chronicle.

Lichtenheld, T. (2010). *Bridget's beret.* New York: Holt.

Lillegard, D. (1994). *Frog's lunch.* New York: Scholastic.

Littledale, R. (1966). *The magic fish.* New York: Scholastic.

Marshall, J. (1972). *George and Martha.* Boston: Houghton Mifflin.

Miranda, A. (1997). *To market, to market.* Orlando, FL: Harcourt.

Mora, P. (2009). *Gracias/Thanks.* New York: Lee and Low.

Munsch, R. (1985). *Thomas' snowsuit.* Buffalo, NY: Annick.

Nielson, L. F. (2008). *Mrs. Muddle's holidays.* New York: Farrar, Straus and Giroux.

Palatini, M. (2004). *Moo who?* New York: HarperCollins.

Prelutsky, J. (1981/2008). *It's Christmas!* New York: HarperCollins.

Prelutsky, J. (1982/2007). *It's Thanksgiving!* New York: Harper Collins.

Prelutsky, J. (1984/2006). *It's snowing! It's snowing!: Winter poems.* New York: HarperCollins.

Reid, B. (2009). *Perfect snow.* Chicago, IL: Albert Whitman.

Rogasky, B. (1994). *Winter poems.* New York: Scholastic.

Rosenthal, A. K. (2009). *Yes day!* New York: HarperCollins.

Shannon, D. (1998). *No, David!* New York: Scholastic.

Shannon, D. (2002). *Duck on a bike.* New York: Scholastic.

Shilling, T. (1997). *Mr. McCready's cleaning day.* New York: Scholastic.

Silvano, W. (2009). *Turkey trouble.* White Plains, NY: Marshall Cavendish.

Smith, L. (2010). *The inside tree.* New York: HarperCollins.

Soto, G. (1993). *Too many tamales.* New York: Putnam.

Stevens, J., & Stevens Crummel, S. (2005). *The great fuzz frenzy.* Orlando, FL: Harcourt.

Van Dusen, C. (2005). *If I built a car.* New York: Penguin.

Van Leeuwen, J. (2009). *Chicken soup.* New York: Abrams.

Venable, C. AF. (2011). *The ferret's a foot.* Minneapolis, MN: Lerner.

Whitman, S. (2008). *Under the Ramadan moon.* Morton Grove, IL: Albert Whitman.

Chapter 5: January—Retelling, Comparing, and Contrasting Stories

Auch, M. J., & Auch, H. (2009). *The plot chickens.* New York: Holiday House.

Browne, A. (2009). *Me and you.* New York: Farrar, Straus and Giroux.

Cleary, B. P. (2010). *Punctuation station.* Minneapolis, MN: Millbrook.

Clement, R. (1997). *Grandpa's teeth.* New York: HarperCollins.

Coffelt, N. (2009). *Big, bigger, biggest.* New York: Holt.

Crews, N. (2011). *Jack and the beanstalk.* New York: Holt.

Danneberg, J. (2000). *First day jitters.* Watertown, MA: Charlesbridge.

Elya, S. M. (2010). *Rubia and the three osos.* New York: Hyperion.

Emberley, R. (2009). *Chicken little.* New York: Roaring Brook.

Emberley, R. (2010). *The red hen.* New York: Roaring Brook.

Fleming, C. (2002). *Muncha! Muncha! Muncha!* New York: Simon & Schuster.

Fleming, C. (2007). *Tippy-tippy-tippy, hide!* New York: Simon & Schuster.

Fleming, C. (2010). *Clever Jack takes the cake.* New York: Schwartz & Wade.

Galdone, P. (1968). *Henny penny.* New York: Clarion.

Galdone, P. (1972). *The three bears.* New York: Clarion.

Galdone, P. (1973a). *The little red hen.* New York: Clarion.

Galdone, P. (1973b). *The three billy goats gruff.* New York: Clarion.

Gardner, C. (2011). *Princess Zelda and the frog.* New York: Feiwel and Friends.

Gibb, S. (2010). *Rapunzel.* Chicago, IL: Albert Whitman.

Graves, K. (2010). *Chicken big.* San Francisco, CA: Chronicle.

Hopkins, L. B. (2010). *Sharing the seasons: A book of poems.* New York: Simon & Schuster.

Jackson, A. (1994). *Cinder Edna.* HarperCollins.

Jackson, A. (2008). *Thea's tree.* New York: Dutton.

Kasza, K. (2003). *My lucky day.* New York: Putnam.

Kellogg, S. (1985). *Chicken little.* New York: Morrow.

Kellogg, S. (1986). *Pecos Bill.* New York: HarperCollins.

Kellogg, S. (1991). *Jack and the beanstalk.* New York: Morrow.

Kellogg, S. (1997). *The three little pigs.* New York: HarperCollins.

Kimmell, E. A. (2009). *The three little tamales.* New York: Marshall Cavendish.

Kloske, G. (2005). *Once upon a time, the end (asleep in 60 seconds).* New York: Atheneum.

Laminack, L. L. (2007). *Snow day!* Atlanta, GA: Peachtree.

LaRochelle, D. (2007). *The end.* Arthur A. Levine.

Latimer, A. (2011). *The boy who cried ninja.* Atlanta, GA: Peachtree.

Lester, H. (2002). *Tackylocks and the three bears.* New York: Houghton Mifflin.

Long, E. (2011). *The book that Zack wrote.* Maplewood, NJ: Blue Apple.

MacDonald, M. R. (2011). *The boy from the dragon palace.* Chicago, IL: Albert Whitman.

Marshall, J. (1987). *Red riding hood.* New York: Dial.

Marshall, J. (1989). *The three little pigs.* New York: Dial.

Martin, R. (1985). *Foolish rabbit's big mistake.* New York: Putnam.

Martin, R. (1992). *The rough-face girl.* New York: Putnam.

Munsch, R. (1998). *Andrew's loose tooth.* New York: Scholastic.

Palatini, M. (2002). *Earthquack!* New York: Simon & Schuster.

Palatini, M. (2005). *The three silly billies.* New York: Simon & Schuster.

Palatini, M. (2011). *Goldie and the three hares.* New York: HarperCollins.

Paul, A. W. (2004). *Mañana, Iguana.* New York: Holiday House.

Paul, A. W. (2009). *Tortuga in trouble.* New York: Holiday House.

Perrault, C. (1990). *Puss in boots.* New York: Farrar, Straus and Giroux.

Pinkney, J. (2007). *Little red riding hood.* New York: Little Brown.

Rylant, C. (2001). *Poppleton in winter.* New York: Scholastic.

Scieszka, J. (1989). *The true story of the three little pigs.* New York: Penguin.

Spinelli, E. (2007). *Polar bear, Arctic hare.* Honesdale, PA: Wordsong.

Stein, D. E. (2010). *Interrupting chicken.* Somerville, MA: Candlewick.

Steptoe, J. (1987). *Mufaro's beautiful daughters: An African folktale.* New York: Lothrop, Lee & Shepard.

Stevens, J. (1995). *Tops & bottoms.* Orlando, FL: Harcourt.

Stevens, J., & Steven Crummell, S. (2011). *The little red pen.* New York: Harcourt.

Trivizas, E. (1993). *The three little wolves and the big bad pig.* New York: Simon & Schuster.

Wilcox, L. (2003). *Falling for Rapunzel.* New York: Putnam.

Wilcox, L. (2008). *Waking Beauty.* New York: Putnam.

Willey, M. (2001). *Clever Beatrice.* New York: Simon & Schuster.

Young, C. (2011). *Ten birds.* Towanda, NY: Kids Can.

Young, E. (1992). *Seven blind mice.* New York: Philomel.

Chapter 6: February—Questioning and Determining Importance to Understand Biographies

Aliki. (1965/1988). *A weed is a flower: The life of George Washington Carver.* New York: Simon & Schuster.

Arnold, T. (2010). *Fly guy meets fly girl.* New York: Scholastic.

Aston, D. H. (2008). *The moon over Star.* New York: Dial.

Borden, L. (2000). *A. Lincoln and me.* New York: Scholastic.

Bowdish, L. (2004). *George Washington Carver.* New York: Scholastic.

Bunting, E. (1991). *Fly away home.* New York: Clarion.

Coles, R. (1995). *The story of Ruby Bridges.* New York: Scholastic.

Cook, M. (2009). *Our children can soar.* New York: Bloomsbury.

Cullinan, B. E., & Wooten, D. (2009). *Another jar of tiny stars: Children select their favorite poems.* Honesdale, PA: Boyds Mills.

Edwards, P. D. (1997). *Barefoot: Escape on the Underground Railroad.* New York: HarperCollins.

Evans, S. W. (2011). *Underground: Finding the light to freedom.* New York: Roaring Brook.

Farris, C. K. (2003). *My brother Martin: A sister remembers growing up with the Rev. Dr. Martin Luther King, Jr.* New York: Simon & Schuster.

Friedman, L. (2006). *Love, Ruby Valentine.* Minneapolis, MN: Carolrhoda.

Friedman, L. (2010). *Ruby Valentine saves the day.* Minneapolis, MN: Carolrhoda.

Hopkinson, D. (2008). *Abe Lincoln crosses a creek: A tall thin tale.* New York: Schwartz & Wade.

Houston, G. (2011). *Miss Dorothy and her bookmobile.* New York: HarperCollins.

Hutchins, P. (1968). *Rosie's walk.* New York: Simon & Schuster.

Johnson, A. (2005). *A sweet smell of roses.* New York: Simon & Schuster.

Johnson, J. C. (2010). *Seeds of change: Planting a path to peace.* New York: Lee and Low.

Kellogg, S. (1973). *The island of the skog.* New York: Dial.

King, M. G. (2010). *Librarian on the roof! A true story.* Chicago, IL: Albert Whitman.

Kittinger, J. S. (2010). *Rosa's bus: The ride to civil rights.* Honesdale, PA: Boyds Mills.

Laden, N. (1994). *The night I followed the dog.* New York: Chronicle.

Levine, E. (2007). *Henry's freedom box: A true story from the Underground Railroad.* New York: Scholastic.

Malaspina, A. (2009). *Finding Lincoln.* Chicago, IL: Albert Whitman.

Mason, M. H. (2010). *These hands.* Boston: Houghton Mifflin.

McCully, E. A. (2010). *Wonder horse: The true story of the world's smartest horse.* New York: Holt.

McKissack, P. (2001). *Goin' someplace special.* New York: Atheneum.

Moss, M. (2004). *Mighty Jackie: The strike-out queen.* New York: Simon & Schuster.

Murphy, F. (2002). *George Washington and the General's dog.* New York: Random House.

Newton, V. (2009). *Let freedom sing.* San Francisco, CA: Chronicle.

Obama, B. (2010). *Of thee I sing: A letter to my daughters.* New York: Knopf.

Perdomo, W. (2010). *Clemente!* New York: Holt.

Polette, N. (2003). *Mae Jemison.* New York: Children's Press.

Prelutsky, J. (1983/1996). *It's Valentine's day.* New York: Greenwillow.

Ramsey, C. A. (2010). *Ruth and the Green Book.* Minneapolis, MN: Carolrhoda.

Rappaport, D. (2001). *Martin's big words: The life of Dr. Martin Luther King, Jr.* New York: Hyperion.

Rappaport, D. (2008). *Abe's honest words: The life of Abraham Lincoln.* New York: Hyperion.

Rappaport, D. (2010). *Jack's path of courage: The life of John F. Kennedy.* New York: Hyperion.

Reynolds, A. (2010). *Back of the bus.* New York: Philomel.

Robinson, S. (2009). *Testing the ice: A true story about Jackie Robinson.* New York: Scholastic.

Rosenthal, A. K. (2009). *Yes day!* New York: HarperCollins.

Sami. (2008). *Big, bigger, biggest.* Maplewood, NJ: Blue Apple.

Shannon, D. (1998). *A bad case of stripes.* New York: Scholastic.

Shea, P. D. (2007). *Patience Wright: American sculptor and revolutionary spy.* New York: Holt.

Shore, D. Z., & Alexander, J. (2006). *This is the dream.* New York: HarperCollins.

Slade, S. (2010). *Climbing Lincoln's steps: The African American journey.* Chicago, IL: Albert Whitman.

Turner, A. (2001). *Abe Lincoln remembers.* New York: HarperCollins.

Walker, S. M. (1999). *The 18 penny goose.* New York: HarperCollins.

Weatherford, C. B. (2005). *Freedom on the menu: The Greensboro sit-ins.* New York: Dial.

Wiles, D. (2001). *Freedom summer.* New York: Simon & Schuster.

Winnick, K. B. (1996). *Mr. Lincoln's whiskers.* Honesdale, PA: Boyds Mills.

Winter, J. (2005). *The librarian from Basra: A true story from Iraq.* Orlando, FL: Harcourt.

Winter, J. (2009). *Sonia Sotomayor: A judge grows in the Bronx.* New York: Atheneum.

Winter, J. (2010). *Biblioburro: A true story from Colombia.* New York: Beach Lane/Simon & Schuster.

Winters, K. (2003). *Abe Lincoln: The boy who loved words.* New York: Simon & Schuster.

Chapter 7: March—Visualizing and Inferring to Peek Into Poetry

Agee, J. (2009). *Orangutan tongs: Poems to tangle your tongue.* New York: Hyperion.

Agee, J. (2010). *Mr. Putney's quacking dog.* New York: Scholastic.

Bagert, B. (2007). *Shout! Little poems that roar.* New York: Dial.

Barnett, M. (2009). *Guess again!* New York: Simon & Schuster.

Barretta, G. (2007). *Dear deer: A book of homophones.* New York: Holt.

Barretta, G. (2011). *Zoola Palooza: A book of homographs.* New York: Holt.

Boelts, M. (2007). *Those shoes.* Somerville, MA: Candlewick.

Bruno, E. K. (2009). *Punctuation celebration.* New York: Holt.

Collins, R. (2011). *Doodleday.* Chicago, IL: Albert Whitman.

Cottin, M. (2006/2008). *The black book of colors.* New York: Publishers Group West.

Esbaum, J. (2009) *Stanza.* New York: Harcourt.

Feldman, E. B. (2009). *Billy & Milly: Short & silly.* New York: Putnam.

Franco, B. (2009). *Messing around on the monkey bars and other school poems for two voices.* Somerville, MA: Candlewick.

Hanson, W. (2010). *The sea of sleep.* New York: Scholastic.

Heard, G. (Ed.). (2009). *Falling down the page: A book of list poems.* New York: Roaring Brook.

Hopkins, L. B. (2010). *Amazing faces.* New York: Lee & Low.

Hutchins, P. (1972). *Good-night, owl.* New York: Simon & Schuster.

Katz, S. (2007). *Oh, Theodore! Guinea pig poems.* New York: Clarion.

LaRochelle, D. (2010). *1+1=5 and other unlikely additions.* New York: Sterling.

Larsen, A. (2009). *The imaginary garden.* New York: Kids Can.

Lechner, J. (2009). *The clever stick.* Somerville, MA: Candlewick.

Lichtenheld, T. (2011). *Cloudette.* New York: Holt.

MacDonald, R. (2003). *Achoo! Bang! Crash! They noisy alphabet.* New York: Roaring Brook.

MacLachlan, P. & Charest, E. M. (2006). *Once I ate a pie.* New York: HarperCollins.

Otoshi, K. (2010). *Zero.* San Rafael, CA: KO Kids.

Pashen, E. (2005). *Poetry speaks to children.* Naperville, IL: Sourcebooks.

Pennypacker, S. (2009). *Sparrow girl.* New York: Hyperion.

Prelutsky, J. (1984). *The new kid on the block.* New York: Greenwillow.

Prelutsky, J. (Ed.). (1986). *Read-aloud rhymes for the very young.* New York: Knopf.

Prelutsky, J. (1990). *Something big has been here.* New York: Greenwillow.

Prelutsky, J. (1996). *A pizza the size of the sun.* New York: Greenwillow.

Prelutsky, J. (2000). *It's raining pigs & noodles.* New York: Greenwillow.

Prelutsky, J. (2005). *Read a rhyme, write a rhyme.* New York: Knopf.

Prelutsky, J. (2008). *My dog may be a genius.* New York: Greenwillow.

Raczka, B. (2010). *Guyku: A year of haiku for boys.* New York: Houghton Mifflin.

Raczka, B. (2011). *Lemonade and other poems squeezed from a single word.* New York: Roaring Brook.

Reynolds, P. (2009). *Rose's garden.* Somerville, MA: Candlewick.

Rosenthal, A. K. (2009). *Duck! Rabbit!* San Francisco, CA: Chronicle.

Ryan, P. M. (2001). *Hello ocean.* New York: Charlesbridge.

Sandall, E. (2010). *Birdsong.* New York: Egmont.

Schertle, A. (2009). *Button up! Wrinkled rhymes.* New York: Harcourt.

Seeger, L. V. (2010). *What if?* New York: Roaring Brook.

Singer, M. (2010). *Mirror mirror: A book of reversible verse.* New York: Dutton.

Smith, L. (2011). *Grandpa green.* New York: Roaring Brook.

Teague, M. (1996). *The secret shortcut.* New York: Scholastic.

Wardlaw, L. (2011). *Won Ton.* New York: Holt.

Weinstock, R. (2010). *Can you dig it? and other poems.* New York: Hyperion.

Yolen, J., & Peters, A. F. (2007). *Here's a little poem: A very first book of poetry.* Cambridge, MA: Candlewick.

Chapter 8: April & May—Questioning and Determining Importance to Navigate Nonfiction

Aston, D. H. (2006). *An egg is quiet.* San Francisco, CA: Chronicle.

Aston, D. H. (2007). *A seed is sleepy.* San Francisco, CA: Chronicle.

Aston, D. H. (2011). *A butterfly is patient.* San Francisco, CA: Chronicle.

Barnett, M. (2010). *Oh no! Or how my science project destroyed the world.* New York: Hyperion.

Bishop, N. (2007). *Spiders.* New York: Scholastic.

Bourke, A., & Rendall, J. (2009). *Christian the lion.* New York: Holt.

Branley, F. (1963/1983). *Down comes the rain.* New York: HarperCollins.

Broach, E. (2010). *Gumption!* New York: Atheneum.

Brown, M. (2011). *Arthur turns green.* New York: Little, Brown.

Cherry, L. (1990). *The great kapok tree: A tale of the Amazon rain forest.* Orlando, FL: Harcourt.

Chin, J. (2009). *Redwoods.* New York: Roaring Brook.

Cowcher, H. (1988). *Rain forest.* New York: Farrar, Straus and Giroux.

Cowcher, H. (2011). *Desert elephants.* New York: Farrar, Straus and Giroux.

Davies, N. (2003). *Surprising sharks.* Cambridge, MA: Candlewick.

deGroat, D. (2011). *Ants in your pants, worms in your plants!* New York: HarperCollins.

Dotlich, R. K. (1998). *Lemonade sun and other summer poems.* Honesdale, PA: Boyds Mills.

Drummond, A. (2011). *Energy island: How one community harnessed the wind and changed their world.* New York: Farrar, Straus and Giroux.

Glaser, L. (2010). *Garbage helps our garden grow: A compost story.* Minneapolis, MN: Millbrook.

Hopkins, L. B. (Ed.). (1999). *Spectacular science: A book of poems.* New York: Simon & Schuster.

Hopkins, L. B. (Ed.). (2005). *Days to celebrate: A full year of poetry, people, holidays, history, fascinating facts, and more.* New York: Greenwillow.

Jango-Cohen, J. (2004). *Flying squirrels.* Minneapolis, MN: Lerner.

Judge, L. (2011). *Strange creatures: The story of Walter Rothschild and his museum.* New York: Hyperion.

Lewin, T. (2010). *Stable.* New York: Roaring Brook.

Lewis, J. P. (2002). *A world of wonders: Geographic travels in verse and rhyme.* New York: Dial.

Lewis, J. P. (2004). *Scien-trickery: Riddles in science.* Orlando, FL: Harcourt.

Lichtenheld, T. (2011). *Cloudette.* New York: Holt.

Madison, A. (2007). *Velma Gratch & the way cool butterfly.* New York: Schwartz & Wade.

Mahy, M. (1994). *The rattlebang picnic.* New York: Dial.

McMullan, K. (2002). *I stink!* New York: HarperCollins.

Monroe, C. (2010). *Sneaky sheep.* Minneapolis, MN: Carolrhoda.

Mora, P. (2009). *Book Fiesta! Celebrate children's day/Book day.* New York: HarperCollins.

Morris, C. (2007). *The boy who was raised by librarians.* Atlanta, GA: Peachtree.

Muir, L. (2011). *Barry B. Wary.* New York: Hyperion.

Peet, B. (1970). *The wump world.* Boston: Houghton Mifflin.

Peters, L. W. (2010). *Volcano wakes up!* New York: Holt.

Rathmann, P. (1995). *Office Buckle and Gloria.* New York: Putnam.

Reynolds, P. H. (2009). *Rose's garden.* Somerville, MA: Candlewick.

Rockwell, A. (1998). *Our Earth.* San Diego: Harcourt.

Rockwell, A. (2008). *Clouds.* New York: HarperCollins.

Rosenberg, L. (2011). *Tyrannosaurus dad.* New York: Roaring Brook.

Ryder, J. (2007). *Toad by the road: A year in the life of these amazing amphibians.* New York: Holt.

Seuss, Dr. (1954/1982). *Horton hears a who!* New York: Random House.

Shannon, D. (2000). *The rain came down.* New York: Scholastic.

Showers, P. (1974/1994). *Where does the garbage go?* New York: HarperCollins.

Siddals, M. M. (2010). *Compost stew: An A to Z recipe for the earth.* New York: Tricycle.

Silverstein, S. (1964). *The giving tree.* New York: Harper & Row.

Trueit, T. S. (2007). *Earth day.* New York: Scholastic.

Urbigkit, C. (2005). *Brave dogs, gentle dogs: How they guard sheep.* Honesdale, PA: Boyds Mills.

Van Allsburg, C. (1990). *Just a dream.* Boston: Houghton Mifflin.

Walker, S. (2008). *Volcanoes.* Minneapolis, MN: Lerner.

Ward, N. (1998). *Don't eat the teacher.* New York: Scholastic.

Watt, M. (2006). *Scaredy squirrel.* Tonawanda, NY: Kids Can.

Zweibel, A. (2005). *Our tree named Steve.* New York: Puffin.

CD PRINT RESOURCES

Folder	File Name	Description	Page Reference
Introduction	I.1	Morning Message Menu	5
	I.2	Mini-Lesson Menu	5–7
	I.3	Ten Things to Do Before School	8
	I.4	Questionnaire	8
Chapter 1	1.1	Read, Think, and Respond Book Cover	18
	1.2	Lined Page	18
	1.3	H-Chart	18
	1.4	Web	18
	1.5	Story Map	18
	1.6	Two-Column Notes	18
	1.7	Three-Column Notes	18
	1.8	ABC Guide 1	29
	1.9	ABC Guide 2	29
	1.10	Conferring Notebook Cover	34
	1.11	Conferring Notebook Inside Page	34
	1.12	What Readers Do	35
Chapter 2	2.1	Reading Workshop: The First 25 Days	42
	2.2	Interest Inventory	47
	2.3	Picture Clues Strategy Song	56
	2.4	Decoding Strategy Wheel	56
	2.5	Just Right Books Song	59
	2.6	Reread Strategy Song	61
	2.7	Partner Reading Tips	63
	2.8	Explore the W.O.R.L.D. Wheel	66
	2.9	Be an Observer Response Sheet	68
	2.10	Boost Bag Note to Parents	76
	2.11	Set 1 Sight Word Record-Keeping Form	76
	2.12	Set 1 Sight Word Flash Cards	76
	2.13	Set 2 Sight Word Record-Keeping Form	76
	2.14	Set 2 Sight Word Flash Cards	76
	2.15	Set 3 Sight Word Record-Keeping Form	76
	2.16	Set 3 Sight Word Flash Cards	76
	2.17	Boost Bag Directions for Teacher	76
	2.18	My Reading Autobiography	76
Chapter 3	3.1	Get Your Mouth Ready Strategy Song	85
	3.2	Skip and Read Through Strategy Song	86
	3.3	Look Through the Word for Sounds You Know Strategy Song	87
	3.4	Look for Chunks Strategy Song	88
	3.5	Comprehension Strategy Wheel	90
	3.6	Comprehension Strategy Song	90
	3.7	Schema Strategy Song	90
	3.8	Making Connections Strategy Song	92
Chapter 4	4.1	Decoding Strategy Prompts	112
	4.2	Rereading Strategy Chart	114
	4.3	Making Predictions Strategy Song	116
	4.4	Predicting Strategy Chart	120
Chapter 5	5.1	Retelling Song	139
	5.2	When Readers Retell	140
	5.3	Key Vocabulary Cards	140
	5.4	Antonym Memory Game Cards	147
	5.5	Take Home Book Club Note for Parents	151
Chapter 6	6.1	Questioning Strategy Song	161
	6.2	Questioning the Writer	164
	6.3	Determining Importance Strategy Song	167
	6.4	Determining Importance Response Sheet	167
Chapter 7	7.1	Mental Images Strategy Song	184
	7.2	Questions Prompting Prediction and Inferring	185
	7.3	Inferring Strategy Song	186
Chapter 8	8.1	Read-Aoud/Think-Aloud Questions and Reflections	202
	8.2	Determining Importance in Nonfiction Strategy Song	204
	8.3	Top Ten Facts	211
	8.4	Nonfiction Song	212

Note: To view and print the print resources on the CD, you will need to download Adobe Reader™, version 7.0 or higher. This download is available free of charge for Mac and PC systems at get.adobe.com/reader.

CD INTERACTIVE WHITEBOARD RESOURCES

Folder	File Name	Description	Page Reference
Interactive Whiteboard Morning Messages	IWB_MM_2A	Self-Monitoring/Decoding: Picture Clues	39
	IWB_MM_2B	Vocabulary Building: Labeling Parts of a Book	42
	IWB_MM_3	Vocabulary Building: Compound Words	81
	IWB_MM_4	Reading Response—Can You Guess the Character?	110
	IWB_MM_5	Vocabulary Building—Familiar Words With New Meanings	133
	IWB_MM_6	Reading Response—A Time Line of Our Day	156
	IWB_MM_7	Vocabulary Building—Quiet Words and Noisy Words	178
	IWB_MM_8	Self-Monitoring/Decoding: Decoding Multi-Syllabic Content-Related Words	196
Interactive Whiteboard Resources	IWB_Comp_Wheel	Comprehension Strategy Wheel	90
	IWB_Decoding_Wheel	Decoding Strategy Wheel	56
	IWB_WORLD_Wheel	Explore the WORLD Wheel	66
Interactive Whiteboard Mini-Lessons	IWB_Lesson_3	Look for Chunks Foundation Lesson	88
	IWB_Lesson_4	Adjectives—Making Connections	122
	IWB_Lesson_5A	Learning About Synonyms	146
	IWB_Lesson_5B	Learning About Antonyms—Antonym Memory Game	147
	IWB_Lesson_6	Studying Root Words	170
	IWB_Lesson_7	Understanding Multiple-Meaning Words—Foundation Lesson	181
	IWB_Lesson_8	Categorizing Content-Area Words	208

Folder	File Name	Description	Page Reference
Interactive Whiteboard Songs	IWB_Song_2.3	Picture Clues Strategy Song	56
	IWB_Song_2.5	Just Right Book Song	59
	IWB_Song_2.6	Reread Strategy Song	61
	IWB_Song_3.1	Get Your Mouth Ready Strategy Song	85
	IWB_Song_3.2	Skip and Read Through Strategy Song	86
	IWB_Song_3.3	Look Through the Word for Sounds You Know Strategy Song	87
	IWB_Song_3.4	Look for Chunks Strategy Song	88
	IWB_Song_3.6	Comprehension Strategy Song	90
	IWB_Song_3.7	Schema Strategy Song	90
	IWB_Song_3.8	Making Connections Strategy Song	92
	IWB_Song_4.3	Making Predictions Strategy Song	116
	IWB_Song_5.1	Retelling Song	139
	IWB_Song_6.1	Questioning Strategy Song	161
	IWB_Song_6.3	Determining Importance Strategy Song	167
	IWB_Song_7.1	Mental Images Strategy Song	184
	IWB_Song_7.3	Inferring Strategy Song	186
	IWB_Song_8.2	Determining Importance	204
	IWB_Song_8.4	Nonfiction Song	212

Note: If you don't already have ActivInspire software, you can install the free personal version contained on this disc. Refer to the How-To document on the CD for specific directions and more information on using interactive whiteboard documents.